T0345727

The Art of the Jewish Family

BARD GRADUATE CENTER
CULTURAL HISTORIES OF THE
MATERIAL WORLD

Cultural Histories of the Material World is a series centered on the exploration of the material turn in the study of culture. Volumes in the series examine the ways human beings have shaped and interpreted the material world from a broad range of scholarly perspectives and show how attention to materiality can contribute to a more precise historical understanding of specific times, places, ways, and means.

Peter N. Miller, Series Editor

Antiquarianism and Intellectual Life in Europe and China, 1500–1800
Peter N. Miller and François Louis, Editors

The Sea: Thalassography and Historiography
Peter N. Miller, Editor

Cultural Histories of the Material World
Peter N. Miller, Editor

Ways of Making and Knowing: The Material Culture of Empirical Knowledge
Pamela H. Smith, Amy R. W. Meyers, and Harold J. Cook, Editors

The Anthropology of Expeditions: Travel, Visualities, Afterlives
Joshua A. Bell and Erin L. Hasinoff, Editors

Ex Voto: Votive Giving Across Cultures
Ittai Weinryb, Editor

In Space We Read Time: On the History of Civilization and Geopolitics
Karl Schlögel
Translated by Gerrit Jackson

The Art of the Jewish Family

A History of Women in
Early New York in Five Objects

Laura Arnold Leibman

Bard Graduate Center

New York City

Laura Arnold Leibman is professor of English and humanities at
Reed College.

*This book was published with generous support from the Leon Levy Foundation,
the David Berg Foundation, and donors to Bard Graduate Center.*

Distributed by the University of Chicago Press. This book may be
purchased in quantity for educational, business, or promotional use.
For information, please email marketing@press.uchicago.edu.

Designed by Laura Grey.
This book is set in New Baskerville ITC Pro.
Printed in the United States of America.

Library of Congress Control Number: 2019952463
ISBN 978-1-941792-20-9

A catalogue record for this book is available from the British Library.

10 9 8 7 6 5 4 3 2 1

Dedicated to Jewish women everywhere.
May their voices be a source of light, sustenance, and hope.

Contents

Illustrations

Series Editor's Preface

Jewish Material Culture. For some, those words should be followed by a question mark, or at least ironic quotation marks. For them, it is a straightforward oxymoron, perhaps best embodied by the witticism attributed to Isaac Deutscher, the late great biographer of the Soviet Union's founding fathers. When asked in an Oxford common room for his "roots," Deutscher supposedly replied, "Jews don't have roots, they have legs." Being the "People of the Book" implied that their homeland was portable—this long before scholars talked of the "history of the book" or "material texts."

Of course, all of this is wrong. Even a superficial reader of vast tracts of the Pentateuch would be confronted with a careful attention to material culture. Just to take one example. Bezalel, whom tradition fashions a craftsman, would be better termed architect or designer. And whoever wrote those chapters of the Book of Exodus in which his designing of the tabernacle is narrated paid the kind of attention to materials, spaces, and movement that would warrant its inclusion in any reader on material culture. Multiply this attentiveness to materiality ten-, twenty-, or a hundredfold and you have the discussions of artifacts, spaces, and rituals in the Mishnah, the code of Jewish law promulgated in Roman Palestine in the early second century CE. And multiply that a hundred- or a thousandfold and you have the discussions of things in the Babylonian Talmud, redacted in the sixth century in Sassanian Persia. So, there was no shortage of Jewish attention to the importance of material culture in its formative textual stage.

For a very long time, there was, however, a shortage of attention on the part of scholars to the value of material culture as historical evidence for the life of the past *in general*. This deficiency is a bigger story in which the Jewish angle is but a very small part. It is in the broad cultural insistence on the priority of the head over the hand, and of the idea over the medium, that all sorts of myths were forged—including the nostalgic celebration of dematerialization embodied in a slogan like "the people of the book."

By the same token, when scholars around Europe began to awaken over the course of the nineteenth century to the informational goldmine constituted by material things, it is no surprise that scholars of the Jewish past began to do so as well, though a bit later. Take, for example, Samuel Krauss's *Talmudische Archäologie* (3 vols., 1910). It addresses this question squarely and in the language of the day but is almost entirely textual— exactly the way in which a sixteenth-century northern European philologist like Guillaume Budé might have discoursed on Roman antiquities. The step from philology to archaeology in European scholarship plays out between 1750 and 1850; for the Jews, it is in the decade separating Krauss's publication from one by Ludwig Blau.

For, in 1926, in an essay published in the *Hebrew Union College Annual*, the Hungarian scholar called for the study of the Jewish past through its material remains under the name "Jewish Archaeology." He situated this practice culturally by titling the article in which he proposed it "Early Christian Archaeology from the Jewish Point of View." By this he was referring to the work of an earlier generation of students of ancient material culture—antiquarians—who applied the skills developed for the study of Roman remains to the study of Early Christian ones. They aimed to understand what was not found in books and by so doing broaden their understanding of a religious community.

Blau looked to this Christian example because there was no precedent for the study of Jewish material culture: "In fact, it does not occur to anyone to read about the Jewish monuments, and, as far as I know, such a subject of study figures in no curriculum and there exists no Jewish archaeologist in the sense of the term employed here" (Blau, "Early Christian Archaeology from the Jewish Point of View," *Hebrew Union College Annual* 3 [1926]: 157–214, at 160).

In the twentieth century, an explicitly Jewish archaeology did come into being—and one of the subsequent volumes in this series will examine its pioneering figure, Eleazar Sukenik. But with the creation of the state of Israel, it entered into a complex relationship with archaeological science as taught in Israeli universities and practiced in the field. And while in the past decades there has been an enormous increase in attention paid to artifacts, things, objects, and material culture, specific attention to doing Jewish history through things—despite the work of archaeology—has lagged behind the secular trend. When the Bard Graduate Center approached the Leon Levy Foundation for the lead gift that created the program that gave birth to this book and those still to come, it was with the idea in mind of modeling what a future study of Jewish material culture could look like and inspiring others to carry it forward. This aim is something Bard Graduate Center has been pursuing since its founding and is part of its vision of a collaborative scholarly ecosystem. Before concluding, let me express our gratitude to the Leon Levy Foundation and the David Berg Foundation for their commitment to this project from its start and their recognition that scholarship on the past helps guide our steps into the future.

Peter N. Miller
Bard Graduate Center, New York City
January 2020

Acknowledgments

Many of these chapters were originally given as lectures during Women's History Month, and I am enormously grateful that Bard Graduate Center (BGC), the Leon Levy Foundation, and the David Berg Foundation provided me the luxury to be able to research and rethink the early history of America Jewish women's lives. This book would not be possible without Susan Weber, the incredible founder of BGC, together with its faculty and staff. I am particularly grateful to Peter Miller, dean of BGC, whose phone call about the Leon Levy Visiting Professorship came when I was in the midst of family tragedy and who offered a very welcome lifeboat. Peter, thank you for your patience and believing in me. Among the many, many fine staff members at BGC, Laura Minsky has my particular appreciation for making the complicated transition to New York smooth and painless. The final shape of these chapters owes much to thoughtful feedback from Ellen Smith, Hasia Diner, and Barbara Mann, as well as BGC faculty and students who attended our lunchtime sessions. A heartfelt thanks also goes out to the original audience members who trooped through the snow to hear me speak, particularly Lisa Gordis and Vivian Mann, ז״ל, who provided support and wisdom. I am incredibly appreciative of the time, energy, and insights each one of you brought to this project.

No book is written on its own, and I am beholden to the members of my various writing groups, including Michael Hoberman, Julia Lieberman, Hilit Surowitz-Israel, Gail Sherman, and Walter Englert, as well as Zev Eleff, all of whom gave me detailed feedback and encouragement. My ability to carve out time to revise the manuscript owes much to the powerful women of the Reed Squad: Naomi Caffee, Laura Zientek, Nicole Reisnour, Mónica López Lerma, Gail Sherman, and Sarah Wagner-McCoy. Thank you for reminding me that guilt is not actual work and that when we stand together, we are more powerful than when we are alone. I owe a debt to Laura Klinkner, who helped me get started researching Sarah Rodrigues Brandon and who shared my love affair with Blanche Moses. Chapter 1 would not have been possible without the inspiration of Jeffrey Shandler, who invited me be one of three people at *Celebrating 250 Years of Jewish Life* at Rutgers University, and the helpful feedback of Laura Levitt and Samira Mehta. I am also deeply grateful to Jonathan Sarna, Pamela Nadell, Daniel Lee, and Annika Fisher for patiently reading the entire manuscript and for all of their thoughtful suggestions.

This book is largely about the early women of Congregation Shearith Israel, and I am grateful to the friendship and support shown to me by members of the congregation both during my residency in New York and over the years, particularly Seth Haberman, Zachary Edinger, Jennifer Ash, Lisa Rohde, and Rabbi Shalom Morris. I owe a large debt to Seth Haberman and Rabbi Morris, now of Bevis Marks, for originally bringing me to speak at Shearith Israel about Sarah Brandon Moses. Seth Haberman, whatever good there is in this book is largely due to your ongoing support, and I hope you forgive anything you don't like. Thank you as well for aiding me in becoming a scholar in residence at the synagogue in spring of 2018. Zachary Edinger, I cannot say enough how much I appreciate your providing me access to the congregational archives and for the cemetery visits. I remain in awe of the wealth of historical information you possess about the congregation. Portions of chapters 3 and 5 also owe a debt to conversations with Rabbi Morris in New York, London, and Oxford. My gratitude as well goes out to Rabbi Meir Soloveichik and Barbara Reiss for graciously hosting me at New York's earliest synagogue.

Four of the five objects in this book are from the collections of the American Jewish Historical Society, and over the years I have made that organization my home away from home. I owe a special thank-you to librarian emerita Susan Malbin and to Jennifer Rodewald of the digital media lab at the Center for Jewish History for the incredible close-ups of Sarah Rodrigues Brandon Moses's miniatures, and to Tanya Elder for responding to all my pleas for acquisition information. Annie Polland, Shirly Bahar, Lila Corwin Berman, Riv-Ellen Prell, and Rachel Lithgow all have my deepest appreciation for what they have done and continue to do for the organization, and for the mentorship and comradery they have shown me throughout this project.

In addition to the work completed at AJHS, I am grateful to the American Jewish Archives; the Metropolitan Museum of Art; the Victoria and Albert Museum; the American Philosophical Society; the Barbados Department of Archives; Congregation Shearith Israel Archives; the Jewish Museum in New York; the Library of Congress; London's Jewish Museum; the London Metropolitan Archives; Congregation Bevis Marks; the National Archives of the Netherlands; the National Museum of American Jewish History; the New York City Municipal Archives; the North Carolina Museum of Art; the New-York Historical Society; the New York Public Library; the Winterthur Museum, Garden, and Library; and Yeshiva University. In addition to the Leon Levy Foundation and the David Berg Foundation, research used in this book was completed with help from the American Philosophical Society, Oxford University, Ruby-Lankford Grants, a Joseph and Eva R. Dave Fellowship, the Hadassah Brandeis Institute, and a Sid and Ruth Lapidus Fellowship.

Last but not least, I owe a debt to my family, particularly my parents and sister, who supported me through hard decisions, and to my husband and son, who enthusiastically followed me to New York. Blessings on Park East Day School, Park East Persian Minyan, the Sephardic Synagogue of 5th Ave, and Shearith Israel for making them, and me, feel at home in the city.

Abbreviations

AJA   American Jewish Archives, Cincinnati
AJHS   American Jewish Historical Society, New York
APS   American Philosophical Society, Philadelphia
BDA   Barbados Department of Archives, Bridgetown
BGC   Bard Graduate Center, New York
CSIA   Congregation Shearith Israel Archives, Newark, NJ
FHBS   Female Hebrew Benevolent Society
JM   The Jewish Museum, London
JMNY   The Jewish Museum, New York
KKSI   Kahal Kadosh Shearith Israel, New York
LAC   Library and Archives Canada, Ottawa
LMA   London Metropolitan Archives
Met   Metropolitan Museum of Art, New York
NA   Nationaal Archief (National archive), The Hague
NARA   National Archives and Records Administration, Washington, DC
NPIGS Nederlandse Portugees Israëlitische Gemeente in Suriname
       (Dutch Portuguese Jewish congregation in Suriname)
NYCMA New York City Municipal Archives
NYCRIS New York City Records and Information Service
NYHS   New-York Historical Society, New York
NYPL   New York Public Library, New York
NYSL   New York State Library, Albany, NY
Occident *The Occident and American Jewish Advocate* (Philadelphia)
OED   *Oxford English Dictionary*
PMFNY Papers of the Moses Family of New York, undated, 1767–1941,
       AJHS

Introduction

After weeks of being held captive by mercenaries, Judith de Mereda stepped off the creaky deck of the French ship *St. Catrina* in 1654 and onto the muddy streets of Nieuw Amsterdam. Relief washed over her like new rain. To be sure, the town was smaller, smellier, and less orderly than she was used to, but the air was also cooler than it had been in her most recent home in Recife, Brazil.[1] More crucially, allies awaited her and the rest of the castaways. A few Jewish traders had predated the refugees. According to one account, Solomon Pietersen of the Netherlands, Asser Levy of Vilna, and Jacob Barsimon of the Netherlands arrived from Europe the month before on the *Pereboom* (Pear tree). Yet prior to the *St. Catrina*, there do not appear to have been any Jewish women in the colonial town or even a minyan of men. Now suddenly there were four more men and their wives, thirteen children, and two single women—Judith de Mereda and Ryche Nounes, who was possibly the widow of Moshe Nunes.[2] It was early September, and a new year was upon Judith.

The reprieve was short lived. Rosh Hashanah had started early that year, but already God's judgment seemed against her. The day before the holiday started, Judith learned that the Dutch colonial court had ruled her few remaining possessions would be sold to meet her and her fellow passengers' debts. Although the money owed was *in solidum*, making all the travellers collectively responsible, Judith—or Judicq as she was known—had been able to pay less than the others with the few coins that survived her travels. Thus, Judith's possessions were among the first to be sold.

1

Judith's story is a poignant reminder of how the saga of Jewish women in New York begins with the troubled history of the things they owned. Her story also reminds us of the holes in that narrative, as if a silverfish or greedy moth had feasted on the past.[3] The records do not tell us, for example, *what* Judith was being forced to sell. Perhaps clothing and bedding or a small memento of her previous lives as a Jewish woman in the Caribbean and Amsterdam? Or maybe it was a relic of the more distant past, of the years her ancestors had spent hiding Jewish practices from the Iberian Inquisition's steely gaze? Whatever they were, the objects would no longer be hers; all she owned was sold to strangers to pay a debt she had not asked to accrue.

Depending on her personality, Judith de Mereda must have felt either exceptionally lucky or exceptionally cursed, or both. True, she had escaped the Inquisition that imprisoned, tormented, and even burned at the stake so many Sephardic women of her generation. She had also survived both the long sea voyage from Amsterdam to Recife, Brazil, and the tropical diseases that slew so many of her fellow colonists. At first her lush new home promised riches: warehouses lined the harbor and tall, white houses with red-tiled roofs and balconies stood alongside the synagogue on *Rua dos Judeos*—Jews' street. Glossy spun fantasies of sugar drew Jews to the colonies, the sweet white crystals making fortunes for those who arrived on Recife's shores with little in their pockets.[4]

Yet wave upon wave of misfortune followed. As the Portuguese battled the Dutch for control of the rich port, they set up a naval blockade, and the town's eight thousand inhabitants began to die off, perishing from hunger, heat, and disease. Cats and dogs became delicacies, and slaves devoured the cadavers of horses they dug up. By the time the Dutch ships broke through the blockade in 1646, many people were too weak to walk to the harbor and greet their rescuers.[5] The conflict would continue for eight more years, until finally the Portuguese won out. The one thousand or so Jews living in Recife were given three months to take all their "movable property" and leave.[6]

Most made it successfully back to the Dutch mainland but not Judith. She and twenty-two others chose to make their way on the *Valck* toward New England via Martinique. Crippling winds forced a landfall in Spanish Jamaica, where mercenaries stripped them of most of their possessions. Judith and her companions fled onward to Cape St. Anthony in Cuba, where Jacques de la Motthe offered to take them to New Amsterdam on the *St. Catrina* for 2,500 guilders, triple the usual fare.[7] The twenty-three Jews only had 933 guilders collectively among them. Faced with no other options, the Jewish men signed the papers and found themselves on the way to the Dutch outpost. They would figure out the money later.

So it was that on Thursday, September 10, 1654, the day before Rosh Hashanah, that the master of the *St. Catrina* received permission from the Dutch colonial court to seize and sell off the property of the greatest debtors, Judith Mereda and Abram Israel. Yet their few remaining belongings were not enough to fully repay the debt, and Jacques de la Motthe returned and asked that two of the men—Israel and Moses Ambrosius—be imprisoned until the debt was paid in full. The struggle between the castaways and captain was drawn out for weeks. Finally, with help from the refugees' coreligionists in Amsterdam, the debt was paid, and the evacuees from Recife were free.[8] Some would stay and face the difficulties of being among only a handful of Jews in an inhospitable town; others would return to Amsterdam or set sail for larger Jewish communities in the Caribbean.

We do not know what path Judith took. The call to sell her possessions would be the last time she appeared in the colonial records.[9] The chronicles from Recife are of little help: although, as Arnold Wiznitzer points out, "Mereda" is almost certainly a misspelling of Mercado, a common Jewish surname in Recife, Judicq does not appear in the early manuscripts from that colony.[10] Moreover, the elusive connection between Judith and more famous men of the Mercado family only raises more questions. Why, for example, did she not follow the lead of Dr. Abraham de Mercado, a member of the Recife Mahamad (governing board), who fled to Barbados, where Cromwell gave him and his son David Raphael de Mercado a pass to "exercise his profession" in 1655?[11] Did she return instead to Amsterdam? If so, was she the same Judith de Mercado who was a witness in marriages of her children, Esther and Jacob de Mercado, in 1668 and 1682, respectively?[12]

Judith's pattern of brief appearance and subsequent silence in the written records haunts the history of Jewish women over the next two centuries; it was a harbinger of what was to come. Although a wide range of scholars have written about Jewish American women from the 1880s onwards, discussions of Jewish American women from before 1850 remain rare. Recent scholars have noted how very little material on Jewish women in the early Atlantic World survives.[13] Even the renowned historian Jacob Rader Marcus, who compiled over one thousand pages in *The American Jewish Woman: A Documentary History*, devotes fewer than sixty to women before 1800, and notably not all of these documents are even *by* women. In total, the first 300 years of Jewish women's experience in the Americas receive 15 percent of the space in his book, while the next 140 years receive 85 percent.[14] Given Marcus's tremendous dedication both to the colonial era and to making Jewish American women's history more accessible, the possibility of finding other sources can seem bleak.

Recent histories of Jewish American women edited and written by women have paid slightly more attention to women from the earlier era. Hasia Diner and Beryl Lieff Benderly's magisterial volume, *Her Works Praise Her: A History of Jewish Women in American from the Colonial Times to the Present,* provides a valuable and important contribution to the study of Jewish American women and is particularly democratic in its approach to showing the range of voices across class boundaries. Surprisingly, however, the book still pays more attention to later eras: 15 percent of the book is dedicated to the 170 years before 1820, another 15 percent covers the 60 years between 1820 and 1880, and 70 percent is committed to the final 120 years.[15] *American Jewish Women's History: A Reader* (2001) has almost the same ratio: of the twelve essays, two are prior to 1830 and two more cover 1830 through 1880, leaving 67 percent of the book to cover 1880 through to the present. Although published two years later, *Women in American Judaism* (2003) contains eighteen essays, but only two from the era prior to 1840 and one covering 1840 to 1879. Even Pam Nadell's recent authoritative and insightful study, *America's Jewish Women: A History from Colonial Times to Today* (2019), follows this trend. The first chapter, "America's Early Jewish Women," covers 1654 until the eve of the Civil War (two hundred years), leaving the remaining four chapters for later eras (less than 160 years). Certainly there were fewer Jews living then in early America than in later eras, but this did not stop Jacob Rader Marcus from writing three volumes with 1713 pages about *The Colonial American Jew, 1492–1776* back in 1969. What has made women's contribution to that voluminous history so hard to trace?

I do not mention these groundbreaking scholars' works in order to denigrate them. On the contrary: my own scholarship is deeply indebted to the paths these authors have forged and would not be possible without their insights. I bring them up instead to highlight how my approach differs and to foreground a central question for my work:[16] Why have important scholars dedicated to women's voices, who wield new methods dedicated to understanding women's role in Jewish history, neglected the earlier era?

To be sure, this lack of attention by scholars of American Jewish women prior to the Civil War reflects the very real paucity and fragmentary nature of evidence about women from this early era.[17] With the rare exception of the letters of Abigail Franks and female members of the Gratz family, most records about Jewish women from this time come in disconnected fragments that seem almost impossible to piece back together. Yet ever since the women's studies movement took off in the American academy in the 1970s, scholars have been trying.[18]

In the past fifty years, scholars have had a range of responses to the lack of evidence about early Jewish American women. The first and most common is to throw up their collective hands in despair. They point to the impossibility of writing a history from so few sources and then move back to sources we do have in abundance, such as those by and about men or by women from later eras.[19] The second strategy scholars have used in grappling with this early era is to talk about two or three early wealthy, privileged Jewish American women who did write, such as Rebecca Gratz and Abigail Franks, without a lot of attention to why records about these women are the ones that survived. While this approach has produced some superb scholarship,[20] it has not really helped us to talk about average women's lives. After the first couple of decades, early Jewish American women typically made up roughly half of established communities, but the vast majority of these women were poor, like their predecessor Judith Mereda. How can we write a history of early American Jewish women that accounts for the economic diversity of their experiences?

I argue in this book that in order to examine the full range of Jewish women's lives in early America we need to (1) expand our definition of evidence and (2) listen to the silences in the archive. What were the structural reasons why women were less likely to create documents? What textual and nontextual sources *did* women in this era create and use? What forces kept these sources out of the archives and silenced early Jewish women's stories in later histories? By thinking about archiving as an active and ongoing process, I suggest that current stories told about Jews in early America are skewed. Expanding our evidence and listening to silences shifts the locus of Jewish identity out of the synagogue and political arena and into the familial sphere.

Why Material Culture?

In order to rethink early Jewish American women's lives, *The Art of the Jewish Family* examines five objects owned by Jewish women who lived at least a portion of their lives in early New York between 1750 and 1850. Each chapter creates a biography of a single woman through her object but also uses her story to shed light on larger changes in Jewish American women's lives. The women I discuss are diverse: some rich, some poor; some Sephardi, some Ashkenazi; some born enslaved, some who were slave owners themselves. In creating these biographies, I propose a new methodology for early American Jewish women's history, one that could be applied to other areas in Jewish history for which records are sparse. This method looks at both material objects and fragmentation as important evidence for understanding the past. What social and religious structures, I ask, caused early Jewish women to disappear from the archives?

First, looking past texts to material culture expands our ability to understand early Jewish American women's lives and restores some of their agency as creators of Jewish identity. While the vast majority of early American texts about Jewish women were written by men, with men as the primary intended audience, objects made for and by Jewish women help us consider women as consumers and creators of identity. Everyday objects such as cups, portrait miniatures, commonplace books, and silhouettes provide windows into those women's daily lives, highlighting what they themselves valued, how they wanted their contemporaries to see and understand them, and how they passed identity on to their children and grandchildren.

Studying Jewish women's material culture also augments how we understand Judaism as a religion. As Janet Hoskins notes, "Gendered religious objects are 'statements' addressed not only to the eye but to the emotions, and part of a complex cultural field in which things can play important roles in people's lives."[21] Focusing on Jewish women's everyday objects can help us understand the role of emotion and subjectively experienced feelings—what theorists call "affect"—in Jewish religious life. Objects like Reyna Levy's silver cups and Sarah Ann Hays Mordecai's commonplace book, for example, clarify the vital but shifting role love played in creating Jewish families.

Turning to Jewish women's material culture shifts the study of religion from the synagogue to the family and, in doing so, clarifies a key change in Jewish life as "Jewishness" began to dance on the borderline between religion and culture. At first, my choice of objects for understanding Jewishness between 1750 and 1850 may seem odd, as the "Jewishness" of each object I have chosen is subjective or questionable rather than obvious. Typically, early American Jewish artifacts typically found in museum collections or still used by Jews today tend to be ritual artifacts handled by men, such as the matzah board owned by the Touro Foundation in Newport, Rhode Island; a shofar from colonial Surinam; and the silver

Torah finials made by colonial Jewish silversmith Myer Myers, which are still used every Rosh Hashanah by Congregation Shearith Israel (fig. 1). In contrast, the objects in this book are quotidian objects that were most likely not used in religious rituals.

This choice is strategic. Each object in this book is more like the nineteenth-century teacup held in the Jewish Historical Museum in

Fig. 1. Myer Myers, Torah finials, 1766–76. Silver; height: 14½ in., base diam.: 1⅓ in. Congregation Shearith Israel.

Amsterdam than the 1803 coconut kiddush cup found in London's Jewish Museum (figs. 2–5). The kiddush cup not only has a known owner but also a clear Jewish ritual purpose that is mirrored in both the images and the inscriptions carved into the coconut shell. In contrast, the teacup did not fulfill an obvious religious purpose. Whereas kiddush cups were commonly used during the colonial period to mark the beginning of the Sabbath and holidays, teacups were not. Like the teacup, however, the objects in this book think of Jewishness as something domestic, feminine, and plagued by loss. While all three scenes carved on the kiddush cup are from the Torah, the scene on the teacup is of a contemporary town. Also like the teacup, the objects I use in this book gender Jewish identity differently. Kiddush rituals were typically performed by men between 1750 and 1850, and each scene of the coconut kiddush cup is centered on men. Indeed, the only female is the biblical matriarch Sarah, who waits in the shadows while Abraham interacts with the visitors (fig. 5). In contrast, the person presiding over the serving and distribution of tea in nineteenth-century tea ceremonies was typically the most senior woman in the household or her designee, also typically female.[22]

Focusing on quotidian objects used by women help us understand not only their experiences but those of Jews more generally during this era, including men. Like the objects discussed in this book, the teacup represents an alternate way of thinking about Jewish identity that more accurately reflects Jews' daily struggles to understand what it meant to be Jewish in an era when legal restrictions against Jewish men were increasingly eliminated and Jews were often asked to cleanse themselves of Jewish difference in order to become citizens. The teacup's scene is of the plantation town, Jodensavanne, the only semiautonomous Jewish community in the Americas. As such it depicts an ideal space where Jews had the power to govern themselves. The cup also celebrates the town and the Jews' prosperity, as it was designed for imbibing the crops grown in Jodensavanne, such as coffee and sugar, which sweetened the tea. Yet this prosperous, autonomous ideal no longer existed by the 1820s. By the time the cup was made, the town was no longer the center of Surinamese Jewish life. Plantation crises in the 1770s and maroon uprisings had caused most inhabitants to relocate north to the port of Paramaribo. By the 1830, the synagogue—the largest and most elaborate building represented on the cup—had been burnt to the ground.

Thus, despite being the depiction of the town that most strongly correlates to the archeological record, the image is steeped in nostalgia. At the same time, the cup is inherently modern. Most likely made either in

Fig. 2. Jodensavanne teacup, ca. 1800–1840. Height: 3½ in, diam.: 4⅓ in. Courtesy of the Collection of the Jewish Historical Museum, Amsterdam.

Fig. 3. Men in early nineteenth-century dress performing kiddush, kiddush cup, 1803. Coconut shell. Jewish Museum, London, JM 401.

Fig. 4. People drinking from goblets, kiddush cup, 1803. Coconut shell. Jewish Museum, London, JM 401.

Fig. 5. Abraham giving hospitality to the three angels, kiddush cup, 1803. Coconut shell. Jewish Museum, London, JM 401.

Paris or Vienna, the cup reflects the stylish cosmopolitan nature of elite Jewish families in the early nineteenth century. Tea, coffee, and chocolate drinks are quintessentially modern beverages, brought to Europe and the colonies as part of the transoceanic trade.[23] Originally limited to society's elite, tea and coffee sets as well as furniture were purchased in order to "reproduce the ceremonies of respectability" and functioned as "signs of wealth or relative standing in class hierarchies."[24] Old Parisian porcelain, particularly with scenic vistas, was fashionable among American elites in the 1820s.[25]

Owning Old Parisian–style porcelain was also supercharged for early American Jews. In the era following the French occupation of the Netherlands, writing, reading, and speaking French was a marker of elite Surinamese Jewish status, in part because of the role the French played in Jewish emancipation. Likewise, Jews signaled their worthiness as full citizens by positioning themselves as part of the planter elite. When leaders of the Jewish community wrote to the Dutch king in August of 1816 regarding Jewish privileges in the colony, they noted that "to exclude the Israelites in the colony from any office or to place any distinction towards them, [would] make their condition in this way relatively worse than it has been before . . . [and] such a distinction would be doubly humiliating and without doubt would produce defiance which in a colony of plantation owners would be even more disastrous and could take away their prestige, without which it would be much more difficult to rule over the subordinates."[26] Failing to recognize Jews as planter elites threatened the safety of the colony.

Although used in everyday family life, the cup belongs to a key moment in Jewish history when Jews wanted to remind themselves and visitors to their homes of the central role Jews played in keeping the colony productive, safe, and respectable. The encoding of this message in a teacup is not incidental. Tea meals were "consciously regarded as a device for training in proper language and manners: for adults, a kind of refresher course (especially for men) . . . for children, education on how to act in the broader rituals of respectable society."[27] It was the job of the older women present and running the tea ritual to police this politeness. As such, the cup reminds us that the creation of Jewish identity was not self-evident, nor was it solely in the domain of the men, who tended to write petitions. Rather, as this book's title suggests, there is a certain *art* to the creation of both families and the stories people tell about their families, especially Jewish families. Women and the objects they owned were essential to the staging and performing of those stories.

If turning to everyday objects can help us challenge the silence regarding early American Jewish women, a second new strategy for rethinking the early history of American Jews is to address the reasons behind the silence in the archive. Here again the teacup is useful. While the coconut

Fig. 6. Broken handle of Jodensavanne teacup, ca. 1800–1840. Courtesy of the Collection Jewish Historical Museum, Amsterdam.

kiddush cup remains whole, the Jodensavanne teacup is broken, missing its handle (fig. 6).

The objects in this book are similarly plagued by fissures and silence. Like the broken Surinamese teacup, even when texts related to early American Jewish women do appear in the archives, they often come in the form of fragments. They represent random moments in what were surely complex lives. The lives they evoke are missing pieces that will most likely never be found. Yet, as Marisa Fuentes notes, "the very call to 'find more sources' about people who left few if any of their own reproduces the same erasures and silences they experienced . . . by demanding the impossible."[28] For Fuentes, the historian's job is not to find all the pieces but to explain what caused the splintering and erasure of lives.

To this end, I have deliberately chosen women about whom little has been written. In some cases, such as that of Reyna Levy Moses, all that exists is a sentence defining her death and birth dates, and the names of two men in her family, her father and husband. I was drawn to these women in part because of the objects they owned but also because of the overwhelming sense of loss regarding their life stories. Theirs is, as Fuentes puts it, a "history of silence."[29] To be sure, not all silence is alike, as the women in this volume demonstrate. Some silence results from a lack of interest by people at the time in the perspectives of the poor or enslaved. Other silences—like the broken handle of the cup—seem to be the result of accidents. Other absences arise from what descendants chose to throw away and what to keep—and, just as crucially, what they considered was worth donating to archives.

At the same time, silence is not altogether random. Like social history more generally, the history of silence is one of patterns. As Steffi Hobuß explains, "Silence is not only absence of speech or absence of activity, but also a socially constructed space."[30] The decision of "who gets to speak and who remains silent, which stories are chosen and which are sidelined," is always subject to negotiation between archivists, curators, academics, and descendants.[31] However, archival silence is also a function of who in any particular era has the ability to write and has the money for ink and paper. The present volume pays particular attention to the role poverty, education, and health played in keeping women's voices from being recorded, and the way early American laws, economies, and religious institutions often kept women from being able to become part of the written record or from writing in the genres that tend to be valued by archives. These social structures changed between 1750 and 1850. As women's opportunities transformed, so did the objects they owned and created.

Yet despite the advances in women's rights by 1850, the fragmentary nature of the textual archive is still present in material culture from this era. Although the Jodensavanne teacup contains a rich brew of information, there are questions about it and its owner that will probably never be answered. Vital information about women's objects from this era is often missing or subject to conjecture. In the case of the teacup, the handle is literally missing, but so too is information about who bought it and used it and how it was passed down to the person who donated it to the Jewish Historical Museum in Amsterdam before the start of WWII. The teacup itself also has years missing from its history. Following the Nazi occupation of the Netherlands, the cup was confiscated by the Germans, only to be returned after the war. Where did it go? What did the confiscators think it meant? Why did they take it? While we know who owned each of the five objects this book is concerned with, we are missing critical *facts* for each of them. Rather than obscuring these holes in the record, I have chosen to highlight those absences and consider their significance.

Most studies of early American Jews have relied upon the types of Jews who were liable to leave written records. These records were written primarily by wealthy men and a small handful of elite women, and they often focus on the synagogue that kept track of Jewish lives. Looking at objects and archival fragments and addressing the structural nature of silences provides a different vision of early American Jews. Relying on objects as well as texts helps recenter Jewishness in the family rather than the synagogue and enables us to talk about women who began (and sometimes ended) their lives in abject poverty. Emphasizing objects, fragments, and silences also nuances our sense of women's agency in the past. On the one hand, it makes visible the social forces that worked to silence women's voices. On the other hand, it underscores the very real ways women shaped how they would be remembered. Despite the significant constraints on their lives, eighteenth- and nineteenth-century women made decisions about what objects were worth keeping and passing along and to whom. These choices expand our understanding of the spatial dimension of acculturation. Examining the lives of these women and the objects they owned can help change our understanding of a place often seen as the heart of Jewish American life—New York.

Gender and the Changing Landscape of Early Jewish New York

Between 1750 and 1850, New York went from being one of many small Jewish communities on the Atlantic seaboard to the largest Jewish community in the Americas, a community whose size rivaled or surpassed many of the historic Western European Jewish centers. The population surge was only one part of the story; over the course of the century, the community shifted from Sephardic- to Ashkenazi-centered, and family structure metamorphosed as Jews adapted their marriage patterns to American life. The role women played in Jewish communities became more public. *The Art of the Jewish Family* looks at how Jews of early New York mediated the radical changes in their lives through material culture, particularly objects associated with displaying and maintaining the family.

Back in the 1750s, most colonists would have been hard pressed to predict New York's later popularity among Jews. It was not just that the town itself was small. In 1750, the largest, best-educated, and wealthiest Jewish American communities were all in the Caribbean. Both Surinam and Curaçao had somewhere between one and two thousand Jews living in their main ports, while New York's Jewish community hovered around three hundred. The French and Indian Wars and the American Revolutionary War changed New York's status. The wars not only disrupted trade but made life difficult in Caribbean colonies that tended to specialize in only a few crops and relied on trade for everyday essentials including food. In contrast, New York's diverse economy allowed the city to regenerate more quickly. Moreover, new technologies made the city a mercantile hub. The newly built Erie Canal, along with the Erie Railroad that connected the city to the waterway, gave New York City a tremendous advantage over other nearby ports.[32]

Thus when the collapse of Caribbean economies forced Jews to seek out new homes, New York beckoned. As a result, Jewish immigrants from the Caribbean as well as Europe sought out the city. While in 1743 New York was only the sixth most populous colony of the original thirteen U.S. colonies and the third largest city after Boston and Philadelphia, with slightly over eleven thousand inhabitants, by 1790 the city had over thirty-three thousand inhabitants and was the largest city in the United States.[33] Immigration continued to fuel its growth, and in 1850 New York was the first U.S. city to surpass five hundred thousand inhabitants.[34] The Jewish population jumped from three hundred to sixteen thousand.[35]

The Jewish communal landscape of the city also metamorphosed. Whereas in 1750 there was one synagogue (Shearith Israel), which served both Sephardic and Ashkenazi Jews but employed the Western Sephardic rite, by 1855 the city was home to ten congregations, with an eleventh in Brooklyn and with 3,825 Jews attending synagogue.[36] The vast majority of these new congregations were Ashkenazi. This makeup made sense, as many of the city's new immigrants were from Germany, though Jews from the Netherlands, England, and the Caribbean also helped remake New York into the largest Jewish city in the Americas. Jewish enlightenment and emancipation helped reshape belief. By 1850 most Jews in New York City did not belong to a synagogue at all, though some continued to purchase seats for the high holiday services.[37] One response to this increasing secular pull was the rise of the city's Jewish Reform movement, which emphasized ethical rather than ceremonial acts and thus denied the prerogatives of Talmudic and Torah law. Among traditionalists, a new "Orthodox" movement emerged to counteract the trends of increasing secularization and reform. These changes would also impact how the Jewish family was understood, ironically by increasing women's visibility.

Between 1750 and 1850, Jewish American women in New York

experienced radical changes in marriage and kinship patterns. In the first part of the eighteenth century, Atlantic World Jews used marriage strategically to create trade networks and maintain religious ties. Married women provided the necessary social glue that connected families across colonial towns. Many men married their daughters to merchants in other ports in order to ensure trading partners. Thus, while the rise of the Enlightenment had caused Christian marriages to shift from "arranged marriages as a social ideal" to partnerships in which "individuals were encouraged to marry for love," early Jewish American marriage contracts remained deeply tied to economics and social relations throughout the eighteenth century.[38] Jewish marriages tended to be more conservative because in the Atlantic World, women mattered deeply to kinship and Jewish culture. While wider New York society passed down property primarily through primogeniture, Jewish kinship was emphatically bilateral. Relatives on both a person's mother's and father's side were important for transferring property and wealth at death and marriage, as well as for the emotional networks they fostered. Yet despite this conservatism, by 1850 most Jewish marriages had changed dramatically. As Jewish immigrants became Americanized, they stopped seeking yoke mates (arranged marriages) and sought soul mates (love matches).[39]

The change in marriage patterns fundamentally altered Jewish kinship in America. The shift from arranged to romantic marriages changed the definition of what constituted the primary kin group. Just as marriage became less about fulfilling obligations to one's blood relatives, so too after women married, kinship with blood relatives began to carry less weight than kinship with one's spouse and his family. Jews were not alone in experiencing this change. Early American Christian women used fiction to respond to the anxieties caused by the shift in kinship from blood to conjugal ties. The novels they wrote rather unrelentingly dramatized problems with biological relatives.[40] Although Jewish women tended to write more in the genre of personal letters than fiction, early Jewish American literature shares this anxiety about biological obligations. Nineteenth-century Jewish American women who came from letter-writing families, such as the Gratzes and Mordecais, depict the struggles over where women's obligations lay.

The writings of early American Jewish women also wrestled with a second and parallel anxiety regarding kinship: namely, the breakdown of the Jewish people as they were traditionally defined. As marriage gained supremacy over biology, American Jews' sense of their kinship to the metaphoric Jewish family, the B'nei Yisrael (children of Israel), began to hold less sway—at least for men. Intermarriage rates doubled following the Revolutionary War, with intermarriage reaching a quarter to a third of marriages made by Jews between 1776 and 1840. This change in kinship was gendered. Men intermarried more frequently than women, and Jewish women disproportionately remained single, while their brothers married out.[41] Letters by Jewish American women respond to this marriage crisis and help redefine kinship during the era following the Revolutionary War. Letters by *single* Jewish women were particularly key in developing a new vision of Jewish kinship—a kinship that stressed the conjugal ties of their male relatives. At the same time women's roles in the Jewish nation became less about producing biological kin and more about nurturing the Jewish poor, educating Jewish youths, and fostering Jewish orphans. Women held the Jewish nation together through affective as much as biological bonds. Throughout this history, I explore how objects shaped the emotional landscape of American Judaism.

If focusing on objects reminds us of the role emotion played in New York Jewish history, so too the telling of Jewish American women's lives through the lens of New York challenges how we think about the city's place in Jewish studies. Of the five women featured in this study, all but one came to New York as adults. Each new wave of arrivals found themselves contributing to the city and Jewish life. While most discussions of Jewish immigration have focused on the impact of immigration from Europe to the city, migration *within* the Americas was equally crucial for reshaping the Jewish family. Early American Jewish women were incredibly mobile, relocating because of wars, marriage, and economic opportunity. None of the women in this book lived all of their lives either in New York City or New York State. Even Reyna Levy Moses, who like her mother was born in New York City, found herself fleeing to nearby Philadelphia during the Revolutionary War. Some of the women I feature, such as Sarah Ann Hays Mordecai, made the journey in the other direction, coming to New York State from Philadelphia after her marriage. Sarah Ann Hays Mordecai's story reminds us that New York was more than a city. Even as metropolitan New York grew, some women found themselves at its margins in smaller Jewish communities or in towns that lacked Jewish infrastructure altogether.

Migration from other parts of the Americas helped reshape Jewish women's lives in New York. While recent histories such as Philip Kasinitz, *Caribbean New York: Black Immigrants and the Politics of Race* (1992); Nancy Foner, *Islands in the City: West Indian Migration to New York* (2001); and Tammy L. Brown, *City of Islands: Caribbean Intellectuals in New York*

(2015) analyze the impact of Caribbean culture on the North American metropolis, few studies have thought about the impact of Caribbean migration on early America or on early American Jewish communities. Yet, as Yolanda Martínez–San Miguel points out, intracolonial migrations impact the way gender and sexuality as well as ethnicity and race are understood.[42] Chapters in this volume such as "Portrait in Ivory" underscore the Caribbean diaspora's key role in New York Jewish life.

Looking at changes in Jewish women's lives through the archetypal Jewish city of New York helps us better understand how that place came to be but also asks us to consider how gender has underlain previous histories of the city, if for no other reason than by virtue of those histories having centered their analysis on texts written by men. The modes of gender presented in women's texts and objects from this era are equally a product of their time. While the vision of women as emotionally rich nurturers may not appeal to us today, it played into the rise of the cult of true womanhood prominent in larger American society in the first half of the nineteenth century. Yet unlike antebellum Christians who often saw the domestic sphere as a "counterpoint to the competitive . . . marketplace, making the home a private refuge from the hustle and bustle of public life,"[43] Jews increasingly expanded the boundaries of the private domestic space into Jewish "public" spaces previously dominated by men.

Changes in Jewish women's lives over this century underscore how a binary model of gender came to dominate Jewish American life. According to Thomas Laqueur, between 1750 and 1850 a new discourse on gender began to replace the old "one-body" model of human anatomy that held "men and women had a common physiological existence."[44] Under the one-body model, gender was revealed and created through clothing and deportment rather than being rooted in the biology of the body. Objects helped mediate and create these changes. While clothing still supported gendered identities in the century around 1800, women began to be seen as "inherently different" in terms of anatomy and biology. Male and female bodies were suddenly "radically incommensurable."[45] By the 1840s, women's dress—particularly corsets—helped remake the ideal female body as radically different from that of both men and working women, whose physical activity precluded the "privilege" of tight lacing (figs. 7–9). Jewish women were neither immune from nor oblivious to the physical toll corsets took on their bodies. "Our Hetty Seixas has been in a poor way these 3 weeks past, bringing up Blood," Grace Seixas Nathan remarked, "which the Doctors say is the Consequence of *tight Corsets*, and I believe it firmly to be the case."[46]

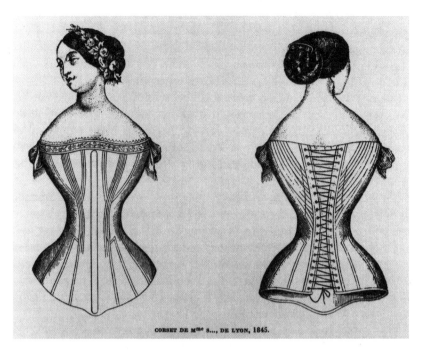

Fig. 7. "Corset de Mme S . . . de Lyon, 1845." Montpellier, 1847.

Physically rebuilding their bodies was only one of the ways Jews in early America participated in the rethinking of gender. Whereas the regency style of Sarah Brandon Moses's 1815 gown (chapter 3) relied on long, relatively loose stays, the narrow waist and full skirt of the 1840s dress worn by Jane Symons Isaacs (chapter 5)—like that of Rachel Jacobs—relied on petticoats and corsets (fig. 10). The changes in portraiture addressed in this volume, such as the surge in popularity of silhouettes, highlights this new incommensurability by emphasizing women's profiles shaped by corsets. That is, just as Jewish women took on more public roles, society increasingly marked their bodies as inherently other. Thus, when Jane's husband, Samuel Myer Isaacs, argued for women's importance to traditional Judaism, he did so based on claims of women's *difference* rather than their equality.

This tension between rights and difference was part and parcel of the experience of Jews in antebellum New York. Jews' legal status had changed between 1750 and 1850, most notably with Jewish men regaining the right to vote and hold public office in 1777. Yet as Jews gained civil equality, anti-Semites increasingly depicted Jewish difference in physical

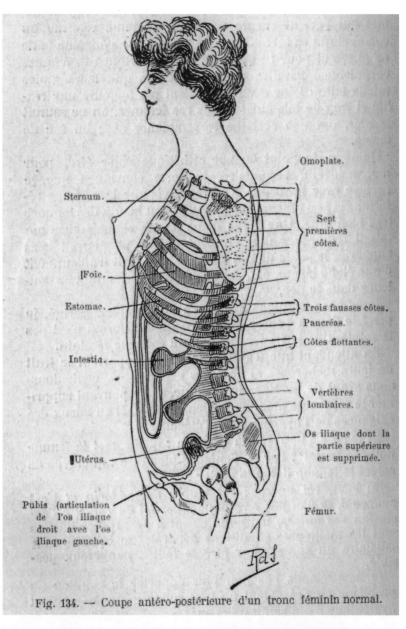

Sternum.

Omoplate.

Sept
premières
côtes.

[Foie.

Estomac.

Trois fausses côtes.
Pancréas.

Côtes flottantes.

Intestia.

Vertèbres
lombaires.

Os iliaque dont la
partie supérieure
est supprimée.

Utérus.

Pubis (articulation
de l'os iliaque
droit avec l'os
iliaque gauche.

Fémur.

Fig. 134. — Coupe antéro-postérieure d'un tronc féminin normal.

Fig. 8. Before: How corsets reshaped and remade female bodies to be "radically incommensurable" with male bodies. From Ludovic O'Followell, *Le corset: Historie—Médicine—Hygiène* (Paris: A. Maloine, 1908), 278.

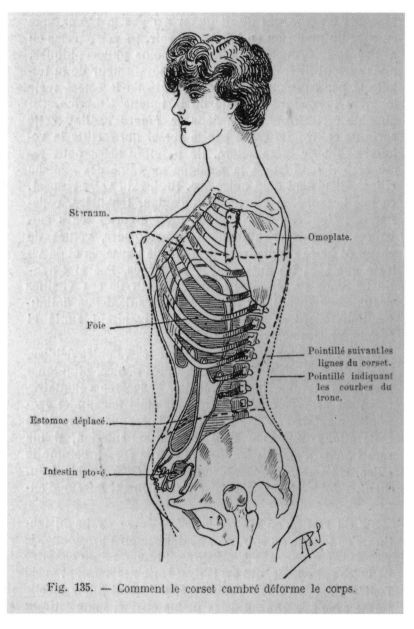

Sternum.

Omoplate.

Foie

Pointillé suivant les
lignes du corset.

Pointillé indiquant
les courbes du
tronc.

Estomac déplacé.

Intestin ptosé.

Fig. 135. — Comment le corset cambré déforme le corps.

Fig. 9. After: How corsets reshaped and remade female bodies to be "radically incommensurable" with male bodies. From O'Followell, *Le corset*, 279.

Fig. 10. Augustin Amant Constant Fidèle Edouart, *Silhouette of Rachel Jacobs*, 1843, showcasing the new female body made possible by tight lacing. 9⅓ × 7⅓ in. Courtesy of AJHS.

rather than spiritual terms. Jewish inferiority was often evoked through comparisons between Jews and African Americans, a comparison hotly refuted by at least some New York Jews. As the editor of the *National Advocate* newspaper, Mordecai Manuel Noah openly distrusted so-called Africans and argued, "It is perfectly ridiculous to give them the right of suffrage—a right which in this city, particularly in the federal wards, is a mere vendible article."[47] Thus Noah complained about "black" New Yorkers who tried to "'ape' the 'respectable' whites" through their dress. Noah's attempts to distance "black" New Yorkers from recently emancipated Jews relies upon a binary that all Jews were "white" and all "blacks" were Christian, yet, as the story of Sarah Brandon Moses and her portrait shows, this was not the case. In important ways, these biographies should help remind us that "Ashkenormativity" (the assumption Jews are either by default Ashkenazim or white[48]) came into being during this era as a function of changes in immigration and culture.

Overview of the Chapters

Prioritizing the changes Jewish women's lives underwent in New York between 1750 and 1850 alters our understanding of Jewish history, women's history, and the history of religion. The century marks a key change in the lives and self-conception of both women and Jews, as fundamental changes displaced prior understandings of kinship, gender, and race. The chapters that follow look at how five Jewish women used objects to grapple with these changes.

The first chapter, "Paper Fragments," examines a letter written in 1761 by Hannah Louzada requesting financial aid from Congregation Shearith Israel, the city's oldest synagogue. The letter represents one fleeting moment from the life of a woman who would most likely have been forgotten had her letter not accidentally survived. I suggest that to best understand her life and the average Jewish American woman's life in the 1750s to 1760s, we should read her letter and talk about four structural sources of fragmentation that contributed to her erasure: poverty, education, laws, and mental illness. These four forces, I argue, were not unique to Hannah but rather contributed to the gaps in the archive. They are key to understanding that overwhelming lack of evidence about early Jewish American women that scholars have noted. This study presents the benefits of taking a structural approach to silence. Sometimes silence itself must testify.

"Pieces of Silver," the second chapter, looks at six silver beakers owned by Reyna Levy Moses (1753–1824). Forged by Reyna's uncle, silversmith Myer Myers, the cups were given to Reyna and her husband, possibly to mark their wedding, and then were passed down through their family for generations. Today the cups are recognized as significant works of Jewish art: two of the beakers are housed in the Winterthur Museum in Delaware, three at the Metropolitan Museum of Art in New York, and one in private hands. Yet most studies of the cups have focused on the Jewishness of the beakers' maker. In contrast, I shift the discussion of the silver away from maker to owner, from the ritual space of the synagogue to the Jewish home, and from men to women. I also put the marriage that inspired the cups back at the center of the discussion. Atlantic World Jews had used marriage strategically to create trade networks and maintain religious ties, and women provided an essential social glue that connected families across colonial ports. Like the large dowry of silver that passed between her father and husband, Reyna's cups reveal the compelling way early American Jews used silver both ritually and domestically to bind generations together.

The third chapter, "Portrait in Ivory," focuses on an ivory miniature made around 1815 of Sarah Brandon Moses (1798–1829). Born enslaved in Barbados, Sarah travelled to early Suriname to convert before arriving in London, where she was educated and met her husband, Joshua Moses, an Ashkenazi Jew from New York. After her marriage, she moved to New York. By her death in 1828, Sarah had reached the pinnacle of New York's wealthy Jewish elite. Once labelled "mulatto" or "colored" by her own enslaver and record keepers,[49] by 1820 Sarah and her children had been recategorized as "white" by New York's census and accepted as such by the New York Jewish community.[50] Her miniature was key to this transformation. In general scholars have ignored the style of miniatures of early American Jews. I argue this is a mistake. Genre and technique not only matter but are inextricably linked to the biographical story that the miniatures were designed to convey. In Sarah's case, her miniature was tied to racecraft in this era and helps us understand how Jews navigated whiteness as they built their families.

"Commonplace Things," the fourth chapter, examines a commonplace book written by Sarah Ann Hays Mordecai (1805–1894) on and off between 1823 and her death. Unlike the previous women I discuss, Sarah Ann Hays married for love and without the dowry or prior permission that traditionally signaled parental interference.[51] Her commonplace book provides a unique vantage point for viewing the shifts in Jewish women's lives that made her choices possible. Commonplace books are collections of quotes, images, and ideas valued by an individual. Antebellum women's commonplace books were highly social: women used them to build and establish friendships and to place other women at the center of their emotional lives. Through her book, Sarah Ann created a series of networks and relationships that would last her a lifetime. In later years when her marriage bore an almost unbearable stress, those networks proved to be a safety net. Sarah Ann's book and story mark a key change in marriage structures and women's use of affective bonds to create kinship.

The fifth and final chapter, "Family Silhouettes," looks at a portrait Auguste Edouart, the world's most famous silhouette maker, created of Jane Symons Isaacs (1823–84) and her young family. Although born poor in London's East End, Jane married Samuel Myer Isaacs, a rising star of traditional Judaism, when she was barely sixteen. Her husband would take on leadership roles in two key early Orthodox congregations in New York, B'nai Jeshurun and Shaaray Tefila. The Isaacses' family portrait displayed the values they held dear, particularly a highly visible attention to mitzvot and a new emphasis on women's roles in maintaining Jewish traditions. In addition to making women's roles in perpetuating Jewish families more public, Samuel placed women at the center of Jewish education and encouraged elite women to form Female Benevolent Societies, forerunners of today's synagogue sisterhoods.[52] Jane helped showcase the new ideal woman's role as "a most perfect helpmate."[53] Her role in her family marked the long road Jewish women had travelled since the 1750s. Once silenced by poverty, lack of education, and financial dependence, Jewish American women of the 1840s now found that changes in Jewish communal structure and American law meant women of the next generation would make their way into the archives in greater numbers.

Taken together, these five chapters reveal the shift in the Jewish family toward conjugal kinship and the new role women and emotions played in the Jewish family writ large. Although only five individual lives, the stories of Hannah, Reyna, Sarah, Sarah Ann, and Jane give voice to the forces that have kept Jewish women silent and the changes that shaped their lives.

ONE

Paper Fragments

To gather in this great harvest of truth was no light or speedy
work. His notes already made a formidable range of volumes,
but the crowning task would be to condense these voluminous
still-accumulating results and bring them, like the earlier vintage
of Hippocratic books, to fit a little shelf.
—George Eliot, *Middlemarch*

After the Reverend Jacques Judah Lyons was laid to rest in the hallowed
ground of Beth Olam Cemetery in Queens in August of 1877, his wife,
Grace Nathan Lyons, and their three children were left with the long process of sorting through his library at the three-story house at 7 West 19th
Street, adjacent to the monumental fourth Shearith Israel Synagogue
(fig. 11). The task must have been overwhelming, as Jacques was one of
the most passionate early collectors of American Judaica.[1] Like a char-
ismatic Jewish Casaubon, his interests were wide ranging, and his note
taking formidable. Born in Suriname in 1813, Jacques had been the spiritual leader of both Paramaribo's Neveh Shalom and Richmond's Beth
Shalome before settling in for thirty-eight years as the rabbi of New York's
premier synagogue, Congregation Shearith Israel. Sadly, like Eliot's unfortunate cleric, Jacques died before he could begin writing his *Key to All
Early American Jews*. Eventually the family gave up on organizing his notes
and boxed away his collection for over forty years. Yet in time, those boxes
would shape the way New York Jewish history was written, and particularly
women's role—or lack thereof—in early American Jewish life.

Fig. 11. House of Jacques Judah Lyons and Grace Nathan Lyons, to the left of the domed building of Congregation Shearith Israel's Fourth Synagogue on West 19th Street. From William S. Pelletreau, *Early New York Houses* (New York: F. P. Harper, 1900), 175.

It is hard to know to what extent Grace abetted or despaired of her husband's obsession. To be sure, their 1842 marriage had made the collection all the more personal. Grace's lineage was at the intersection of most of the prestigious genealogies of early American Jewry. Named for her maternal grandmother, Grace was closely related to the congregation's most important early leader, Gershom Mendes Seixas. Moreover, large numbers of papers from Grace's family ended up in Jacques's collection, though certainly some items—such as the poems written by Grace's beloved grandmother—had escaped either Jacques's interest or grasp.[2] Grace may have helped finance her husband's hobby as well, albeit perhaps inadvertently. As the sister of stockbroker Benjamin Nathan, she certainly brought money to their marriage.[3] She also inherited an additional $5,000 after her brother's murder in 1870.[4] Grace's feelings about her husband's collection, however, are noticeably absent from his voluminous records.

Whatever Grace's thoughts were, for the final sixteen years of his life, Jacques had balanced collecting trips against his pastoral duties. Members of his congregation were not immune to his obsession. Shearith Israel's oldest families, including the Philipses, Gomezes, Noneses, and Judahs, all donated valuable relics to the growing collection. Jacques was nothing if not methodical. Precious items crossed his desk only to be tucked away in his vast notebooks: correspondence of Jews with George Washington, early circumcision registers, books of *slichot* from Suriname, as well as hundreds and hundreds of small scraps of writing. Although interested in Canada, the Caribbean, and other parts of the United States, Jacques's favorite topic was early New York, and every historian of the city's Jews henceforth would be indebted to what he compiled. Eventually materials related to Jacques's role as minister of Shearith Israel would be sequestered in the congregation's archives, and his print library would be housed at what is now the Jewish Theological Seminary. But in 1908, the couple's three children specifically donated Jacques's manuscripts, newspaper clippings, scrapbooks, notebooks, and photographs to the American Jewish Historical Society, the country's oldest ethnic historical organization, which was also located at the Jewish Theological Seminary at the time. Five years and much work later, the papers would be published as the Lyons Collection.[5]

While most of the Lyons Collection relates to famous men in early Jewish communities, nestled in the albums are a few records by or about early Jewish women, typically in dialogue with the KKSI (Kahal Kadosh Shearith Israel) synagogue. There is a 1796 note, for instance, from Mrs. G. Philips regarding her husband's punishment by the congregation, an

1819 letter from Grace's great-aunt Anne Seixas acknowledging a $200 allowance, and a copy of a 1751 marriage contract between Haym Myers and Rachel Louzada. Also somewhat astonishingly, there is a list of girls who had attended the KKSI school in 1795. Most of New York's earliest Jewish records—those prior the 1770s—do not survive. Miraculously, of those that do, one of the very earliest is a small petition penned by Rachel Louzada's mother, Hannah, to Congregation Shearith Israel requesting financial aid on November 9, 1761 (fig. 12). Like many of Jacques's precious scraps, Hannah's letter provides a small window onto the everyday lives of Jewish women belonging to New York's first congregation. Unlike the records of Grace's family, however, this scrap offers a glimpse into the world of New York's Jewish poor.

Hannah Louzada writes:

Sir,

j [I][6] take the liberty to wright to yow now[.] j [I] think the at [that] is time for yow to get my Wenters [winter's] ase Provisions[,] likewise a little money to bay some Wood for the Wenter[.] j [I] would a Come down my self to feetchet [fetch it], but ben desebled[,] my legs heving swelds [swellings.] but j [I] hope [sir] that at ensent [ancient proverb] not aut a sigt aut of mind [will apply to me.] sir[,] hier j [I] lay suffering for the [ ] want of wood and provisions[.] j [I] Remende sir your

   Most humble servent

      hanne Lezade

Remember My Love to your Espouse and the Reste of your familey

Hannah's letter is at once extraordinary and utterly mundane. Perhaps what is most obvious is that the fragment is from what was surely a complex life. It reflects a seemingly random moment in the life of a woman, who would most likely have been entirely forgotten had her letter not accidentally survived. What is not random, however, is the lack of evidence about Hannah herself. Texts by early American Jewish women are rare, and the records that do survive are often fragmentary. Their lives feel almost impossible to piece back together.

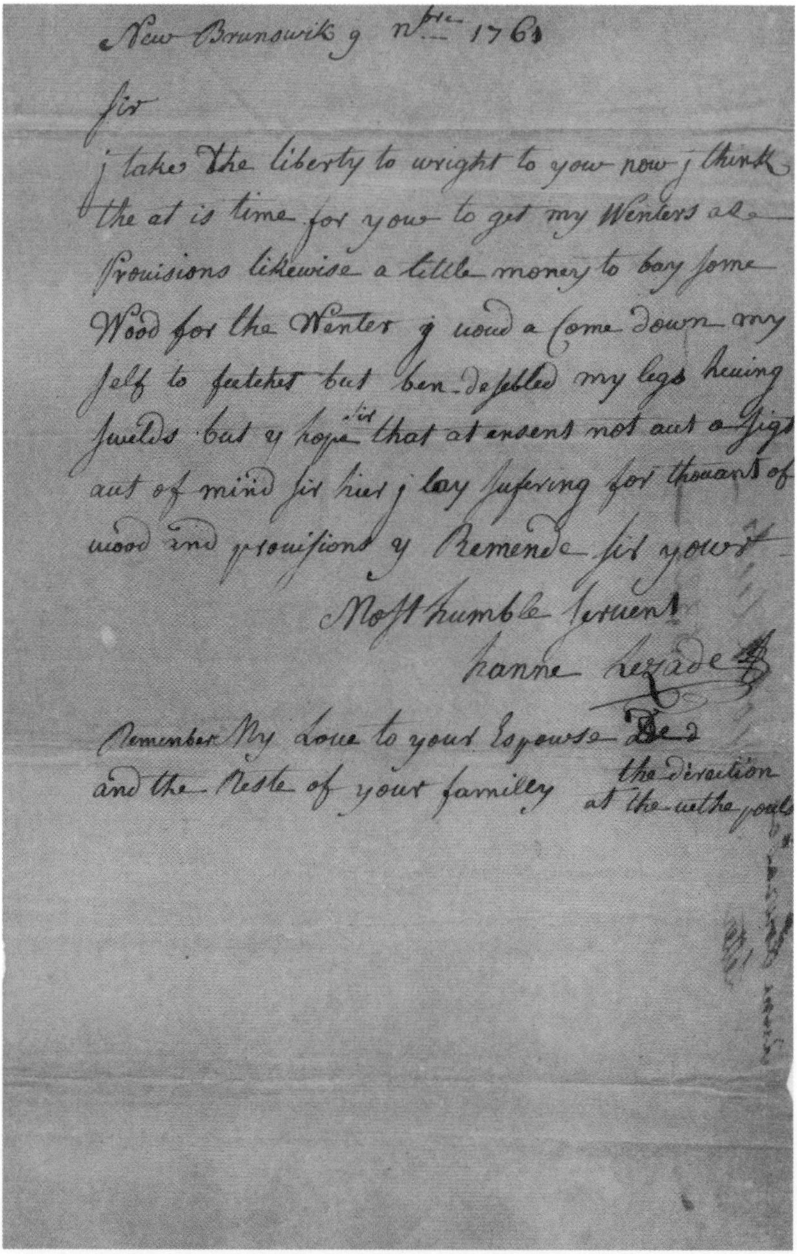

New Brunswick 9 n[ber] 1761

Sir

j takes the liberty to wright to you now j think
the at is time for you to get my Winters al
prouisions likewise a little money to bay some
Wood for the Winter j woud a come down my
self to fatches but ben desbled my legs heuing
sweld but y hope[s] that at ensent not aut a sig[t]
aut of mind sir hier j lay sufering for thousand of
wood and prouisions y Remende sir your

                    Most humble seruant

                         hanne lezade

Remember My Loue to your Espowse
and the Reste of your familley   the direction
                                      at the uether souls

Fig. 12. "Application for assistance from Hanna[h] Louzada, New
Brunswick, N.J.," Nov. 9, 1761. Papers of Jacques Judah Lyons, P-15.
Courtesy of AJHS.

The fragmentary nature of Hannah's letter is a poignant reminder of the way in which archives resemble archeological sites. Museums tend to display only the best-preserved artifacts, even though fragments make up the majority of what is found during excavations. When I was doing archival research in Barbados in 2016, for example, I went by the synagogue complex, which was currently under renovation. One of the great discoveries revealed during the project was a set of luminous marble gravestones of leaders of the synagogue: men like Isaac de Piza Massiah the *shamash* (warden), Israel Abaddy the *hazzan* (synagogue official), and Aaron Pinheiro the "Ruler of our Congregation and a Merchant of this Island."[7] The tombstones were exquisite, in nearly pristine condition, having lain under the floorboards of shops for over a century and a half. Less exquisite but much more numerous were the other debris uncovered by the nearby construction: hundreds of shards of blue-and-white pottery known as delftware, lying just beneath the topsoil.

Since at the time I was then busy tracing the lineage of a Jewish family who had begun their lives enslaved to other Jews, I was intrigued by these broken serving utensils, which surely had been touched by the hands of enslaved people. There were originally four houses in the synagogue compound, and I knew from synagogue records that several enslaved women either lived or worked in the complex. Most likely they had served people with these very plates. Yet, when I visited the archives in both Bridgetown and London, it was nearly impossible to find even the most basic information about the enslaved women who labored in the complex. Only the smallest shards of their lives were left.

From what objects did the fragments on the cemetery's floor come? Plates, cups, bowls? Maybe the dishes had once been used to serve elegant meals amidst silver and lace on a mahogany table in Bridgetown. Yet somehow their remains had ended up in a trash pit—broken either by accident or perhaps by the 1780 or 1831 hurricanes that toppled the houses in the complex. The fragments are symbols of the fabric of daily life, the things people typically think are not worth keeping.

Hannah Louzada's letter is like one of those sharp fragments. I could hunt and sift through the synagogue complex for weeks and never find the rest of the dish from which the one shard in my hand came. Likewise, we will probably never know all of Hannah's story—too many pieces are simply gone.

We can ask, though, what forces ruptured Hannah's life and broke it into pieces. Hannah was a poor woman asking for charity. Why was she impoverished, like so many Jewish widows of the time? To best understand her life and the lives of average Jewish American women in the third quarter of the eighteenth century, we should reexamine her letter and consider four structural sources that splintered her life: poverty, education, laws, and mental illness. These four forces were not unique to Hannah but rather contributed to the gaps in the archive, that overwhelming lack of evidence about her and other early Jewish American women that scholars have noted. Silence is its own kind of evidence.

Women and Poverty

Petitions for charity played a decisive role in early American Jewish life. Jews have long placed a value on caring for their own, and giving *tzedakah* (charity) is considered an important mitzvah (obligation, good deed) that has the power to heal the soul and overturn negative decress from heaven. Yet petitions for charity were also important because poverty was rampant among early American Jews. Early scholarship on colonial Jews written in the 1930s to 1970s often focused on "merchant princes"— men who ruled Jewish communities and wielded great power by virtue of their wealth and economic prowess. This makes sense: successful merchants left extensive records. The princes also exemplified the American dream, thereby creating a pleasing and usable past for later Jewish arrivals.[8] Yet by the second half of the eighteenth century, most major Jewish communities in the Atlantic World were overwhelmed by caring for the poor. The Inquisition and natural disasters like the 1755 Lisbon earthquake had set Iberian refugees in motion. They were joined by Jews from Italian and German states fleeing war and hostilities and those from Eastern Europe escaping pogroms.

Their arrival meant that the vast majority of Jews even in "wealthy" communities like Amsterdam and London were predominantly poor. For the first two hundred years, only 4 to 7 percent of Amsterdam's Sephardic community owned more than 2,250 guilders. Even this wealth was moderate (by way of contrast, Rembrandt's house on Jodenbreestraat— only two blocks from the Portuguese Synagogue—cost 13,000 guilders in 1639). Sixty to 84 percent of Amsterdam's Sephardim possessed less than 500 guilders, and 16 to 31 percent of congregants lay somewhere in between these two extremes of wealth and poverty. By the end of the eighteenth century, this middle group had shrunk further, swelling the ranks of the impoverished such that by 1780, 65 percent of the community was on poor relief. European centers solved the problem by giving poor Jews a one-way ticket to the colonies, thereby passing the problem along.[9]

Many congregations that were drowning in poor had singled out women as part of the problem. From 1740 to 1741, nearly half of Shearith Israel's budget went toward helping the poor, with women receiving the largest amount of aid and for the longest periods of time.[10] This gendered trend reflected that of the feeder communities to the colonies. As early as 1619, Amsterdam's Portuguese Jewish community identified women as a substantial part of the burden posed by the poor.[11] Poor women, however, continued to flood into Jewish metropoles and quickly outnumbered men needing poor relief from synagogues. Widowed women had a particularly hard time escaping the circle of poverty.[12] By the eighteenth century, some Jewish congregations had specific *hevrot* (organizations) to help impoverished women, a development that would be reflected in the Americas in the rise of Jewish women's aid societies in the early nineteenth century.[13]

Not surprisingly, then, requests for money are one of three main types of writings by or about early Jewish American women. Most early records about these women were written by men. Typically, women appear in the minutes of synagogue boards in what I refer to as the "triangle of discontent": either they are mentioned in passing in association with life cycles; they have allegedly "misbehaved"; or (like Hannah) they are requesting charity. With the exception of weddings and marriage contracts, these records are almost all painful. The most common life event for which women are mentioned are death records. These records are all the more poignant when women die in childbirth or of diseases that today are easily preventable.[14]

Rarer but more fun to read about are moments of "misbehavior." Although these moments stand out to us because the perpetrators seem delightfully rebellious, they were clearly painful for those involved, as the instances are almost always recorded because the women were censured or punished. Two cases in point involve a bath attendant who allowed enslaved women to use the Surinamese or Barbadian *mikva'ot* (ritual baths)[15] and Mrs. Gomes of Bridgetown, who grew tired of her aging husband and took to the town. When confronted by the synagogue board with how she had "disgraced" the community, "Mrs. Gomes came up and behaved in a most scandalous & indecent mann[er]" and declared she would continue to do whatever she wanted.[16]

Sadly, such instances of rebellion are few and far between. Although Laurel Thatcher Ulrich famously remarked, "Well-behaved women seldom make history,"[17] in early Jewish communities, women *had* to "behave well" to get money to eat. Congregants often needed to prove formally or informally that they were "a deserving object of charity"—a category that not only encompassed need but also moral worthiness.[18] It was not enough to be old, infirm, or unable to work. One had to keep out of trouble, be of good standing in the synagogue, and stay away from vice. In London, for example, Sephardic women who received free medical attention needed to submit themselves to regulations regarding "order and good behavior."[19] Gaming or alcohol and tobacco use could lead to punishment by the *parnassim* (leaders) of the charitable institution.[20]

Yet many women could not afford *not* to ask for help. Their petitions were often to cover the most basic of necessities. Mrs. Fonseca of Barbados, for example, pleaded for clothes for her son; Mrs. Abrams of New York requested funds to leave the colonies after her husband died; Hannah Louzada requested money to buy food and wood in order to survive a cold northeastern winter.[21] They pleaded because women had extremely limited options for making money without losing social standing.[22] While colonial American women might increase their fortune as storekeepers, actresses, or hoteliers, the most lucrative of these options was negatively correlated with the "womanly virtue" and the piety associated with white female privilege. Jewish widows whose husbands had run profitable businesses, like Esther Pinheiro, Esther Brown, Rachel Luis, Simja De Torres, and Rebecca Gomez, were often able to prosper.[23] Those whose husbands had failed to thrive had less to build on after their husbands' deaths. Hannah, for example, appears to have kept a store, but was unsuccessful and had to request funds from Shearith Israel to pull herself out of debt.[24] Cut out of colonial economies, women's pleading relied on ritual abasement to powerful men.

Hannah's letter only exists because of how charity worked in early America. Although the poor could often receive a pension from state and local governments, it rarely was enough to live on. Those who could not get by on the pension had two options. Prior to the 1730s, the poor were commonly cared for in the homes of their neighbors, with Jews caring for other Jews. Economic depressions, surges of poor immigrants, and outbreaks of measles and smallpox had changed the "in care model."[25] Starting in 1734, New York City ran an almshouse adjacent to the city common, with shelter for the "deserving poor" and a workhouse for the "unworthy" (figs. 13 and 14). Yet even the deserving were expected to work if able, performing tasks such as "sewing, spinning, laundering, cooking, baking, caring for orphans, or picking oakum in return for food, clothing, and shelter."[26] Collecting oakum was a terrible task that involved "picking apart old salt and tar incrusted ship lines so that hemp fibers could be then sold and used for calking in ships."[27] It was a recipe for painfully cracked, raw hands. Although there has been heated debate about just how bad the new institutions were, at least some scholars have suggested they represented a "new, more mean-spirited attitude" toward the poor, which many found "intolerable."[28] Those who set up such institutions clearly saw them as places for those of extremely low social standing; one colonist described an almshouse as "a sort of calaboose [jail] for unruly slaves."[29] New Brunswick was hardly any better: the poor were officially at the mercy of the town, and poor women could expect their children to be taken from them and apprenticed.[30]

Those who could not get by on city pensions alone but still wanted to escape the indignity of the almshouse or workhouse needed to supplement their payments with firewood, food, or extra stipends from the congregations to which they belonged.[31] For Hannah, this meant she would

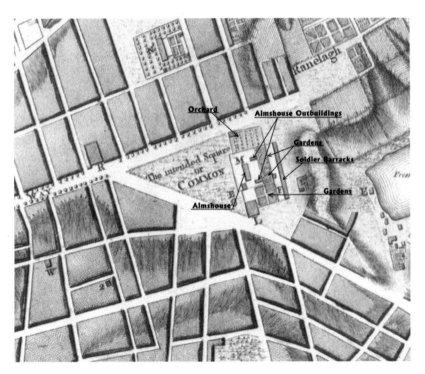

Fig. 13. Site of the New York City almshouse on John Montresor's *Plan of the City of New-York*, 1775. Based on Sherene Baugher, "Visible Charity: The Archaeology, Material Culture, and Landscape Design of New York City's Municipal Almshouse Complex, 1736–1797," *International Journal of Historical Archaeology* 5, no. 2 (2001): 182.

Fig. 14. David Grim, *New York City Almshouse, 1722–44* (1813). From Stokes, *The Iconography of Manhattan Island, 1498–1900* (New York: Robert H. Dodd, 1915), vol. 1, plate 32a.

need to rely on the good graces of the Jewish community. Back when New York was New Amsterdam, the West India Company had made it clear that Jews could immigrate only so long as "the poor among them [the Jews] shall not become a burden to the Company or the community, but be supported by their own [Jewish] nation."[32] As there were no Jewish congregations in New Jersey at the time,[33] Hannah applied for assistance to the closest synagogue, of which her husband and brother-in-law had both been members.

Hannah's application is an important reminder that Jewish communities did not adhere to colonial boundaries but rather encompassed people who flowed into surrounding areas. From Shearith Israel's point of view, Hannah was a member of the New York Jewish community and, as such, was their responsibility. Remaining a member of nearby congregations was important not only because synagogues provided essentials like matzah for Passover and kosher meat but also because synagogue membership functioned as a sort of "insurance" of the day. Since her husband had been a member of the congregation, Hannah should have been virtually guaranteed the right to a pension for reasons of poverty, old age, or illness. Indeed, she was given a grant in 1756 after her husband died and then remained on Shearith Israel's pension rolls at least as late as 1774.[34] By 1770 she was living in New York.[35] The letter from 1761 has her making a request for her "usual grant." Yet she still feels the need to argue her case of poverty, illness, and age using the language of supplication.

A supplicant is a fervently religious person who prays to God for help with her problems, but the term can also refer to someone who respectfully makes a humble plea to a person in power or authority.[36] In her letter, Hannah made sure to present herself as both. "I *take the liberty to wright to yow*," Hannah opens, as if she did not rest secure in the synagogue board's benevolence.[37] Likewise, she ends her letter with a colonial formula that underscores her subordinate status: "[I] remende sir your most humble servent." In making these gestures, Hannah relied upon eighteenth-century norms for letter writing. Although scholars have tended to focus on how the "middling sort" used the rules and conventions of letter writing to "pursue their claims to social refinement and upward mobility," letter writing was also necessary for the lower classes or those like Hannah who had fallen into poverty.[38] Even impoverished youths attending Eleazar Wheelock's "Indian School" (Moor's Charity School) in Lebanon, Connecticut, in the 1760s and 1770s were "schooled" in the art of proper letter writing.[39]

Both Jews and non-Jews in eighteenth-century America paid close attention to the marks of social deference when responding to charitable gifts from religious bodies. While signing a letter "your humble servant" or "your obedient servant" was to a certain extent a cliché, it was also an important means by which "inferiors signified their dependence on their Superior."[40] Polite eighteenth-century letters called attention to the social debt owed to those in power in ways that later generations might find painful. A case in point: in addition to signing her epistles "Your Most Obedient and Very Humble Servant," Montauk Indian Mary Occom wrote to Minister Eleazar Wheelock that it is "with Joy to hear that my Son has behaved himself so well" and thanked the minister "for taking so hard a task upon yourself as to take such a vile Creature as he was into your Care."[41] Eighteenth-century ministers in the northeastern colonies understood such self-abasement to be *positive* indicators of the "appropriate" humility the poor should display before God and his congregations.[42]

Minutes of various colonial synagogue boards similarly implied that the worthy poor should be grateful when receiving an *obra pia* (charitable gift). Moreover, synagogue boards assumed the poor's appreciation would be enduring. One board, for instance, railed against a man who was "so intoxicated with prosperity as to forget that he ever felt the chill gripe of Penury, and . . . is now ungrateful to God and Man."[43] Future wealth did not end the need for gratitude, it only reshaped it as an obligation to contribute to synagogue funds. At least one early Jewish congregation underscored that the *private* nature of religious charity magnified the debt the poor should feel.[44] Importantly, Hannah calls attention to her subordinate position in both her salutation and her valediction.

But being humble and grateful was not enough: Hannah also underscores her suffering. By including physical laments in her petition, Hannah accentuates her needs and aligns herself with the "deserving" poor. Analyses of English pauper letters have sometimes focused on how the poor failed to achieve the refined "schooled English" of the upper and middle classes by focusing on the poor's use of monosyllabic words, inadequate punctuation, Anglo-Saxon lexis, and clause tone groups (rather than sentences) as the major discourse units.[45] To be sure, Hannah's letter shares these attributes. Yet focusing on Hannah's linguistic flaws underplays the letter's rhetorical cleverness. Historian Claire Schen notes that the "men and women who beseeched parishes for relief sought to emphasize their genuine need by weaving 'true' stories of suffering . . . in[to] their accounts."[46] Such suffering aligned their bodies with biblical models like Job, who stood at the nexus of suffering, humility, and redemption.[47] We see this strategy at work in Hannah's letter when she reminds her reader that she is "desebled, my legs heving swelds." She also calls attention to how feeble she is: she is decrepit and lies "suffering for the want of wood and provisions." Hannah seems extremely aware that the synagogue board was more likely to fund the infirm, aged, and sick, and she presents herself as worthy of their attention.

Hannah's abasement was not all show. Women could not be elected to synagogue boards that distributed funds, and prior to the 1820s they did not play central roles in organized charities aimed at women and orphans. As someone dependent upon the congregation, Hannah lost much of the agency over her life. In 1756, for example, the congregation voted to help support her and her youngest son, Benjamin, but also "Resolved that Mrs. Hanah Louzada should be dispatched to Lancaster & her son Benja: should be maintain'd here [in New York] by the Congregation."[48] They could either starve together or live apart. Receiving charity shaped Hannah's life and the way she wrote.

Charity is the reason for Hannah's letter, but it also points to a structural reason our understanding of early Jewish women in New York is so fragmented. Although stylized in its pleas, Hannah's letter reflects real disparities in power between men and women and between those with and without means. Most impoverished early American Jews appear in synagogue records *only* when soliciting or receiving funds, the rest of their lives vanishing under the stigma of poverty. Yet the letter's survival is also surprising. Synagogues rarely held on to petitions written by the poor themselves, preferring instead to summarize the requests in board minutes.[49] Even board minutes got lost. Although Lyons was a dedicated collector of Shearith Israel's minute books, the first he found was numbered twenty-five, suggesting twenty-four earlier volumes had been misplaced or destroyed over time, though one would miraculously later turn up in London.[50] In this context, Hannah's letter is fairly phenomenal, a lone voice representing the hundreds of pleas now lost.

Perhaps its survival was due to the one rhetorical ploy Hannah made that I have not yet discussed: affection. In her postscript, Hannah asks that the unnamed Sir "Remeber My Love to your Espowse and the Reste of your familey," suggesting the families had once been close. Perhaps this is why the synagogue official who catalogued the letter under "accounts" decided to keep this scrap written by the woman he apparently knew better as Anne (fig. 15). In the end, Hannah's petitions for charity seem to have been successful in keeping her out of the almshouse, which started keeping track of arrivals and departures in 1758. Although the records are sketchy for the period before the Revolutionary War, Hannah's name does not appear.[51]

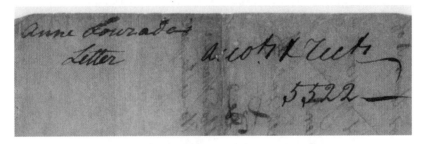

Fig. 15. Detail of verso, "Application for assistance from Hanna[h] Louzada, New Brunswick, N.J.," Nov. 9, 1761. Papers of Jacques Judah Lyons, P-15. Courtesy of AJHS.

Women and Education

Just as Hannah's letter showcases how charity disenfranchised Jewish women's voices, so too it calls attention to the role education played in creating the silences of early Jewish American women in the archives. Hannah's letter is "unschooled" in ways that resemble non-Jewish paupers' letters but arises out of a more distinctly Jewish—and Sephardic—history.

As I noted before, Hannah's letter uses an "open" rather than "schooled" form of English typical of other paupers' letters. Whereas refined or schooled English had been passed on for centuries "from master to apprentice in a scriptorium or printing workshop, or from teacher to pupil in a school or drawing room, using books as authority for what might be called 'best practice,'" open (or nonstandard) English was "free of Schooling but Open to other influences."[52] As one reader put it, Hannah writes in "phonetic and almost unintelligible English."[53] More specifically, her letter favors monosyllables, has no punctuation, rarely relies on Latinate vocabulary, and lacks the kind of sentence construction favored in elite eighteenth-century education. We see this in charming phrases like "j would a Come down my self to feetchet." Yet strangely her handwriting is actually quite lovely and fluid, differing markedly from the letters of other English paupers of the era, who often had to erase and start words again.[54] I would argue that Hannah's language was shaped by her not being a native speaker. The first hint of her linguistic history comes from her signature (fig. 16).

The curlicue under her name has a special name: *rúbrica*, meaning "flourish." It was an essential part of official signatures in Iberia and the Spanish colonies, such that a signature without a *rúbrica* was deemed less

Fig. 16. Signature from "Application for assistance from Hanna[h] Louzada, New Brunswick, N.J.," Nov. 9, 1761. Papers of Jacques Judah Lyons, P-15. Courtesy of AJHS.

authentic than a *rúbrica* alone. Those who could not sign their names used a *rúbrica* instead.[55] The *rúbrica* underneath a name was also typical of signatures of Sephardim who learned to write in Spanish and Portuguese during this era, though it was sometimes passed down for a generation or two after leaving Iberia.

More evidence that English was not Hannah's first language comes from other surviving letters. In the 1770s, Hannah wrote two more surviving petitions, both addressed to Aaron Lopez, one of the wealthiest Jews in early America. The first of these she wrote in the elegant baroque Spanish that was typical of Spanish and Portuguese Jews of the era. Once again, the letter's longevity is due largely to the fluke of a nineteenth-century male collector, in this case George G. Champlin (1862–1937), a librarian who created an autograph collection that he later donated to the New York State Library (figs. 17 and 18).[56] Ironically, the letter most likely caught Champlin's eye because of her famous addressee, Aaron Lopez.

In many ways the 1770 letter from New York is familiar, as it uses the same rhetorical ploys Hannah used a decade earlier in English: she is old (seventy and some years old at this point) and greatly in need (she owes money to a doctor and for rent). Lopez, in contrast, is powerful and good. Not only is his family noble, but his character is stellar: "I have heard of your good reputation, and that you were Father of the poor and a Good Jew." His heights and her worthiness are emphasized through her ritual abasement. Once again she "dares" to write him (*tomo el atribimiento de Escribirlo*). Her valediction repeats her subservience by signing off "Your Servant who kisses your hands" (*Servidora de vmd Q.S.M.B. [Que Sus Manos Besa]*). She positions herself as devout—while simultaneously reminding Lopez of his religious obligations—by repeatedly emphasizing that it is God who will move Lopez to perform charity. These are the same strategies that appear in her English epistle.

Yet linguistically the letter presents us with a Hannah we have not previously met: one schooled in the arts of baroque Spanish. To be sure, the letter has some marks of hesitance or poverty. The letter is not just missing pieces along the edges, it has errors that are crossed out and rewritten, as if the piece of paper was too precious to waste. Letters are likewise inscribed above the line, suggesting time and care put into rereading and correcting—mementos of the anxiety over what was at stake. While critics have suggested that such moments are typical of the "unschooled" poor, Hannah's use of Spanish is anything but uneducated.[57]

First, it is worth noting Hannah need not have written to Lopez in

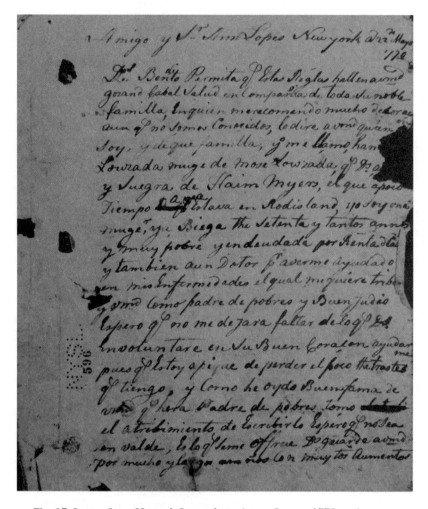

Fig. 17. Letter from Hannah Louzada to Aaron Lopez, 1770, p. 1.
Champlin Collection of Autographs, no. 596, NYSL.

Spanish. She could clearly write in English, and while Lopez was born
in Portugal, he maintained an extensive correspondence in English.
Even his own children wrote to him in English. Indeed, Lopez's only
correspondents who wrote to him in Spanish and Portuguese were other
immigrants—Jews who were born like him in Iberia, such as his cousin
James Lucena, or in non-English-speaking Sephardic communities, such
as Rabbi Isaac Carigal.[58] Hannah's use of Spanish, then, functions as a deliberate, rhetorical plea. It stresses kinship: she, like Lopez, is a member

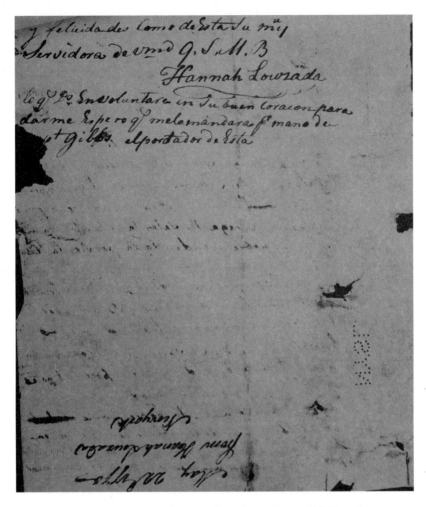

Fig. 18. Letter from Hannah Louzada to Aaron Lopez, 1770, p. 2.
Champlin Collection of Autographs, no. 596, NYSL.

of the *nação,* Jews of the Portuguese nation. Hannah further underscores this affinity in her opening by saying she will tell him something
of her family and that she is "Hannah Louzada, wife of Moses Louzada"
(*han[na] Louzada muge[r] de Mose Lowzada*). Furthermore, by writing in
Spanish, she makes clear that she is a *nação* by birth rather than merely
by marriage, a distinction that carried great weight, as some Western Sephardic communities demoted members who married Ashkenazim during
this era.[59] Hannah's use of Spanish provides us with valuable information

about her life history. Not only do we learn for the first time that she was born sometime between 1690 and 1700, as she is seventy something years old (*setenta y tantos annos*), but also that she was most likely born in Iberia.

She also appears to have been educated there, for unlike her English, Hannah's Spanish reveals many of the inflections of "schooled" discourse proper to elite Spanish education during the eighteenth century. First and foremost, her Spanish style reveals the impact of Iberian letter-writing manuals. As historian Rebecca Earle notes, "Writing to a new correspondent . . . involved a complicated series of etiquettes."[60] Hannah negotiates these etiquettes through formulas such as the *Servidora de vmd Q.S.M.B.* with which she closes her letter. In one of the most popular letter-writing primers, *Manual de escribientes* (1574), Antonio de Torquemada "devoted nearly 20 percent of the entire discussion of letter-writing to the art of choosing the correct salutation and closing."[61] Hannah had either read manuals such as Torquemada's or was trained by those who had.

Second, while Hannah's English is monosyllabic, lacking punctuation, and without the touches of neoclassicism favored during the era, her Spanish is the opposite. It is formal and graceful and punctuated by abbreviations that show a remarkable fluency. We see all three of these elements in her opening, in which she prays, "May God grant that these lines find you enjoying perfect health" (*D^s [Dios] Bendito Permita q^e [que] Estas Reglas hallen a vmd gozand[o] Cabal Salud*). The phrases are melodious as well as elegant, with three pairings of end or beginning rhymes: *Bendito Permita; Estas Reglas; Cabal Salud.* Hannah's letter also shows the marks of a native speaker, as in the substitution of *Biega* for *viega*.[62] Using Spanish rather than Portuguese might suggest that Hannah was born in a city in Spain, such as Seville, which was known for its large population of *nação*.[63] However, since elegant Spanish was a mainstay of elite Portuguese education during this era as well, she might equally likely have been born in Portugal and been trying to impress upon Lopez her high origins.[64] What her Spanish does suggest, however, is that she chose to represent herself linguistically as a woman of quality who had fallen on hard times.

Sadly, the appeal does not seem to have worked, as on July 26, 1770, Hannah wrote to Lopez again from New York, this time in English. She returned to key themes from her previous English plea to Shearith Israel: subservience, age, infirmness. Necessity drives her to write, she explains. So does fear. She is "unable to do anny thing for my self," and yet "Quarter day" (when her rent was due) was rapidly approaching. Her friends have "helpt" her, but it was not enough. For the first time, we see Hannah invoke the bonds of sympathy outright: "I hope your heart," she writes, "which is Naturally tender will be moved with Kind Compassion for a Poor Fellow Creature who is laboring under great distress."[65] It is unclear if the new plea worked and if Lopez came to her aid.[66] It would be the last letter she wrote that was saved by collectors.

The third piece of evidence about Hannah's education comes earlier, from 1750 when she had to help make an inventory of her husband's estate. Hannah's first known signature is in Hebrew, which the court reporter seems not to have recognized as writing and hence put as "her mark" and translated for her (fig. 19). She similarly signed the court's form in Hebrew (fig. 20).

Hannah's Hebrew signature is interesting for several reasons. First, it suggests that she identified strongly as Jewish, so much so that she signed

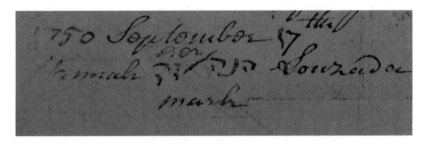

Fig. 19. Signature of Hannah Louzada in Hebrew, estate inventory of Moses Louzada, filed Oct. 10, 1750. County of Middlesex, New Jersey. Photocopy AJA.

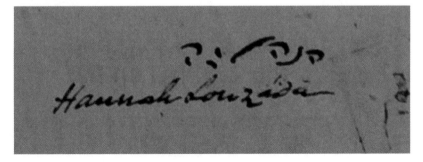

Fig. 20. Signature of Hannah Louzada in Hebrew, court's form in estate inventory of Moses Louzada, filed Oct. 10, 1750. County of Middlesex, New Jersey. Photocopy AJA.

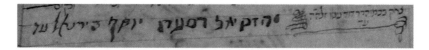

Fig. 21. Groom's and witnesses' signatures from the *ketubah* of
Jehezquel Sehadya and Ribca Lealtad, September 30, 1734 (14
Tishri 5495), London. Bevis Marks *ketubah* registers, V. 116,
LMA/4521/A/02/03/005, LMA.

her name in Hebrew rather than the Roman alphabet, at least when faced
with non-Jews who would not judge her handwriting. When compared to
signatures on Western Sephardic *ketubot* (marriage contacts) from London from the second half of the eighteenth century, Hannah's signature
falls midway between those who could not sign in Hebrew at all and those
who were very well educated and signed their names in elegant Rashi
script (fig. 21). While her *nun* conforms to the Sephardic Solitreo script,
her *heh* resembles block lettering more than Rashi or Solitreo.

Thus, like the bridegroom Jehezquel Sehadya who writes in a mixture
of block and Rashi script (fig. 21), Hannah's signature suggests a rudimentary Hebrew education typical either of those too poor to attend
school for much time or of first-generation Iberian immigrants who arrived in London, Amsterdam, or Hamburg at an age when their schooling had already substantially begun (but was not complete). Hannah's
expertise in Spanish suggests the latter scenario. Thus, while Hannah
and Moses's *ketubah* has not been located (suggesting a colonial marriage), it is reasonable to assume Hannah came from one of the main
Western Sephardic feeder communities to the colonies when she was
between eight and twelve years of age, that is, somewhere between 1705
and 1711, depending on her date of birth. After arrival, she appears to
have received a rudimentary Hebrew education, perhaps one that focused more on reading than writing.

Taken as a whole, Hannah's letters and signatures suggest English
was most likely her third written language. By the 1770s, when her last
letter was written, Hannah had become more comfortable with English
but never completely fluent. However, Hannah was not the only early
Jewish American woman who was not fluent in the authoritative language of the colony in which she lived. There was no public education
in colonial America, and women were less likely to be educated in the
language of business.[67] This lack of schooling was a problem encountered by other Sephardic women throughout the Americas. We find, for

example, Jewish men in Suriname complaining that many Sephardic women spoke the Afro-Surinamese creole language of Sranan and could not read or write Dutch at all; they were forced to sign wills with an *X*.[68] Likewise, when Sara Pardo and Abraham Andrade carried on an illicit love affair in Curaçao in 1775, Sara wrote her letters in the local creole language known today as Papiamentu but referred to in colonial sources as *creoles taal* or *Portugeese neegers spraak* (Portuguese Negro speech), a dialect that Dutch authorities had to pay to have translated for the official records.[69] Non-elite Jewish women's lack of literacy in the language of colonial authority and business made it harder for them to support themselves. It also made it harder to create documents that were likely to be preserved. This pattern did not begin to change until the nineteenth century, when public education became available.[70]

Women, Property, and Colonial Laws

Just as charity and education disenfranchised colonial Jewish women, so too laws regarding property rights provided a third structural issue that led to petitions for *tzedakah* like Hannah's being so rampant. British common law about coverture meant that upon marriage, all of a woman's movable property, as well as cash brought to the marriage, inherited, or earned, belonged to her husband. Moreover, she could not make any contract—or even a will—without his permission.[71] Although Jewish women who married with a *ketubah* were guaranteed the money they brought into the marriage, the contracts did not always seem to trump local laws.[72] When a woman married in the colonies, all of her property belonged to her husband. Indeed, this was true in New Brunswick until 1852, when a statute guaranteed that married women could continue to own any property they brought to a marriage.[73]

Certainly Hannah's husband, Moses, could have written a will that left some of his money to her. Hannah's sister-in-law Blume, for example, inherited £200 and the use of her husband's real and personal estate to bring up their children.[74] Unfortunately Moses did not have the foresight to write a will. This oversight was not all that atypical. People often died unexpectedly of sudden illness. Moreover, it cost money to have a will written and witnessed, and most people could not afford it.[75] Had Hannah lived in West Jersey, a 1676 law would have guaranteed that, as a widow, she would receive a third of her husband's estate, even if he died intestate.[76] Hannah's husband died, however, in East Jersey. Thus, like residents in most British colonies before the revolution, she was subject to English law and custom. Based on primogeniture, these laws held that if an individual died intestate, all his estate devolved on his eldest (legitimate) son.[77] His widow and younger children did not receive a penny.

This law had horrible repercussions for Jewish women like Hannah. Prior to her husband's death, she had been reasonably well off. Like Cora Wilburn nearly a century later, who would write from firsthand experience about "Jewish Women Without Money," Hannah's poverty affected someone who had once been used to a full stomach; yet, unlike Cora, Hannah was not so "genteel" that she was afraid to beg for food after her fall.[78] The estate inventory of Hannah's husband indicates a distinctly middle-class existence: among his items were nineteen pewter plates, a mahogany desk, a chest of drawers, a looking glass, twelve common chairs, a table, curtains, three feather beds with sundry sheets, and a wide range of food provisions. He also owned two enslaved people—a woman named Jenny and a man named Tom.

Owning enslaved people was not unusual. Slavery was not abolished in New Jersey until 1804, and even then emancipation was only gradual.[79] Little is known about Jenny and Tom, but it is possible they were born in New Jersey, as many enslaved people were by the second half of the eighteenth century. Enslaved men and women in New Jersey were asked to do a wide range of skilled and unskilled work. It is unclear what happened to either Jenny or Tom after Moses's death, though Jenny was possibly sold north into Canada by Hannah's son-in-law, Haym Myers.[80] Owning enslaved people meant Hannah was used to having help both with housework and manual labor.[81] Moses's whole estate was valued at over £240.[82] Had Hannah inherited even a widow's third, she would have been at least not completely impoverished. Alternatively, this fate would have been avoided if she could have relied upon her oldest son's affection to support her in her poverty. Unfortunately, however, her oldest son, Jacob, had been declared insane.

Jews and Mental Illness in Early America

This leads me to the fourth issue that fragmented Hannah's life. Hannah's oldest son's mental illness had a devastating impact on her life as the family struggled to care for him, declare him incompetent, and regain access to the house, furniture, and belongings that Hannah would have once thought of as her own.[83] While today the role Jacob Louzada played in his mother's poverty may seem like random bad luck, mental illness was on the rise during this era. Was it a particular problem, though, for early American Jews?

Although we do not know the particulars of Jacob's case, at least one author has noticed what seems to be a "disturbing pattern of insanity" among early American Jews, conveniently listed by Malcolm Stern in his monumental *First American Jewish Families: 600 Genealogies, 1654–1977* (fig. 22).[84] Dr. Stern's propensity to mark individuals as "insane" seems "to verge on the libelous."[85] Later scholars' reticence in addressing Stern's findings is not without reason: during the very era Stern covers, anti-Semitic discourse—and even some assimilated Jews—equated Jewishness with illness.[86] By the late nineteenth century, anti-Semites depicted Jews as an "essentially 'ill' people and labeled the origins of that illness as incest/inbreeding. . . . The illness dominating the discourse of the anti-Semitic science was madness, and its origin was in the 'dangerous' marriages of the Jews: their refusal to marry beyond the inner group . . . even when such 'inbreeding' was not consanguineous."[87] Concerns about reinforcing anti-Semitic stereotypes may have led scholars to neglect Stern's annotations as a resource in their analyses.

So, how should we understand Stern's annotations? For example, even if we reject Jewish endogamy as a source of mental illness among Jews, could the extremely small pool of possible Jewish spouses in the colonies and the legacy of cousin and uncle-aunt marriages caused by the Inquisition be to blame?[88] To be sure, Iberian refugees from families who had

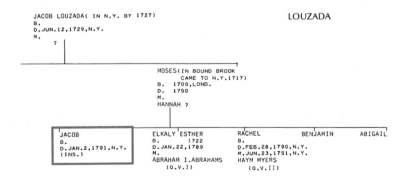

Fig. 22. Detail of Stern's Louzada family tree, with Jacob marked as "Ins[ane]." From Malcolm H. Stern, *First American Jewish Families: 600 Genealogies, 1654–1977* (Cincinnati: American Jewish Archives, 1978), 179.

maintained Jewish practices in secret had often married close relations in order to ensure that the offspring would have Jewish bloodlines and to confirm that both parties were sympathetic to Crypto-Judaism, which, if revealed to the Inquisition, could result in death. Other "New Christian" families had married kin because of Iberian prejudice against Jewish ancestry. Moreover, some "New Christians" deliberately married relations in order to safely maintain Crypto-Jewish traditions or Jewish bloodlines. As a result, uncle-niece and cousin marriages were common.[89] Many Sephardic Jews came to the Americas married to close relations: marriages of uncles and nieces were so common that Rhode Island's incest laws had an exception for Jewish marriages.[90] Hannah was of the generation of Sephardic American Jews who had come in waves of clandestine immigration directly from Iberia in the 1720s to 1750s. Thus, while we do not know her ancestry, it is more likely than not that she was related in some way to her husband. Might this be behind Jacob's problems?

Perhaps. But when we compare Jewish rates of "insanity" in early America with other populations, we find Jews were no more likely to be declared mentally ill than anyone else. Today mental illness impacts roughly one in five adults in the United States, and some scholars have suggested Americans are "less often insane or seriously disturbed" in 2000 than in early America.[91] Yet, of Stern's six hundred early Jewish families that span from the colonial period to the present, only twelve had a person *at any time* who was either insane or committed suicide. Committing suicide was only twice as common as dying in a duel, and a person was three times more likely to drown than die by their own hand. Moreover, drowning was more likely to "run in families" than either "insanity" or suicide, even if one sets aside the incidents in which multiple family members died in the same shipwreck.[92]

All this suggests that Jews were not disproportionately prone to mental illness during this era, and that, in fact, Stern's data most likely greatly underrepresents what we would consider incidents of mental instability today. Stern indicates suicide or "insanity" only when it is noted in the records, typically because of a court case or questions at the time of burial. As one scholar notes, "To get officially noticed as insane . . . people had to act bizarrely or repeatedly endanger lives."[93] Even then, others—typically family or neighbors—had to testify that the person was "delusional, violent, and, perhaps most critically, unable to manage his or her normal affairs."[94] People who were mentally disabled but did not become a public burden were unlikely to have been noted.

Recent genetic studies also suggest that we should interpret Stern's annotations with caution. Geneticists have found that the actual risks of consanguineous marriages (such as between cousins) vary tremendously.[95] While nineteenth-century scientists were more likely to ascribe "madness" to "inbreeding," today's genetic studies are more likely to focus on genetic mutations causing inherited diseases or mental disabilities, such as "remarkably low intellectual functioning."[96] This shift in designation says as much about changing visions of "insanity" between the nineteenth century and today as it does about advances in genetics as a science.

We might also question what exactly either Stern or the colonial records meant when they deemed an individual such as Jacob Louzada "insane." Colonial designations of mental illness varied considerably and encompassed a wide range of issues. Other than "insane," commonly used terms and phrases were "crazy," "distempered," "distracted," "crazy brained," "out of their wits," "deluded," "overcome with melancholy," "not in his right mind," "completely bereft of his senses," and "one part off the moon," the latter echoing the equation of "lunatics" with the moon.[97] Yet also included in the insane category were people who were "simple" or "idiots"—people deemed "too dumb" to manage their own affairs.[98] Other problems that we would rarely today associate with mental illness were often conflated with insanity during this era, including epilepsy, "vice" (women's nonreproductive sexual activity), and substance abuse.[99] Gender bias in determining who was insane may explain why women were twice as likely to be placed in this category in Stern's records.[100] Poverty, class, marital status (all but one of Stern's "insane" were single),[101] and ethnicity all made one more vulnerable to being labelled mentally ill. Moreover, the "cosmic loneliness" of life in the colonies, widespread alcoholism fed by diluting water with spirits to prevent disease, and chronic pain were as much to blame as anything else.[102]

Though Jews did not suffer mental illness more than other people and "insanity" covered a wide range of issues, the problems that confronted the afflicted and their families still had a detrimental impact on the Jewish poor. Because state and local communities only stepped in to help when "insane" people were a danger to themselves or their families could not care for them, "insanity" disproportionately impacted families like the Louzadas, who lacked resources. Indeed, while some things improved for Sephardic Jews when they migrated to North America, care for the mentally ill was not one of them. Early modern Iberia had a well-developed support system for people—and their families—grappling with mental illness. There were a large number of institutions specifically dedicated to caring for the mentally ill, who were distinguished from the poor and infirm.[103] The mentally ill had a privileged place in both "Catholic theological teaching on charity . . . and in reform programs."[104] Insanity also may have worked to the advantage of certain crypto-Jews: more than a hundred trial transcripts from Inquisition records include defendants "who either pled insanity or for whom insanity was alleged."[105] To be sure, being deemed insane was not a free ride: "a determination of *locura* (madness) by any judicial or civil authority was grounds for economic dispossession, annulment of marriage, and prohibition of exercise of a trade."[106] Nonetheless, it could save a person's life.

Given the extensive support system for mental illness in Iberia, the treatment of mental illness in the British colonies must have struck Sephardic refugees as debilitating. Unlike Spain, which opened its first insane asylum in 1419,[107] the first "freestanding hospital [built] for the insane" in the colonies that would become the United States did not open until 1770,[108] twenty years too late to help Hannah with her inheritance issues. Before then, communities were legally responsible for their own mentally ill, but only if the afflicted had no relatives or property. Many early American Jews with means cared for their mentally ill relatives at home, a trend which may account for their not appearing in court and legal records as "insane." Harmon Hendricks's sister Sally, for example, who suffered from "a very unsettled disposition," spent her life "shuffled back and forth between relatives, none of whom was ever particularly overjoyed to see her."[109]

However, if like Jacob Louzada those who were deemed mentally ill (rather than their relatives) had inherited a home and all its belongings, their money was managed by the town's selectmen and was used to pay all the expenses the "insane" person incurred. The town would not assume fiscal responsibility until all of the inheritance had been depleted.[110] Even then, towns often dealt with the problem by running the mentally ill person out of town so that they would become someone else's problem.[111]

In Jacob's case, his family attempted to gain control of the estate in 1762 by making his brother-in-law, Haym Myers, Jacob's legal guardian. This ploy only held for a couple of years before Jacob came of age, vacated the ruling, and took full possession of the estate.[112] Whatever the nature of his illness, it did not hinder his ability eventually to prosper. When the Revolutionary War broke out, Jacob sided with the British, serving as the master of the ship *Pool(e)* and overseeing four men.[113] As the revolutionary forces took New Jersey, however, Jacob was forced to flee the family's homestead, first to New York and then Nova Scotia. The property had flourished since his father's death. There were eighty-eight acres and a couple of "goodly dwelling houses," valued at roughly £880, with furniture adding another £68 4s. In the end it was for naught. The New Jersey state legislature confiscated and sold all Jacob had, and the British refused his pleas to reimburse him.[114] Even before he lost everything, however, Jacob did not seem inclined to help out his mother, who had played a role in ensuring his original designation of "insane." When Hannah wrote asking for help from Lopez in 1770, she mentioned she was Moses Louzada's widow and the mother-in-law of Haym Myers but conveniently neglected to mention her first son.

Indeed, throughout the struggle, Hannah was destitute. In all, three "begging letters" from Hannah survive: one from 1761 and two from the summer of 1770. While one has been anthologized, her name was unfortunately mistranscribed as "Hannah Paysaddon," an error repeated by later scholars.[115] Given that all of the scholars involved are typically meticulous, the mistake says more about the systematic fragmentation of women's lives in this era and in the surviving archives than the quality of their scholarship. Lack of communal care for the mentally ill, along with British inheritance laws, unequal education of Jewish women, and religious structures all contributed to break up Hannah's life, necessitating her letters. The same structural forces kept most early Jewish women on the brink of poverty. Yet by 1774, Hannah's frantic petitions had stopped, as her name moved from the *tzedakah* to the *escava* list, finally joining the women the congregation chose to remember, yoked together in the memorial prayer for the dead.[116]

Conclusion

Thinking about the 1761 letter Hannah wrote to Congregation Shearith Israel as an object owned by Hannah is by some reckoning odd. After all, Hannah possessed her letter only briefly before it made its way north and across the Hudson River, toward the city that Hannah would sometimes call her home. Yet the very transience of the letter as Hannah's property is also revealing, as it underscores how forces combined to keep all of Hannah's things constantly in motion to others, slipping out of her hands.

My goal in focusing on Hannah's letter has been to think about what it reveals about the lack of women's voices in the colonial archive. On some level this focus on silence may seem grim. For a long time, early American Jewish studies has focused on Jewish versions of rags-to-riches stories, of men who escaped the Inquisition's flames and started vast mercantile empires or help fund the Revolutionary War. These tales were evidence of early Jewish patriotism and provided a sort of hope that Jews had a place in the American dream.

There is a downside to this dream story, though, as it suggests that people who do not succeed have themselves to blame. One historian, for example, suggested Hannah was unable to succeed because she was "incompetent" at business and "a chronic complainer."[117] I would argue, however, that while Hannah died poor and alone, there were a lot of reasons for her lack of success, almost none of which were her fault. Moreover, the structural processes that splintered Hannah's life continue to impact American Jewry. Despite being a "model minority," many Jews today face the same problems Hannah did.[118]

Myths of Jewish success both today and through histories that focus solely on wealthy Jews undercut our ability to understand the structural sources of poverty. Model minority myths promote the idea that certain ethnic groups naturally achieve "universal and unparalleled academic and occupational success."[119] To be sure, one of the most nefarious problems with model minority myths is that they suggest other, "inferior" minorities are poor by choice or lack of effort.[120] Yet model minority myths are also harmful for those identified as "good" ethnic others, as they suggest that individuals within the group who do not succeed have only themselves to blame—that is, that Jewish women like Hannah were "incompetent" rather than coping with structural issues not faced by everyone else. Jewish success, however, was universal neither in the past nor in the present. Jews in early America were a diverse lot, and Hannah's life story reminds us that other factors such as age, gender, and education played key roles in determining who required resources and support. While Jewish poverty is less rampant today than in 1761,[121] many, like Hannah, are elderly immigrants whose ability to access services is impeded by language barriers.[122] Focusing on the gaps in our stories about the past widens our sense of what it meant to be Jewish in America and can help us begin to break some of the silences about struggles that Jews have always faced in the United States.

TWO

Pieces of Silver

One cold January day, I found myself fighting through the crowds in the Grand Hall of the Metropolitan Museum of Art. I was in search of colonial silver. After pushing past the lines of people snaking through ancient, European, and showcased exhibitions, I arrived in the monumental atrium of the American wing. The objects of my affection were on the eastern balcony. High above the main floor in their airy glass display cases, they nestled among the finest pieces from the Met's collection of American silver, pewter, and ceramics.

The setting was sublime. Ethereal light from the skylights above rained down, creating geometric rectangles on the shiny surfaces on display. Designed to detract as little as possible from the objects themselves, the display cases emphasized the pieces' simple grandeur. Unlike the period rooms to the north of the main hall, where objects are seen in situ in American domestic interiors, here the aesthetic was a sort of miniature "white box." Each free-standing case or wall display positioned the precious objects on neutral, soft gray platforms, with simple white descriptors below, creating a "non-space, ultra space, or ideal space where the surrounding matrix of space-time is symbolically annulled."[1] The result was a focus on the objects' timeless beauty, each piece refracting the museum's original agenda of making "American cities more civilized, sanitary, moral, and peaceful."[2]

I was there to see three silver cups, beakers to be precise, once part of a set of six owned by Reyna (Levy) Moses (1753–1824) (fig. 23). The beakers had earned their place in the atrium not because of her, however, but because of who made them: her uncle, the silversmith Myer Myers (1723–95). Myers was a favorite of New York elites, and his silverwork has long been considered a pinnacle example of the American rococo style, exemplified by his Torah finials.[3] The beakers, however, are more classical revival style. They emphasize symmetry, order, and restraint, and the display brought all of this out in spades. Like all of the silver on the breezeway, no fingerprints or smudges marred the beakers' beauty. The flawless silver was polished in all its glory. Myers's design was elegantly simple, with two purposefully incised lines below the cup's lip and a molded ring at the foot, showcasing the silversmith's talent.[4] Standing only four inches high and weighing slightly over five and a half ounces, each beaker was worth a small fortune.[5] Who was Reyna, and how had three of her cups made their way into New York's premier art museum?

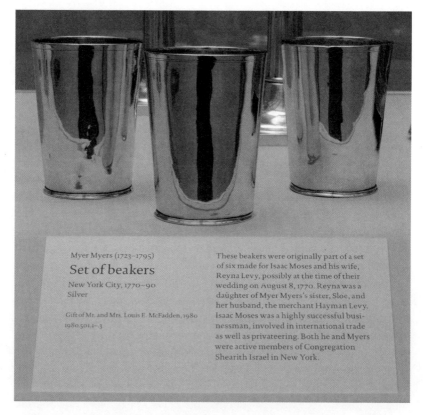

Myer Myers (1723–1795)

Set of beakers

New York City, 1770–90
Silver

Gift of Mr. and Mrs. Louis E. McFadden, 1980
1980.501.1–3

These beakers were originally part of a set of six made for Isaac Moses and his wife, Reyna Levy, possibly at the time of their wedding on August 8, 1770. Reyna was a daughter of Myer Myers's sister, Sloe, and her husband, the merchant Hayman Levy. Isaac Moses was a highly successful businessman, involved in international trade as well as privateering. Both he and Myers were active members of Congregation Shearith Israel in New York.

Fig. 23. Museum display of silver beakers, 1770–90. Height: 4 in. Metropolitan Museum of Art 1980.501.1–3. Photo by author.

Reyna was the daughter of the silversmith's sister Sloe Myers and her husband, Hayman Levy, a colonial merchant. The Levys were extraordinarily rich and were related to most Jewish families worth knowing in the colonial town.[6] The Met's description recounts that both Reyna's father, Hayman, and Reyna's uncle, silversmith Myers, "were active members of Congregation Shearith Israel." This understates things a bit. Reyna's family sat on the synagogue governance board that ran the congregation and gave out charity, sitting in judgment on women like Hannah Louzada who came pleading. Hayman Levy had just finished his term as the *parnas presidente* when Hannah's 1761 letter came before the board, and both Hayman and Myers sat on the very board that responded to Hannah's plea.[7] Beakers were not the most extravagant of colonial possessions, but the set of six of which the Met's three were a part bespeaks something of the distance between Reyna Levy Moses's life and that of Hannah Louzada. Born in early New York just three years after Hannah's husband, Moses, died, Reyna was everything Hannah was not.

Yet, like Hannah, Reyna's life story is largely missing from Jewish American histories. The Met's bare-bones description points to this problem. According to the museum's plaque, Reyna is first and foremost a daughter and wife. In contrast, Reyna's husband, Isaac Moses, has inspired a fair amount of prose in displays, histories, and collections referring to early American Jews. He was, as the Met notes, a "highly successful businessman, involved in international trade as well as privateering," and as such his portraits appear in private collections and in the Museum of the City of New York.[8] His gravestone is highlighted on cemetery tours. He is well represented in multiple archives. His letters with Stephen Girard—arguably the wealthiest man in early America—are at the American Philosophical Society (in Philadelphia), while the American Jewish Historical Society has Isaac's personal correspondence, his business papers, a receipt book, and his will and estate inventory.[9] This treasury means we know not only Reyna's husband's own views on key moments in his life but also trivia about him, such as who shaved him, when, and how much it cost. (For the curious, he paid John Marette 1 pound 10 shillings for a shave on May 20, 1785.)[10] Yet despite her husband's prowess, when one looks up Reyna in the *Biographical Dictionary of Early American Jews*, one finds even less than the Met provides: "LEVY, Reyna. April 15, 1753–June 24, 1824. Daughter of Hayman Levy, she was married to Isaac Moses on August 8, 1770, in New York City (*Publications of the American Jewish Historical Society*, IV, 210; SIR)."[11] Fairly underwhelming.

Reyna's story parallels Hannah's in another way: it was a strange mix of privilege and constriction. Hannah had been a slave owner, but when her husband died, the synagogue board took control over where she could live and with whom. Reyna similarly lacked agency over key decisions in her life. When she married her first cousin Isaac Moses on August 8, 1770, Reyna was just seventeen, and in all likelihood, she had little say in the matter of her marriage. At least for the upper classes, most Jewish marriages were arranged.[12] It is here that her beakers symbolically come into play, as silver was key to the ceremony.

Since late antiquity, silver has played an important role in creating Jewish spouses. According to the marriage contract Reyna's husband signed, silver needed to ritually change hands, marking the couple's change in status and Reyna's change from virgin maiden to a wife who it was hoped would bear legitimate heirs. Silver may have similarly marked the gifts given to the couple. Sometime after the wedding, Reyna's uncle Myer Myers made the young couple at least six plain silver beakers, stamped underneath with Myers's mark and engraved with the couple's initials. Were the beakers a purchase or a gift? Record books from Myers's silversmith shop have long disappeared, but using silver gifts to mark Jewish marriages was certainly not unusual: in various times and places, silver has been given at Jewish weddings.[13] Such gifts often became associated with the union itself. Indeed, the Myers beakers helped establish the family's identity. Long after the ritually exchanged money was spent or converted into real estate investments, the beakers lived on in family tradition, becoming a key heirloom passed between the generations before falling into non-Jewish hands.[14] Five of the beakers eventually became museum trophies: three are highlighted in the collections of the Met, while two others are at the Winterthur Museum in Delaware, one of the most significant collections of Americana in the United States. The last of the six would fetch large sums of money as it moved from one elite collector to another.

Reyna's beakers are unusual because most museums and scholars focus on ritual rather than domestic silver Judaica. Indeed, despite the ubiquity of silver used by early American Jewish families, almost nothing has been said about silver's significance or its role in constructing Jewish identity outside the synagogue. I will argue that this is due in part to the way that Jewish silver has been collected and displayed in the twentieth and twenty-first centuries. Likewise, when discussing what makes Myers's silver "Jewish," scholars have commonly focused on the Jewishness of the silversmith himself—as if something about his spiritual or ethnic essence was transferred to each object he made[15]—or on ritual objects Myers made, such as the beautiful Torah finials currently housed at the Boston

Museum of Fine Arts.[16] The result is the deemphasis of the lives of women like Reyna and the use of silver for constructing Jewish families.

Yet the role of silver in family legacies and the creation of Jewish families themselves is not accidental. If there was an art to the creation of families and the stories people tell about their families, silver was key to that art for early American Jews. Jewish law requires silver for certain life-cycle events, and silver is important in the form of threshold gifts, that is, gifts made of silver "mark the time of, or act as the actual agents of, individual transformation."[17] For early American Jewish merchant families, silver became a useful heirloom, portable yet valuable, and the objects reminded descendants of the family legacies they inherited.

In this chapter, I shift the discussion of silver away from maker to owner, from the ritual space of the synagogue to the Jewish home, and from men to women. I also put the marriage that inspired the cups back at the center of the discussion. Over time, the beakers went from being everyday objects in Reyna's house on 37 Great Dock Street[18] to being precious heirlooms passed down from generation to generation, finally becoming early American collectibles in private hands and the Met. As the cups moved through time and space, their role in Reyna's history changed. Silver was entwined with each stage of Reyna's life: first her childhood as the daughter of a merchant prince, then her marriage to Isaac Moses, then her role as a mother, and finally her afterlife as an ancestor. At each stage, marks, engravings, and scratches were left on the beakers. They are a mute testimony to the cups' transformation and the slow erasure of Reyna's place in their story.

Reyna's Cup

Reyna was born in the Jewish community living on the very tip of lower Manhattan in the middle of the eighteenth century. Her family combined two important and entangled strands of early Jewish American life: artisans and merchants. The silver her mother's family made helped merchants weave family stories that would last for generations. The wealthy elites of Europe had landed estates on which to stamp their names. The wandering Jews of early America did not. They had to make their own fortunes and family stories, and silver was critical to displaying the legends they created. For Jews, silver also had religious symbolism, as it was part of the traditional way marriages were ritually enacted. If you turn over any of the six cups in Reyna's set, you will find two marks made by

Fig. 24. "Myers" mark stamped on the underside of Myers's beaker.
Courtesy of Metropolitan Museum of Art, 1980.501.2.

Myers: first, the "Myers" stamp certifying the cups were from his workshop (fig. 24), and second, "IMR"—Reyna and her husband's initials
(see fig. 28). For Reyna, the marks had special significance, as they at-
tested to her two worlds—the kinships of blood and marriage.

The first kinship network stamped into the cups was one of blood. Although the *Biographical Dictionary of Early American Jews* identifies Reyna as
the "Daughter of Hayman Levy," early on it was her mother's family that
would make the greatest difference in her life. Before Reyna's mother
had married Hayman in 1750, Sloe had been a Myers, and that extended
Myers family surrounded Reyna during her earliest days in New York. The
first mark stamped into the cups' silver attests to this kinship. The *M* of
the Myers's name is small compared to the other letters, and the end of
the *y* almost kisses the *M*'s right foot.[19] This label is somewhat mundane,
as it was a style of stamp that Myer Myers would add to most of his work
made between 1765 and 1795. Silversmiths were responsible for the quality of silver used, and for renowned craftsmen like Myers, a maker's mark
added value to the object.[20] Yet for Reyna, the mark had emotional implications as well. When Reyna turned over her six silver cups, the stamp
"Myers" underneath did not just signal the cups' maker; the stamp symbolized Reyna's belonging within the larger kinship of the Myers family.

When Reyna was born in 1753, the Myers were a large school in a small
New York pond. New York was still quite modest in the 1750s: roughly
thirteen thousand souls lived in the town,[21] still located at Manhattan's
lower tip with farmlands spreading out to the north and east (fig. 25).[22]

New York's Jewish community was even smaller, numbering about three hundred people.[23] Being a Myers meant being nestled among kin. Unlike Hayman Levy, who came to New York closer to 1750 from what is now Germany, Reyna's grandparents, Judith and Solomon Myers, had come to Manhattan from Holland in the 1720s.[24] By Reyna's birth, the Myers were essential to New York Jewish life. Solomon not only served as a *shochet* (ritual slaughterer) for the congregation, he pledged crucial money to build the town's first synagogue.[25]

Like most Jews in the early town, the Myers clan settled around the first Mill Street synagogue complex, the hub of Jewish life, with a school, *mikveh*, and *hazzan*'s house (see fig. 25). On the blocks nearby lived not only Reyna's grandparents and her own parents but the four other Myers siblings. Sloe's brothers were metalworkers, and her sisters married key men in the congregation: Michael Moses Hays (a Dutch

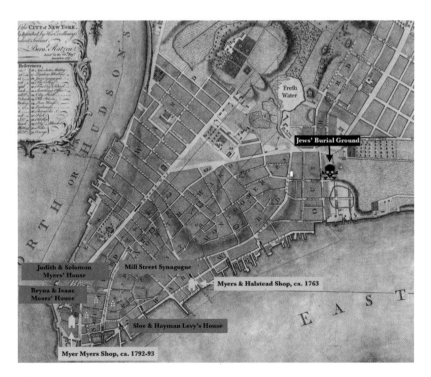

Fig. 25. Location of Shearith Israel's Mill Street synagogue and Myers-Levy-Moses family houses and store on Bernard Ratzer's *Plan of the City of New York* (London: Jeffreys and Faden, 1776). Courtesy of the Library of Congress, 74692118.

Jew born in New York) and Solomon Marache (a Dutch immigrant from Curaçao). Like Hayman Levy, Hays was an influential Jewish merchant in the bustling town.[26]

To marry a merchant was a risky gamble for a woman. On the one hand, good winds and fortune could shower the family with riches. Yet, the next year, a lost ship or a blockade during a war might bring ruin and bankruptcy. Sloe experienced both.[27] In contrast, the husband of her younger sister Rebecca, Marache, seemed a safer bet. Marache—like his Myers in-laws—was an artisan, most commonly listed as a watchmaker, though on occasion he would engage in trade as Hayman Levy's partner.[28] Little risked, however, meant little gained. After his wife's early death, Marache remarried a non-Jew,[29] and the extended Myers clan were left to pick up the pieces, making sure Rebecca's unmarried daughter, Judith, could live comfortably.[30]

Of all the Myers clan, however, none is so famous today as Sloe's eldest brother, Myer Myers. He is the reason the silver beakers are stamped "Myers" underneath. He made a decent living because silver was important in early American life. As silver collector Ruth Nutt notes, "From the 17th century on, silver was an overt way of saying to your neighbors and guests, I am important, I have money. Silver was and is for display."[31] Beyond its desirability as a beautiful, shiny, and malleable metal, silver indicated that people had money to waste. Most of the original thirteen colonies had property requirements for men to vote. In early New York, only real estate fulfilled this requirement.[32] After Jews regained the right to vote in 1747, silver must have been a particularly conspicuous way of showing that the family owned more than enough to participate in politics.[33] "I have so much money," silver said, "I don't even have to use it to buy real estate."

For a luxury item, silver was also interactive. Paintings and rugs just hung or sat there, but silver could be brought out for guests during the tea and coffee ceremonies so central to eighteenth-century American life, ceremonies which, importantly, were the domain of women. Silver was also easily relocated. This transportability was critical, as early American Jews were particularly mobile. Most New York Jews were displaced during the Revolutionary War, many of them fleeing to nearby Philadelphia, but disease, work, marriage, and misfortune also meant that nearly all early American Jews lived in multiple locations during their lifetimes. When Reyna had to flee her home in 1776, the silver survived. She must have travelled ahead with it. Her husband, Isaac, waited until the very last minute. When the British cannons and musket fire finally drove him from the city, he fled on foot so as not to desecrate the Jewish Sabbath.[34]

Sloe's daughter was not the only member of the extended Myers clan to end up with Myers silver.[35] As the reward posted after a 1767 robbery demonstrates, Myers silver was also owned by the mother of Moses Michael Hays, the husband of Reyna's aunt, Rachel Myers (fig. 26).[36] The missing tablespoons were not the family's only Myers-made domestic silver. Rachel and Moses also likely owned a sauce spoon made by Myers and his sometime partner Benjamin Halstead. The couple additionally owned ritual items made by Myers, such as the Myers Torah finials once used in Newport.[37] Other extended family members purchased ritual items from the Jewish silversmith: the Myers circumcision shield and probe now housed at the Jewish Museum in New York, for example, is believed to have once been owned by Moses Seixas (1744–1800), Myer Myers's nephew by marriage as well as a relation through his sister Sloe (fig. 27).[38]

The Myers stamp underneath Reyna's six beakers reminds us of the importance of female lines in early New York Jewish history. Women were the glue connecting family lines. Today people sometimes say when a daughter marries, "I didn't lose a daughter, I gained a son-in-law." This gain was meaningful for Reyna's grandfather. When Hayman Levy came

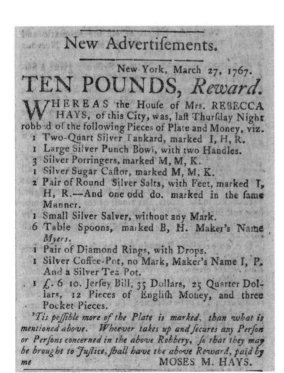

Fig. 26. Advertisement, *New-York Gazette*, March 23–30, 1767. Courtesy American Antiquarian Society, Worcester, MA.

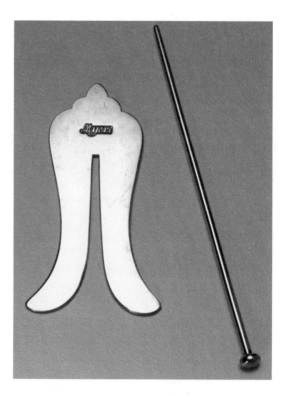

Fig. 27. Myer Myers, circumcision shield and probe, 1765–75. Silver; 2⅗ × 1½ in. Courtesy of the Jewish Museum, New York.

to New York, thousands of miles separated him from his kin. The first step in changing his kinless status was to marry into the Myers clan. The second step, however, was to bring over his biological kin from the Old World and marry his first child to that relation. That marriage inspired the second mark on Reyna's cups.

All six beakers are engraved underneath with the three initials "IMR" along with the "Myers" stamp (fig. 28). When Reyna was seventeen, she married Isaac Moses, her first cousin. He was eleven years her senior, a fairly typical age spread.[39] The silver beakers were engraved in capital letters underneath to reflect their union. The highest letter, *M*, engraved directly above the Myers stamp, signifies Reyna's new last name: Moses. On either side, forming a triangle, are the couple's first initials. To the left, in the most prominent spot, stands the *I* for Isaac, and to the right, the *R* for Reyna. Together the "Myers" stamp and "IMR" engravings form a sort of arrow. The marks and engravings would be an omen, a prayer of sorts that the marriage would last and prosper. It did.

The marriage was a long time coming. Like Reyna's father, Isaac Moses had been born in what is now Germany in a town called Giessen.[40]

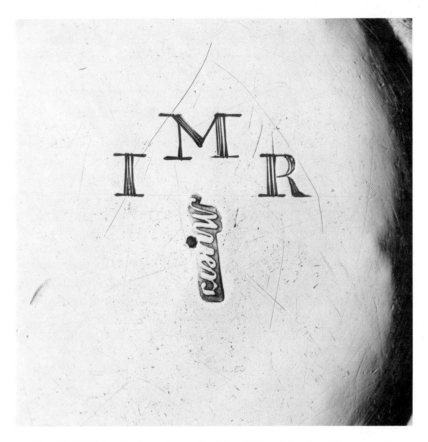

Fig. 28. "IMR" etched on the underside of Myers's beaker. Courtesy of the Metropolitan Museum of Art, 1980.501.3.

In 1764 he came to New York seeking "business opportunities."[41] Most likely he was brought over by Reyna's father.[42] For Hayman, having a nephew in town—a male child who shared his own bloodline—was essential. Although Hayman and Sloe had eleven children, the first five were girls.[43] Hayman had brothers whose sons he might call upon to make up for his early lack of male offspring—some were even located in the colonies by the 1760s. Hayman turned instead, though, to his sister Rischa's son, showing yet again how female lines mattered in early Jewish New York.

Isaac Moses came to the colonies to succeed in business, and he did so spectacularly. Between 1764 and 1775, "he developed numerous business skills, working in Levy's lucrative Bayard Street firm and the fur trade. During these years . . . [Isaac] sold deerskins, bearskins, Indian blankets, spermaceti oil, and logwood to European merchants. He also distributed English woolens, Irish linens, French wines, and West Indian rum in domestic markets."[44] Advertisements for his stores reveal the incredible breadth of goods he carried, ranging from luxury items to everyday staples like soap, candles, tea, and cordage.[45] By 1768, he had become a naturalized citizen of New York, giving him "equal rights to the native born with rights to property, inheritance and civic responsibilities."[46]

Isaac's marriage to his uncle's oldest daughter, Reyna, on August 8, 1770, wed him to the Levy family business. Although cousin marriages were not unheard of among Western European Ashkenazi Jews, they were also not the norm. Business alliances tended to motivate marriage in the Old World, particularly among wealthy and socially mobile Ashkenazi Jews. Fathers were responsible for marrying their children into "respectable" families," and men often exceeded their means to provide a dowry to ensure a good match.[47] Although some men made matches for their children while travelling on business, others relied on contacts made through relatives or via a matchmaker. Only poor women like servants could choose their spouses, as there was less to be gained by their alliances.[48]

Reyna was probably luckier, then, than her Aunt Rischa regarding marriage. At least Reyna had met her groom before the ceremony. Because German Jewish marriages were often arranged across space and via proxies, commonly not only the bride but also her parents would not have met the groom before the marriage.[49] We do not know how old Rischa was when she married, but like Reyna, Jewish women in German lands were typically close to twenty when they married (and their husbands were five to seven years older); some Jewish girls, however, married as young as twelve and often under duress.[50]

In using silver to mark a marriage, the beakers represented Old World ways. When Reyna and Moses's union was etched into silver with their initials, the marks reflected the traditional role silver played in creating Jewish spouses. Their ceremony was most likely similar to the Jewish marriage colonist Dr. Benjamin Rush described a few years later. The wedding was probably held in Reyna's father's parlor rather than at the synagogue, with special benches brought in for the guests. A beautiful chuppah (marriage canopy), likely made of silk, would have been hoisted up on poles by young men wearing white gloves. As soon as it was aloft, female relations would have escorted the bride, a veil covering her face. After prayers in Hebrew and sips of wine, Isaac would place a ring on Reyna's finger.[51] Ever since the custom of rings had been introduced into Jewish tradition in the seventh and eighth centuries,[52] silver rings (along with gold) were favored because they echoed "the ancient custom of purchasing a bride," a transaction the Talmud explicitly required be made with silver.[53]

Silver implied that technically the wedding had already been enacted before the bride and groom even reached the wedding canopy. Men would have arrived early not only to take part in the prayers but also to witness the reading and signing of a "small piece of parchment"—the *ketubah*, or marriage contract.[54] The contract ensured Reyna was provided for after Isaac's death in case she survived him and protected the bride in case of divorce.[55] If the marriage were to end, Reyna and her money could return to her birth family. Thanks to Congregation Shearith Israel's excellent record keeping, Isaac Moses and Reyna Levy's *ketubah* survives today (fig. 29).

Between the Talmudic era and 1770, only a few things had changed in the form of this contract. One that had not was the exchange of silver. According to her *ketubah*, Reyna's cousin gave her father (as mandated by Jewish law) the equivalent of 200 silver *zuzim*, an ancient Jewish silver coin. This amount would weigh about 700 grams (22.5 oz.) of pure silver, or slightly over four of the Myer Myers silver beakers.[56] It was the amount required for a "pure virgin," whereas a divorcee or widow would only receive 100 *zuzim*. Because this wedding joined not only a couple but merchants in particular, Reyna's father, Hayman, also provided a dowry of £1000 in silver, gold, jewelry, and household furnishings, and Isaac brought to the marriage a groom's gift of 1000 *litra monies* of the city of New York.[57]

Although *litra monies* was the antiquated way of saying "local currency" in Aramaic, it also referred to the small silver coins used in antiquity worth 60 shekels.[58] It was unusual during the eighteenth century for the father and groom to bring equal amounts, let alone such large sums, to the marriage. Although technically this money was "set aside" for the bride in case of death or divorce, in reality the money (framed as silver) ensured that the couple had the funds to start married life, money that was Isaac's to spend in colonial New York.

Wedding gifts and the silver exchanged in the *ketubah* epitomize what anthropologists refer to as threshold gifts. These items "mark the time of, or act as the agents of, individual transformation."[59] Threshold gifts accompany rites of passage or moments of great change and are commonly given at life-cycle events such as weddings, funerals, and coming-of-age ceremonies.[60] In Jewish tradition, silver threshold gifts specifically mark the redemption of the firstborn (*pidyon haben*). During this ceremony

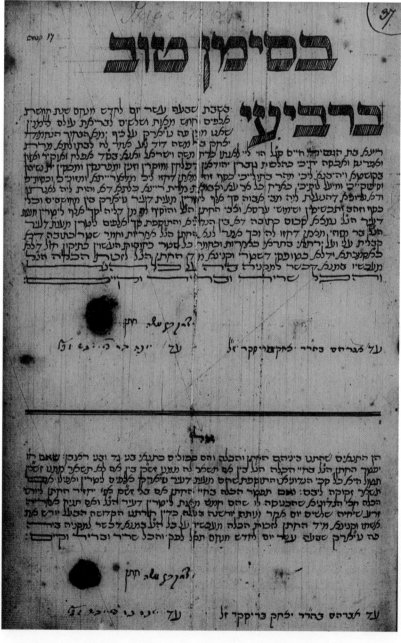

Fig. 29. *Ketubah* of Isaac Moses and Reyna Levy, 1770. Records of
Congregation Shearith Israel, 1759–1932, MF-1e, microfilm, reel 3,
microdex 1, AJA. Courtesy of Congregation Shearith Israel and AJA.

the father "redeems" his firstborn son when the child is at least thirty-one days old (fig. 30). The purpose of the ceremony is to transform a firstborn son from someone who, according to Jewish law, belonged to God and was obliged to fulfill the duties of the priests in the Temple into a person once again belonging to his family. The ritual does this by transferring the child's obligation to serve in the Temple to members of the priestly caste via the exchange of five silver coins, originally *sheka-lim*. Over time, the ritual silver coinage associated with the threshold rite accrued to other items used to perform the ceremony. During the eighteenth century, five local (silver) coins could be given to the *kohen* (member of the priestly caste) during the ceremony, but so could other objects such as a ring, silverwork, or a pewter tray.[61]

In Bernard Picart's depiction of a *pidyon haben* ceremony in an elite Amsterdam household, we see the use of silver coins to enact the

Fig. 30. Claude Du Bosc, after Bernard Picart, *The Redemption of the First Born*, engraving from *The Ceremonies and Religious Customs of the Various Nations of the Known* World, vol. 1 (London: William Jackson and Claude Dubosc, 1733). Courtesy of Special Collections, College of Charleston Libraries.

transformation of the child. The baby's cradle lies to the far left, while the *kohen* stands at the center with a book (A), and the father (B) reaches into a dish of coins held by a slave (figs. 30 and 31). Importantly, the ceremony moves the child from the margins of the family, in the "female" corner with his mother (C) and midwife (D), to center stage, below the framed portrait of a patriarch. In undergoing the ceremony, the child is transformed from one who serves, like the slave holding coins or the nurse opening the door (E), to one who stands at the center of familial life. The ritual exchange of coins enacts this metamorphosis. When the child has grown up and married, the exchange of coins between men would once again mark the threshold ceremony.

It is not accidental that two men are placed at the center of the engraving of the *pidyon haben* and at the center of exchanges in marriage contracts. As anthropologist Annette Weiner notes, giving threshold gifts marks the transformation of the giver as well as the receiver: "On the one hand, some older person—the donor who is leaving that stage of life—dis-invests himself of an old identity by bestowing these same gifts upon the young."[62] Notably, in eighteenth-century Jewish marriage contracts, the people actually transferring goods are the two men; in the

Fig. 31. Detail of Du Bosc, *The Redemption of the First Born.*

case of Reyna's marriage contract, the two men ritually exchanging items were her father, Hayman, and her groom, Isaac. By gifting Isaac with the dowry, Hayman disinvested himself of his old identity as the primary male in charge of maintaining Reyna and bestowed that role upon Isaac. By returning a gift (the groom's gift), Isaac bestowed his old role as auxiliary kin on Hayman.

Like the ritualized exchange of silver in the *ketubah*, the event leading Myer Myers to create the beakers was the couple's union. Details about the acquisition of the cups have been lost: the rough date of 1770–90 reflects only the style of the "Myers" stamp and the other marks on the cup.[63] It is even unclear whether the couple were gifted the beakers by Myers himself or whether they bought them from his store and had them inscribed. Yet either way, the beakers were a fitting remembrance of the couple's marriage, as early American Jews often used silver as threshold gifts and to mark unions. Perhaps the most classic instance of the use of silver by colonial Jews to form a union is a silver circumcision shield and probe (1765–75) made by Myers and used to mark the binding of male children with the Jewish people and the divine (see fig. 27).[64] Myer Myers's silver beakers echo the *ketubah*'s use of silver to bind new families to old ones. The stamping on the cups with "Myers" and the engraved "IMR" would wed not only the silversmith to client but uncle to niece and uncle to nephew-in-law.

If Myers did choose the beakers as a gift for the young couple, he was not merely advertising his wares or wishing them well in their new life together; he was also helping transform Isaac Moses into closer kin. The wedding marked a new, closer relationship between the men. Myers and Isaac would establish ties as fellow Freemasons, as coreligionists, and as leaders of Congregation Shearith Israel. Myers would also stand beside Isaac as a witness on April 25, 1771, when Isaac was naturalized, "with Myer Myers testifying as to his required residency."[65] When in 1785 the two men helped form a burial society, Isaac Moses donated a pair of silver candlesticks after he first paid Myer Myers 16 shillings to inscribe the silver with Hebrew. The silver candlesticks would be used to mark the transition of the dead from one world to the next.[66] The familial connection would serve the Myers family well. As artisans, the Myers were a class below the newly wealthy Moses and Levy clans. During the Revolutionary War, however, Isaac Moses took on Myer Myers's son Samuel as his business partner.[67] This help was central to Samuel's development as a merchant, and when he died, he "left the largest estate in Richmond up to that time."[68] His granddaughter Caroline would become an important benefactor of the Touro synagogue, leaving them an exquisite set of neo-classical Torah finials made by her great-grandfather.[69]

Reyna and Isaac were not the only early American Jews to use locally made household silver in gifts exchanged to mark thresholds. Families used silver to mark the transition between weekdays and the Sabbath and often willed those objects when they died. Indeed, prior associations of silver with Jewish tradition made the beakers the perfect objects to be transformed into heirlooms, passed down through Reyna and Isaac's descendants. Silver wedded together generations of the Moses clan. At almost every stage in the objects' descent through the family, the beakers were re-marked with new initials and names. These scratched names and inscriptions wound the new owners into a legacy. As the beakers were transformed into heirlooms, they helped maintain memory and Jewish lines. The first marks also recorded Reyna's transition from bride to mother.

A Cup's Second Life: Mothers and Heirlooms

As Reyna's life progressed, the family acquired other silver, including a silver watch for her husband and a silver coffee pot bought at auction.[70] Unlike Hannah Louzada, whose husband was too poor to think about his wife's lot after his death, Reyna's husband, Isaac Moses, died prepared with a will that made careful provisions for his wife and children yet left much to Reyna's discretion in case her wishes were—as Isaac put it—"contrary to my own" due to "any cause which I cannot anticipate."[71] When Isaac passed in 1818 at the couple's country estate in Mt. Listen, all of the silver and furniture both in New York and Philadelphia became Reyna's to use until her death. These goods were substantial: Isaac's estate inventory ran to three pages and included over $300 worth of silver and silver plate in their house near the Shearith Israel synagogue alone. By the 1820s, silver dishes like the set of beakers, once displayed on dining parlor shelves or sideboard tables, would have been relegated to locked cupboards. The silver was hers and passed to her descendants when Reyna died six years after Isaac.[72] Just as Reyna changed over the years from bride to mother and then grandmother, so too the nature of the silver transformed from intimate objects into well-guarded heirlooms, imbued with family memory. The scratches marked underneath aided in this metamorphosis and tell us something important about Jews and family legacies in early America.

Unlike Moses Louzada's estate that went in good British style to his oldest son, Reyna and Isaac treated each of their sons equally and each of their daughters equitably when it came to money and real estate. The daughters each received a small fortune. The house in which Reyna lived and the furniture would be passed down to her unmarried daughters to use for the rest of their lives. The rest of the estate, including the vast amounts of property that Isaac had accumulated over the years, would be divided equally among the couple's five sons, Moses, Solomon, David, Joshua, and Hayman.

This legacy was substantial. By 1816 Isaac was a real estate baron with some of the largest holdings in the emergent city.[73] These properties included not only the house on Pearl Street and fifteen acres in Greenwich Village along Fitzroy Road[74] but also the family's self-described "Estate in the Country" at Mt. Listen, valued at $25,000.[75] It was to here that the family would retreat when a yellow fever epidemic swept the city, holding a private minyan during the high holy days in the fall.[76] For old New Yorkers, this was known as the "old Cooper farm"—a vast property that covered what is today the area between 32nd and 35th Streets and from Seventh Avenue all the way to the Hudson River (fig. 32).[77]

If the Moses family had resided in England, their country estate might have helped them emulate landed gentry. British Jews of Isaac and Reyna's generation, such as Naphtali Franks (son of Abigail Franks), were busy buying up land in scenic towns outside of London like Richmond, where they built houses to emulate the aristocracy.[78] In New York, the city overtook the country much faster, transforming rural estates into urban blocks. By the 1830s, Mt. Listen was already on the city's rapidly expanding grid and was home to a chemical company (see fig. 32). By 1860 it had become prime urban real estate, in part owing to the 8th Avenue railroad line that ran across it starting in 1854, taking New Yorkers from Vesey to 59th Street and later all the way north to Harlem, Manhattan's new rural neighborhood.[79]

In England, country estates and heirlooms were part of being upper class. Like country estates, heirlooms were items specifically entailed to oldest sons (by "will, settlement or custom") and hence could not be sold.[80] By 1700, the English government overseeing New York had legally shifted the colony's inheritance system from the Dutch one (equal distribution of goods among kin) to the English system of primogeniture (descent of all real estate to the oldest son). In the colony this only applied, however, when there was no will, and early New Yorkers like Reyna and Isaac got around these issues by not entailing their newly made estates

Fig. 32. Location of the Moses family's "country estate." J. H. & Co., *Topographical Map of the City and County of New-York*, 1836. Courtesy of the Library of Congress Geography and Map Division, 2007627512.

and by writing wills to share wealth more equitably among their children. In doing so, they deliberately rejected English aristocratic customs.[81] In New York, real estate created riches but was not intended to be passed down untouched through the ages. Silver, however, functioned differently: it became a way of creating a legacy and family story.

Unlike real estate, which was sold or rented, silver heirlooms could be etched with the names of those who inherited them, creating a living memorial to the past and a chain of family history. Three of Reyna's original six beakers were scratched underneath with the initials "SM" for Solomon Moses (1774–1857), Reyna's second-oldest son (fig. 33). A fourth was scratched "Keep for Saly for her only" (see fig. 35). In designating a cup for a specific child, Reyna and her husband began the beakers' transformation into heirlooms, that is, into objects to be passed down through family lines. For anthropologists, heirlooms are serious business, wrapped up in gift giving, inheritance, and identity. Over time, these heirlooms become associated with the family's sense of itself, signifying their rank and class as much as heraldic symbols, aristocratic titles, or family trees might. Typically, heirlooms are highly valuable or rare in some way, thereby ensuring not only their transmission to another generation but also their continued possession and display. Owning and

Fig. 33. "SM" scratched lightly in script on the underside of Myers's silver beaker. Winterthur Museum, 1961.0957.002.

exhibiting heirlooms allowes the living to distinguish themselves from their "social inferiors" and thereby helps the next generation maintain inherited social and class distinctions.[82]

Giving heirlooms serves as a form of self-curation: objects like the Myerses' beakers would have allowed family members to preserve ideas about why their family mattered, as well as key aspects of the family's sense of "self." As archeologist Katine Lillios explains, "Heirlooms serve to objectify memories and histories, acting as mnemonics to remind the living of their link to a distant, ancestral past."[83] As they rose into the merchant class, Jews like the Moses family had a palpable need for new heirlooms. Whereas the landed gentry or aristocrats in England relied on titles, land, or country houses to carry on a sense of the family, Jewish merchants tended to move frequently during this era and hence sought out small, transportable goods to pass to the next generation. Heirlooms connected future descendants to the past their ancestors had worked so hard to create.

For Jews arriving in New York in the late eighteenth and early nineteenth centuries, heirlooms, particularly silver, became an important way to shape the family and create new visions of the past, present, and future. Western Sephardic Jews tended to be nostalgic about their own aristocratic lineages, and the few Jews who had titles or heraldic symbols tended to display them on gravestones and sometimes even above the doorways to their houses.[84] For most merchant families, however, the wealth they gained in the Americas could be transformed in part into heirlooms. Silver heirlooms symbolized the "ancestral power" Isaac Moses and his wife Reyna sought to pass along to their children. For men, the power was to be great merchants and money lenders. For women, the power was to be the crucial solder welding merchant houses together. Indeed, it was not until Reyna's descendants *stopped* being merchants that Reyna's silver beakers ceased to have a powerful hold over posterity as heirlooms.

The choice of Solomon as the recipient of half the cups speaks to the importance of merchant houses and family lines in heirloom production.[85] Although not professionally made like the initial etching "IMR," the scratched initials are in elegant cursive. They are marks of pride. The cursive "SM" loops below the original marks, forming a larger triangle with the past. Born at the cusp of the Revolutionary War, Solomon would inherit his father's and grandfather's legacy. More than just a son, Solomon was part of Isaac's mercantile empire. Like members of the *nação*, Ashkenazi Jews in the Atlantic World created merchant houses whose members "maintain[ed] tight and lasting bonds among themselves even if they were often physically separated from one another by the span of oceans and continents." Merchant houses like Isaac Moses & Sons were composed of "a highly interconnected network of houses created by the extension of both affective and business ties between different houses. Individual merchants were not only one another's associates, partners, and commission agents, but, more often than not, were also related by varying degrees of kinship. The tight-knit interrelation of these houses had clear advantages in the world of Atlantic trade."[86] Like his father, Solomon would learn to balance mercantile interests with a life tied to the synagogue. In his early years, Solomon worked alongside his father in the company Isaac Moses & Sons, importing fur, wine, mahogany, cloth, jewelry, and porcelain.[87] In the early nineteenth century, he and his younger brother Joshua continued the family's tradition by serving as international brokers for the wealthy Stephen Girard. Throughout his life, Solomon served as a hub for his father's network.[88] He also played a central role in Congregation Mikveh Israel, the synagogue his father had helped start in Philadelphia during the Revolutionary War.

Solomon's marriage choice reflected both his mercantile and religious interests but involved a new aspect: love. Solomon's wife, Rachel, was the daughter of a leading Jewish merchant, Michael Gratz, giving her a status much like that of Solomon's mother.[89] More famously, Rachel was the younger sister of Rebecca Gratz, an important Jewish philanthropist

and educator. Unlike his father, however, Solomon found himself needing to woo Rachel herself to make the marriage. In keeping with the
younger generation's newfound belief in romantic love, Solomon's marriage prospects depended upon more than his future father-in-law's business needs. Unfortunately for the young New Yorker, when Solomon visited Philadelphia in 1804, Michael Gratz's daughters found Solomon to
be "an insufferable bore."[90] Strikingly beautiful, the sisters were known
as the "Three Graces"—a play on their last name, Gratz. Like her sisters,
Rachel would be the subject of a Gilbert Stuart painting, a Thomas Sully
portrait, and a lovely romantic miniature by Edward Greene Malbone
(fig. 34).[91] The plethora of paintings alone showed the distance of this
new age from Reyna's world, as no known portraits of her survive. The
Gratz women were used to "the best society" and the wittiest men in Philadelphia.[92] Solomon Moses did not measure up. "Thank God for all his
Mercy Sol. Moses left P[hiladelphia] on Thursday last," wrote Rachel to
her sister. Sadly, she noted, "the pleasure of his departure is a great deal
interrupted by the thoughts of his return again soon."[93] Yet like so many
lovers before him, Solomon seems not to have let either the Gratzes' lack
of interest or local competition stop him. Solomon had already fallen in
love with Rachel, who, according to her niece, "was the most beautiful
[sister] of all."[94] We have the Gratz women's wonderful letter writing to
thank for our understanding of their courtship.[95]

Although boorish, Solomon was persistent, and that perseverance
paid off. Upon his return to Philadelphia two years later, Rachel wrote
her sister Rebecca that Solomon had "secured my everlasting Friendship. I think him much improved in every respect."[96] Then only a few
days later, Rachel wrote again, saying Solomon inspired "greater agitation than any other gentlemen ever occasioned me. . . . Every day has
encreased [sic] those feelings and added to them. . . . I cannot myself
account for the change but I have learned from my heart to love him."[97]
Worried her sister still scorned Solomon, Rachel wrote to Rebecca at
the "first gleam of day" after a sleepless night: "You my beloved Sister
shall decide my future fate." She explains, "I will make any sacrifice[,]
every sacrifice[,] to you that I will give up the man my heart has chosen
if you wish it and live for you alone my dear dear sister."[98] Fortunately
for our story, Rebecca not only provided her blessing but also somehow
helped convince their other sister, Sarah,[99] who still disliked Solomon,
to change her mind.[100] On June 24, 1806, when Solomon was thirty-one
and Rachel was twenty-three, they wed.[101] In the end, it was good that the
couple had gained Rebecca's blessing, as when Rachel was laid to rest in

Fig. 34. Anonymous, *Rachel Gratz*, ca. 1806; copy of the miniature by
Edward Greene Malbone. Oil on paper; height: 2⁷⁄₁₀ in. Courtesy of the
Rosenbach Museum, 1995.001.

a coffin in 1823 with her "sleeping infant," Gertrude, beside her, it was
"Aunt Becky" who would "make a home for the motherless."[102] Solomon
and his "seven bereaved children" moved into the Gratz house, where
Rebecca raised the children as her own.[103] Even after his wife's death,
Solomon's life was inextricably interwoven with the Gratzes.

The wedding of the Gratz and Moses lines probably explains why, despite having nine other siblings, Solomon's initials are inscribed on the underside of not one but three of the original six beakers. Although we might expect the silver to pass down to the oldest son, the potential to have Jewish descendants seems to better predict to whom Reyna and Isaac would give their cups. When Solomon married in 1806, only one of his nine siblings was married: his oldest sister, Richea. She had married her maternal uncle, Aaron Levy, six years before. Because her parents were first cousins, Aaron was not only the brother of Richea's mother but also her father's first cousin.[104] Although the marriage lasted a long time, the couple never bore any children of their own. Solomon's inheritance reflected a legacy Reyna and Isaac apparently wanted to preserve: an ongoing family dynasty in synagogue and in trade.

For Reyna's daughters, however, the silver would also hold a power of a new kind—a memento of people to be remembered. Three cups may have been destined for Solomon Moses, but a fourth was marked to indicate that it should go to Solomon's sister Sarah, known by the family as Saly: "Keep for Saly for her only" (fig. 35). Born in 1787, Saly was the second to last of the ten Moses children. Like over half her siblings, she never married.[105] Yet the descent of the silver to Saly tells us something key about changes in Jewish families during Reyna's lifetime and how women's role in maintaining the family legacy had begun to shift. Whereas once women had tied families together through marriage, now women who remained single also helped familial lines through affective ties.

We know little enough about Saly's upbringing, other than that her parents intended for her to be a lady. Her father paid for both music lessons and her secular education.[106] Unlike her brothers, though, she does not appear to have attended Shearith Israel's new coeducational Jewish school.[107] Saly *was* typical of the Jewish girls of her generation in one way: she decided not to marry. To be sure, the new value on romance was partially to blame. The pool of acceptable Jewish partners was small for women of Saly's class. The pool shrunk further if one felt compelled to follow Jane Austen's advice that "a woman is not to marry a man merely because she is asked, or because he is attached to her, and can write a tolerable letter."[108] The new-fledged need to "do anything rather than marry without affection"[109] was further complicated by the disproportionate dearth of available Jewish men.[110] Between 1776 and 1826, intermarriage rates for Jewish men more than doubled,[111] yet few Jewish women opted to marry out. The result was that single Jewish women were as numerous as married ones from the 1790s to the 1830s.[112] As Louisa Hart of Philadelphia noted, remaining single could

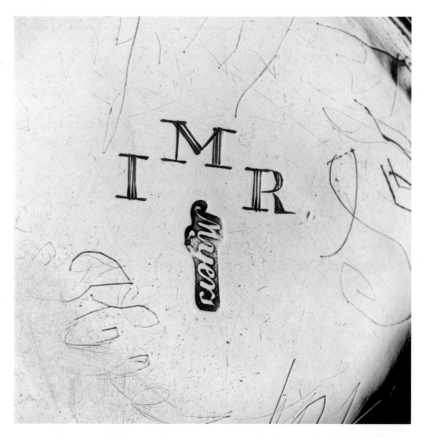

Fig. 35. "Keep for Saly for her only" scratched lightly on the underside of Myers's silver beaker. Metropolitan Museum of Art, 1980.501.1

be frustrating. She explained to a friend that while older single women might be "very happy," "the road is a very sad one to travel before one reaches the climacteric [menopause]."[113]

Not everyone saw the single life as a problem, however. By remaining single, women maintained greater control over their property. Moreover, larger American culture had begun to rethink unmarried women, who, at least as some argued, "as a class, have among them more purity and active goodness."[114] Rather than dismissing them as "old maids," nineteenth-century magazines encouraged readers to think of single women as "silent active doers of good," living in a state of "single blessedness."[115] Nineteenth-century women also embraced their single status, as exemplified by Susan Elizabeth Daggett, whose sewing circle designed a quilt for her to celebrate her single status when she firmly declared she would never marry.[116] Like their Christian counterparts, Jewish women during this era increasingly embraced not marrying as a *virtuous* option. They became involved in helping Jewish children and the poor. They helped found not only Jewish Sunday schools but also orphan asylums.[117] Within families, single women increasingly played a larger role in remaking their brother's wives into kin through exuberant, emotional letters.[118] Like Rebecca Gratz, they also tended to help raise their brothers' children if their wives died young.[119]

Saly's inheritance of a beaker (as well as substantial amounts of cash) reflects single women's new roles in maintaining family lines. When Saly's father, Isaac, died in 1818, the bulk of his estate passed to Reyna, with whom Saly lived, including the household furniture, silver plate, their house near the synagogue, and their country estate at Mt. Listen. Isaac also ensured that Saly had money easily at her disposal to pay for her immediate needs.[120] When Reyna died six years later in 1824, Saly (now thirty-six) was left a fortune: $7,500 to be placed out in stock, with the interest and income going to Saly.[121] Ways of determining the worth of early American money today vary, but using economic status, this would be like inheriting over $6 million today.[122] If Saly married, half would go to her husband, but Reyna safeguarded the remainder for Saly's "own separate use and benefit free from the control and engagements" of her future husband.[123] Reyna did the same for her other daughters. They would also inherit her household furniture, but the rest of her estate—including any silver she still owned—went to her five sons, Moses, Solomon, David, Joshua, and Hayman—Saly's cup excepted.[124]

The transfer of silver from Reyna to her sons hardly left Saly bereft of silver to use in her remaining years. As an unmarried woman of means, she could dispose of her property as she pleased. Her will states Saly's unmarried sister Rebecca would inherit all her money. After Rebecca's death, it was to pass to Saly's "much beloved" nephew, Abraham Rodriguez Brandon. Most of the rest of Saly's will concerns the family silver, the lion's share of which went to Abraham. He received a silver spice box, nine silver table spoons, one silver porringer with cover, spoons marked "ARL" for family members, two silver rings, two silver goblets, one spice box, one sugar pot, one milk pot, eleven knives, and twelve forks. Abraham's recent marriage to a non-Jew did not deter Saly. In fact, she gave him not just one spice box for bringing the Sabbath to a close but two.[125] Census records and Saly's interest in Abraham suggest she probably helped raise him after his mother, Lavinia, Saly's closest sister, died in 1828. Much like Rebecca Gratz, Saly took on this role frequently assigned to women without children of their own: raising their siblings' orphans.[126] Most of the rest of the silver went to Saly's surviving siblings, with instructions as to how the silver should descend through the family line after their own deaths. Other pieces went to younger relations Saly could guarantee would "value them from their association" with previous generations.[127]

Yet a little more than a month after Saly's will was read into the record, her beloved nephew, Abraham Rodriguez Brandon, was dead at only thirty-three years of age.[128] For the first time since his father's ancestors had left Iberia, a Brandon was buried in a Christian cemetery. He lay among his wife's kin in Trinity Cemetery in Morningside Heights. Everything, including the family silver, passed to his young Protestant wife, Miriam, who was left to raise their young children.[129] Saly's beaker, though, made it back to the Moses family. In the year before Abraham's death, he had bought a new silver Tiffany beaker and engraved it as a gift for his newborn daughter, Edith, starting a tradition anew.[130]

Early American Jews who acquired silver during their lifetimes either as gifts or purchases tended to will the silver to descendants upon their deaths. Silver and silver plate often first passed to wives or unmarried daughters for use during their lifetime and then on to other recipients. Both because silver was a luxury item and because it was commonly marked with the initials of the original owners, it made the perfect heirloom for families in the growing city. Silver often was willed with emotional ties. Esther Benazaken, for example, noted that everything should be divided equally "Except a Silver Bell & Correl," which she left as a "token of Remembrance," and a Silver Stone pin, which went to another daughter "as a token of my further Love & affection."[131] Marks that once indicated who owned an object now became tokens of remembrance, a way of preserving a legacy of people now dead and continuing ties after family members "married out." In an age in which the city was rapidly expanding and Jewish neighborhoods kept moving steadily uptown, valuable yet movable goods like silver worked to tie family members to the past and to ancestral legacies more than houses or land. When descendants forsook the family legacy or the heirlooms had more value as antiques than as memorials, they passed into their third lives as objects in museum and private collections.

Museum Collectibles: The Afterlife of an Heirloom

Although the beakers were passed down lovingly for generations, today no one in the Moses family owns *any* of the six beakers. Once used to provide sustenance to a family, today the silver beakers are collectibles in lighted glass cases. Reyna's memory dimmed with this final transition. The erasure of women's stories from displays of Judaica is not an accident: the very way that Jewish silver is collected privileges men's lives.

Reyna's beakers ceased to function as heirlooms when her descendants wrote new family stories. The story of merchant greatness began its decline in the 1870s, a hundred years after the beakers were first made. Reyna was now long dead, and the cups bore mute witness to her afterlife merely as the *R* in "IMR." Reyna's last known descendant to own any of the cups was Lionel Moses Jr., Reyna's great-grandson (appendix 2). His ownership seemed promising at first. The transfer was marked by a new inscription on one beaker: "Lionel Moses FROM UNCLE ISAAC April 16th 1871" (fig. 36).[132] It was the first time a professional silversmith

Fig. 36. Myer Myers, silver beaker, 1770–90. Height: 4 in. Private collection. Photo © Christie's Images / Bridgeman Images.

had engraved the vessels since Myer Myers held them a hundred years earlier. The new engraving once again marked a rite of passage: Lionel Jr.'s first birthday.

The engraved cup aimed to weave Lionel Jr. into a fabric of family associations he would only know by legend. Uncle Isaac (1807–47), Solomon's oldest son, had died unmarried and alone twenty-four years before while working in Mobile, Alabama.[133] When he died, he appears to have owned four of the original six beakers. Upon his death, Isaac's cups would pass to his nephew, Lionel Sr. (appendix 2). It was a solid choice. Tradition was important to Lionel Sr., whose wife, Selina Seixas, was the granddaughter of Gershom Mendes Seixas, Congregation Shearith Israel's most beloved early rabbi.[134] When he inscribed the cup, Lionel Sr. commemorated his Uncle Isaac's part in the family story and thereby explained to Lionel Jr. the tradition he was entering, a merchant's covenant. At one year of age, Lionel Jr.'s inheritance was the legacy of silver.

It would not be enough. Unlike his father and forebearers, Lionel Jr. would not become a merchant but an artist—and a successful one at that. For forty-four years, he worked at the famous New York architectural firm McKim, Mead & White, for whom he helped design several buildings at Columbia University and the Players Club in New York. Later he opened his own office in the Architects' Building and shifted his focus to country houses and residences for New York's new elite. He also designed the DKE Fraternity House at Amherst College.[135] By 1920 Lionel Jr. had become the art director of Gorham Manufacturing Company in Providence, one of the largest and most influential American silver companies, and he is mentioned as an expert resource in early scholarship on colonial silver.[136] Yet somehow the beakers, once precious reminders of the family's gifts in commerce, had lost their sway. Or maybe Lionel just understood their new value as Americana. Despite having several Jewish male heirs, Lionel gave or sold three beakers to his architectural client Josephine Ettlinger McFadden. Her son and daughter-in-law later donated them to the Met.[137] Eventually even the inscribed cup also passed from the Moses family's hands, appearing first in collections of Eric Noah and Mark Bortman and later selling at auction at Christies in 2015 for $17,500, nearly three times the highest expected estimate.[138] The cups had stopped being heirlooms and were now officially art.

This transformation impacted Reyna's legacy. First and foremost, it meant that the cups she owned would be displayed as colonial American silver. Although the Met has long had separate wings for Islamic and Christian art,[139] all Jewish art in the museum is integrated within the surrounding cultures and eras of its creation.[140] Even American silver had a tenuous claim on its status as "art." As the curators at the Met note, "Plain domestic beakers of this type, [were] especially popular during the last quarter of the eighteenth century," and like Reyna's set, they were "often made in pairs or in sets of six or more."[141] Rethinking every-day domestic silver as "art" had not been an obvious process. It was not until 1909 that the museum even displayed early Americana and then only on loan to "test out the question whether American domestic art was worthy of a place in the art museum."[142] Built in the 1920s when the museum was already fifty years old, the glorious American wing on the northwest end was in many ways an afterthought, a result of a gift by Robert W. de Forest and his wife, collectors of American antiques. While ethereal, the "white box" treatment the beakers receive there deliber-ately embodies "an attitude that disconnects art from life" in order to emphasize that Americana *is* art.[143] By becoming art, the history of the items' original owners—including Reyna— would be downplayed.

Being collected as art also meant that Reyna's cups were unlikely to be categorized as Jewish, since the way Judaica has been collected and displayed often limits the dimensions of what it means to be a Jewish object in ways that favor men.[144] As John Cotton Dana explains, collec-tors tend to acquire objects that are "ancient, costly, and imported, that the rich feel they must buy to give themselves a desired distinction."[145] In turn, these objects are "inevitably the kinds that they, as patrons and directors of museums, cause those museums to acquire."[146] Some of the costliest of these items are the silver objects used for Jewish rituals, partic-ularly those taking place in the synagogue. Historical synagogues, after all, were the original collectors of Judaica, and they too were to a certain extent at the mercy of their benefactors.

Precious holy objects were typically bequeathed to synagogues with trifold and overlapping goals: (1) glorifying God and his service, (2) in-creasing the spiritual merit of the donor or person honored by the gift, and (3) displaying and accruing communal prestige and power for the donor. Hence museum-quality collections of silver Judaica typically in-clude Torah crowns, Torah shields, *rimonim* (Torah finials), Torah point-ers, lavers and basins, megillah holders originally given to communities by individuals, as well as spice boxes, Sabbath lamps, *chanukiahs* (Chanu-kah lamps), kiddush cups, seder dishes, and *etrog* boxes used by wealthy families. With the exception of Sabbath lamps, almost all of these objects were primarily used in rituals by men during the eighteenth century. When we ignore things owned by Jews that can activate Jewish identity but in a secular or not explicitly religious context, we significantly limit what it means to be a "Jewish object" in ways that—at least in the eighteenth century—favored men (appendix 6). By becoming "art," the beakers had been stripped not only of much of their original context but of their central role in creating a Jewish family as well.

Conclusion

Reyna's silver beakers remind us how gifts, possessions, and heirlooms help establish and maintain a family's sense of itself, and how women's roles in that history can get lost as heirlooms become collectibles. Silver's presence in this story is not random: silver plays a decisive role not only in objects used in Jewish rituals but also in the symbolic transformation of people from one state to another. Rather than merely seeing silver goods as bright, shiny objects, we should take the metal's role in creating kinship more seriously, even when the objects in question do not seem explicitly "Jewish."

Thinking about the role of silver in Reyna's life can help us look at silver we own or have been given in new ways. Today silver and silver plate are still valued among American Jews as gifts to mark weddings and rites of passage, whether the silver is kiddush cups, candlesticks, or flatware with which family and festive meals will be eaten. As anyone who has obsessed over *just the right gift to give* knows, presents received at life-cycle events are not just mementos but also help establish relationships. As those gifts move down through the generations, each person has the right to sign their name to that legacy or reject it. Women's roles in gift giving are often dismissed as part of a nefarious consumer culture that "dupes" women into purchasing goods they do not need.[147] Yet anthropologists have pointed out that gifts are also a form of "kin keeping"—a way to cement necessary social ties.[148] Rethinking the role objects play in maintaining family lines helps us better understand women's ongoing roles in creating Jewish families.

The function of silver in Jewish family crafting also underwent radical changes not only between Reyna's marriage and today but also between 1750 and 1850. The earliest Jewish women in New York often did not have much choice about whom they married; rather, their partners were predetermined by the limited pool of available men and family needs. The amount of silver exchanged between men's hands in dowries often foreshadowed women's future fortunes. But as the nineteenth century matured, Jewish women—and men—started to embrace the dream of romantic love, and dowries became less significant. The dream of a soul mate changed not only whom they married but also kinship and the Jewish family itself. For Reyna, her silver dowry solidified a partnership between men and laid the groundwork for the family dynasty she would birth. In the next two chapters, we will see how the understanding of Jewish marriage changed as the nineteenth century dawned.

THREE

Portraits in Ivory

The soft white cotton gloves on my hands remind me I am trespassing. They have that flimsy loose weave that make them easily identifiable as archive accessories, reminders that my hands and their natural oils might mar history. Yet when I delicately flip over the photos I am holding, I forget all that. Instead I am awash with the intimacy of the personal notes from one family member to another, left in shaky handwriting. "For Selina with Much Love from Blanche. Dec. 1885," one reads. The front shows Blanche, stylish and young, her hair swooping high and a ribbon hanging down one shoulder. A few photos down is a photo labeled "My dear Mother" that Blanche's sister, Liny, gave "With love" to an unknown friend or relative in 1882. Below her scrawl is the quixotic emblem of Fredricks's Knickerbocker Family Portrait Gallery, with a man in Benjamin Franklin garb in front of a nineteenth-century camera.[1] The photos are all cabinet cards—a genre of late nineteenth-century photographs mounted on thick paper or a card. Like *cartes de visite*, cabinet cards were meant for exchanging. They could cement relationships across distances. They reminded people of social obligations and helped build friendships. Taken together, the photos in the collection I am looking at reveal a web of family affections and interdependencies that would otherwise be lost and imperceptible with the passage of time.

The photos are also an important reminder that while men played decisive roles in the preservation of Hannah Louzada's letter and in the transformation of Reyna Moses's silver cups into museum collectibles, women have also long been essential in the safeguarding of Jewish

Fig. 37. Rockwood Studio, *Blanche Moses*, ca. 1900. Photograph.
Courtesy of AJHS.

family heirlooms. Like work, American leisure activities tend to be gendered, and genealogy and other forms of "family collectibles" are hobbies typically dominated by women.[2] Yet individual women's roles in the preservation of family lore are often as unacknowledged as the women whose possessions they seek to preserve. One such female collector was Reyna Moses's great-granddaughter, Blanche Moses (1859–1946) (fig. 37). Like her great-aunt Saly, Blanche never married, but she became an important guardian of her family's memory. Before she died, Blanche too would pass along her treasures, to the American Jewish Historical Society. If it were not for her collecting and genealogical work—and her dedication to preserving the past—this chapter would not exist.

Blanche collected a lot: photographs, painted portraits, a journal from a sea voyage to Madras and Calcutta, several personal diaries, letters of a Civil War doctor and other correspondence, scrapbooks, Masonic memorabilia, and marriage contracts. Also among Blanche's possessions were items from her two famous great-grandfathers. The first, Rev. Gershom Mendes Seixas, was remembered as one of Shearith Israel's most beloved spiritual leaders. The second, Isaac Moses, husband of Reyna, was a real-estate tycoon and synagogue leader. Blanche had inherited many of the Moses family papers, but unlike that other, more famous collector, Jacques Judah Lyons, the minister of Shearith Israel, Blanche's interest was genealogical rather than institutional. Thus her collection included intimate glimpses into her foremothers' lives. It included daguerreotypes not only of uncles in Civil War uniforms but also of Blanche's beautiful young mother, Selina Seixas, in lacy fingerless gloves (all the rage in 1854), her braided hair wound in heavy loops on the sides of her head like a Victorian Princess Leia (fig. 38). Blanche made room for other family portraits in her collection: early ivory miniatures as well as photos of Blanche's sister Edith in blond ringlets and Blanche herself, pouting with her dolls (fig. 39). She was a diligent researcher, often publishing corrections to printed stories about her illustrious ancestors.[3]

Blanche was not the only Jewish woman of her era to obsess over family history. Today genealogy is the second most popular hobby in the United States,[4] but Jewish American genealogy had important roots in the social and political upheavals of the 1890s, beginning with what Jewish Americans scholars refer to as the Great Migration. Between 1881 and 1924, millions of Jews from Europe and the former Ottoman Empire migrated to the United States.[5] Many sought refuge from financial oppression and religious persecution. They were not alone but were joined by other Europeans from Italy, Ireland, Finland, and the Netherlands,

Fig. 38. Anonymous, *Selina Seixas [Moses]*, 1854. Daguerreotype; 4⅗ × 3⅗ in. Courtesy of AJHS.

Fig. 39. Charles D. Fredricks and Co., *Blanche and Edith Moses*, 1862. Photograph. Courtesy of AJHS.

as well as people from those Asian countries allowed to immigrate following the Chinese Exclusion Act of 1882 but before the Asian Exclusion Act of 1924.[6] These arrivals changed the nature of American cities and challenged the notion of who and what was American; genealogy responded to this identity crisis.

The Civil War had already irreparably shifted American genealogical practices toward nationalism and ancestor worship such that genealogy had become "a political and social tie for some Americans, as well as a way to exclude others"; the trend was only magnified as new arrivals swelled urban populations.[7] While white Protestant nativists used genealogy to emphasize their long-standing position "as members of the great Aryan race" (a fairly new category),[8] Jewish genealogists responded by tracing their long role in American history or alternatively—for new arrivals—their *yichut* (lineage) to famous scholars and rabbis back in their old countries. For Jews like Blanche whose ancestors had been in New York back before it was even a state, genealogy was a way of positioning themselves as part of the Jewish aristocracy of early New York and of differentiating themselves from the impoverished masses crammed into tenements on the Lower East Side. Jewish genealogy "counterbalance[d] . . . the undue weight of Anglo-Saxonism in the United States" by emphasizing Jewish contributions to the nation, but it also positioned certain Jews, namely the groups who had arrived before the 1880s, as elites.[9] The American Jewish Historical Society played a fundamental role in this revisionist history, and Blanche corresponded frequently with the society's early librarians, making corrections to publications based on her own research.[10]

Even Blanche would probably have been surprised, however, by recent interest in one of the artifacts she donated (fig. 40). Amidst papers and images of famous men is a small ivory miniature, painted in watercolor, depicting a relative Blanche never met and knew almost nothing about: her grandmother, Sarah Brandon Moses (1798–1828), a woman who died thirty years before Blanche was born and a mere ten days after the third birthday of Blanche's father.

To be sure, Blanche knew scraps about Sarah's past. Sarah's father was clearly Abraham Rodrigues Brandon of Barbados, the island's wealthiest Jew. Yet despite being a meticulous family historian,[11] Blanche drew an uncharacteristic blank for her grandmother's maternal line. Who was Sarah's mother? Moreover, why was so little known about her, when she had married a man so famous? Among the many documents cluttering Blanche's apartment on West 118th, evidence about Sarah's early life was

Fig. 40. Anonymous, *Portrait of Sarah Brandon Moses*, ca. 1815–16. Water-color on ivory; 2¾ × 2¼ in. Courtesy of AJHS.

notably absent. Blanche was left to guess about Sarah's origins. "Abra-ham Rodrigues Brandon Barbados," Blanche scribbled on the margin of one paper, "married Sarah Esther?"[12] Even Malcolm Stern, the pre-mier genealogist of early American Jews, could do no better, speculating she was part of the Lopez clan of Barbados.[13] They were both wrong. Moreover, the answer to the mystery of Sarah's origins did not fit neatly within the elite history of early American Jews that either researcher had been compiling, both of which resemble something more like a Jewish Daughters of the American Revolution (DAR) than a people's history of the United States.

The genealogists were right about one small thing. Blanche's great-grandmother *had* been raised in the Lopez household in Barbados and sometimes used their last name. She did so, however, because she was their slave. Blanche's grandmother, Sarah, had begun her life poor, Christian, and enslaved in the late eighteenth-century Lopez household in Bridgetown, Barbados. Yet within thirty years, Sarah had reached the pinnacle of New York's wealthy Jewish elite. Whereas once her own kin referred to her as "mulatto,"[14] by 1820 New York's census and the New York Jewish community had reclassified her as white.[15] What makes this change all the more surprising is that it was not a secret during Sarah's lifetime. Although a mystery to Sarah's granddaughter, Blanche, Sarah's partial African ancestry was known by numerous people everywhere she lived. Sarah's ability to change her officially designated race to "white"—despite this knowledge—tells us as much about the early history of how race was made in the Atlantic World as it does about the lives of early American Jewish women.

Today the small portrait of Sarah Brandon Moses, along with that of her brother Isaac Lopez Brandon (also born enslaved), are understood to be among the rarest items owned by the historical society, as they are the earliest known portraits of multiracial Jews (figs. 40 and 41). For over two centuries, the remarkable story of Sarah lay buried in archives across three continents. Were it not for a small, random footnote about her brother's ancestry in the records of Barbados's Nidhe Israel synagogue uncovered by historian Karl Watson, the cocoon of assumptions obscuring Sarah's past might have remained intact. Sarah and her brother would have forever remained the lesser-known members of an illustrious family.

Like the narratives of most multiracial Jews in early America, Sarah's story has largely been hidden from history. In this chapter I use her miniature to unveil that past. In general, miniatures of early American Jews have been used to illustrate the broadest brushstrokes of the biographies of famous early American Jewish men and women. Authors will sometimes employ an illustration and note, "Above: Moses Raphael Levy," as if somehow the portrait and the man were the same thing.[16] Other times scholars use portraits merely as illustrations because certain miniatures are copies that might not stand up to a detailed art analysis (fig.

Fig. 41. Anonymous, *Portrait of Isaac Lopez Brandon*, early 19th century. Watercolor on ivory; 3⅛ × 2½ in. Courtesy of AJHS.

42). However, even when early Jewish American portraits *are* made by famous miniaturists with great skill (such as John Ramage's 1789 portrait of Jacob de Leon), almost no attention is paid to the significance of the style. Sarah's miniature suggests this is a mistake.

Fig. 42. Anonymous, *Portrait of Abraham Rodrigues Brandon*, ca. 1790.
Watercolor on ivory. Private collection. Courtesy of Ann E. Gegan.

Genre and technique not only matter but are inextricably linked to
the biographical story the miniatures were designed to convey. In Sarah's
case, her miniature is linked to the racecraft of this era. "Racecraft" is a
term I borrow from Karen and Barbara Fields. They point out that "dis-
tinct from *race* and *racism, racecraft* does not refer to groups or to ideas

about groups' traits. . . . It refers [instead] to the mental terrain and to pervasive belief. . . . Unlike physical terrain, racecraft originates not in nature but in human action and imagination."[17] Or in this case, in the artist's creative attempt to explain who Sarah was. As Fields and Fields emphasize, "*racecraft* is not a euphemistic substitution for *racism*. It is a kind of fingerprint evidence that *racism* has been on the scene."[18] Racecraft impacted the lives not only of Jews with known African ancestry, like Sarah and Isaac, but all Jews.

Sarah lived at a tipping point in discussions of Jews and race, when Jews were increasingly seen in racial rather than religious terms. In the Caribbean, Jews often existed in a category between slave and free and between "black" and "white," in terms of both their civil rights and their social positions in society.[19] Pierre Jacques Benoit depicts this poignantly in his representation of Jews in Suriname, in which the Jewish shopkeeper is positioned alongside other "nonwhites" in the colony (fig. 43).

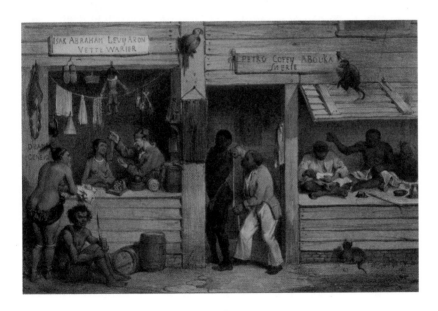

Fig. 43. Pierre Jacques Benoit, *A gauche, la boutique d'un vette-warier ou détaillant; à droite, la boutique d'un snerie ou tailleur; au milieu, un nègre nu se faisant prendre mesure d'un vêtement* [On the left, the shop of a *vette-warier*, or petty grocer; on the right, the shop of a *snerie*, or tailor; in the middle, a naked black slave having his measurements taken for some clothes], ca. 1831, in *Voyage à Surinam . . . cent dessins pris sur nature par l'auteur* (Brussels: Société des Beaux-Arts, 1839), plate xvi, fig. 32. Courtesy of the John Carter Brown Library, Brown University.

Benoit further underscores the Jew's nonwhite status by drawing visual parallels through the hand gestures of the shopkeeper, the "colored" tailor, and the monkey at the top right. As colonial slave regimes crumbled, the categories of "citizen" and "slave" changed, as did how the "body itself [was] invested by power relations."[20] Back in Europe, novelists as well as "racial scientists" took up the idea that Jews were "not quite white."[21] For racial scientists the question was who exactly counted as white? Caucasians? Saxons? Aryans? With the exception of Saxons, these categories were invented by racial scientists themselves, and they meant different things and reflected competing notions of where civilization began. Of the three classifications, only "Caucasian" included Jews.[22] Travel writers, meanwhile, attacked Jews, particularly Sephardic Jews, for being "swarthy" or "black."[23]

Novelists such as William Makepeace Thackeray likewise took up the trope of the Jew as inherently "interracial"—for example, through the character of Miss Swartz in *Vanity Fair*, whom Thackeray describes as a "rich wooly-haired mulatto from St. Kitts," descended from a German Jewish father and an enslaved mother (fig. 44).[24] For Thackeray this "mixed" heritage is a sign of "Jewish degeneracy," and Miss Swartz (whose name means "black") is described as "neither very bright nor very talented."[25] Jews found themselves caught up in debates about where they belonged. Miniatures could act to rebuke attempts to position Jews as something other than white by using the strategies of racecraft.

Between the 1790s and the 1830s, ivory miniatures played a critical part in the construction of Jewish families. Eventually, by the 1840s, silhouettes and daguerreotypes would replace miniatures as the small portrait of choice, but for nearly forty years, miniatures held sway. In order to explain why miniatures were so useful to early American Jews, I explore the steps of how Sarah's portrait was made and bring to light the role of miniatures in creating Jewish families in the early nineteenth century. Jewish miniatures were interwoven with the four main practices of racecraft: that is, ideas that "govern what goes with what and whom (sumptuary codes), how different people must deal with each other (rituals of deference and dominance), where human kinship begins and ends (blood), and how . . . [people] look at themselves and each other (the gaze)."[26] Racecraft infused the process that transformed Sarah from an enslaved person to an elite woman posing for a painter. It also came into play in the work done on the portrait during the three times Sarah sat for the painter and the one time he worked without her between the first and second sitting on detailing her clothing and the backdrop.

Fig. 44. Racial caricature of "Miss Swartz," from William Makepeace
Thackeray, *Vanity Fair. A Novel Without a Hero* (London: Collins, 1848), 182.

In order to draw out the work of racecraft in Sarah's life and portrait,
I rely on new methods for studying miniatures. My argument is based on
digital humanities as much as early nineteenth-century advice manuals for
miniature makers. Advances in digital photography clarify how miniatures
were made, allowing viewers to zoom in on the incredible skill required to
place small specks of paint on the ivory's surface. For Jewish patrons, this
miniature art had far-reaching ramifications for how all Jews—and particularly interracial Jews like Sarah—aimed to present themselves during
an age when their race was increasingly called into question.

From Slavery to the Portrait Studio

Although she was born in Barbados and died in New York, sometime around 1815 to 1816 Sarah Rodrigues Brandon, a young West Indian heiress, found herself in London having her portrait painted. Since Sarah's journey to the portrait maker's gallery was unusually difficult, it deserves an explanation before we turn to how her portrait itself was made. This journey reveals how deeply racecraft impacted Sarah's life before she placed even a toe inside the portrait studio.

Sarah entered the London portrait studio a free woman. Yet when she came into the world in 1798,[27] Sarah was the fourth generation of women enslaved by the Lopez family of Barbados.[28] Like most Bajan Jews, the Lopezes lived in Bridgetown, near the synagogue along Swan Street (fig. 45).[29] Although Sarah's mother eventually gained her freedom and even inherited property, she never legally gained her lover's last name. In fact, throughout her life, Sarah's mother's name varied. Sometimes her first name was Esther and sometimes Sarah Esther, but in this chapter I refer to her as "Esther" to differentiate her from her daughter. Esther's last name also varied in the early years, between Lopez and Gill, the name of Esther's white father.[30] Early on, Sarah and her mother did not share a last name because Esther and Abraham Rodrigues Brandon never officially married.[31] Although intermarriage between "whites" and people of African descent technically was not forbidden on the island, it was not done. Denying marriages between so-called whites and blacks or between whites and "mulattos" helped create racial binaries on the island. The church's unwillingness to sanction interracial marriages underscored that children produced from such alliances should not be considered "real kin" by their white fathers, as offspring typically only inherited when they were legitimate. Anglican church records (which also controlled taxes, the right to vote, and the ability to serve in the legislature) obsessively marked both race and legitimacy.[32]

Yet despite laws and social conventions that encouraged Sarah's father and grandfather not to consider their "interracial" offspring as blood kin, both men took the unusual steps of recognizing their children and financially supporting them. While Sarah's mother, Esther, had to wait until she became an adult and had borne at least three children before she could gain her freedom, Sarah herself was more fortunate. When she was only three she stood before the warden at St. Michael's Church as her father paid for her manumission.[33] Gaining her freedom was the first step on her path to the portrait maker's gallery.

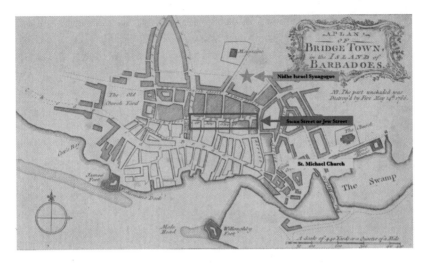

Fig. 45. John Gibson, "A Plan of Bridge Town in the Island of Barbadoes," 1766. 4⅓ × 7½ in. Courtesy of Map Collections from the
University of Texas at Arlington.

The second step took place in 1811, when Sarah and her older brother
Isaac travelled five hundred nautical miles to the southeast to Suriname.
Suriname was in both the wrong and right directions. On the one hand,
the boat ride took Sarah further south, away from the British Isles. On
the other hand, once she arrived in Suriname, she was able to convert
to Judaism. This rite of passage laid the groundwork for her transformation into her father's preferred heir. The records of the Barbadian and
Surinamese synagogues clearly state the journey was spiritual in nature:
Sarah and her brother Isaac had come to Suriname to be made Jews
of the Portuguese nation, as Western Sephardic Jews were known.[34] Although today in Suriname the Jewish community is quite small, in the
first part of the nineteenth century Paramaribo had one of the largest
and wealthiest Jewish communities in the Americas. Suriname was also
home to the first Afro-Jewish prayer group. By the time Sarah landed in
the beautiful port, approximately 10 percent of the city's Jewish community could claim African ancestry.[35]

   When Sarah left Suriname, she was free and a Jew. This status meant
that at that time Sarah and her brother Isaac were also her father's only
Jewish children.[36] Originally not a particularly notable Jew on the island,
Abraham Rodrigues Brandon had established himself as an important
merchant and was on the road to becoming the island's wealthiest Jewish

resident.[37] Just as a generation earlier Reyna Levy had been a resource for her father, Hayman, Sarah too was an asset. For merchants, children were investments that could cement trade alliances with other Jewish merchant families. Hence, like most wealthy Jews, Abraham's vision was toward the future and the kind of match his children might make. Like children of the Montefiores, Barrows, and other prosperous West Indian Jewish families, Sarah was sent to England to be educated.[38] That education was to prepare her for marriage and further strip away her identity as someone formerly enslaved.

In both England and the British colonies, education "was a crucial marker of elite status" during the eighteenth and nineteenth centuries.[39] In the language of racecraft, education taught people "rituals of deference and dominance" and "how different people must deal with each other."[40] Education trained male elites to govern themselves so that they could govern others.[41] Elite girls' education likewise prepared females to take their place in "polite society," including how to deal with servants and the Jewish poor. Beyond reading, writing, and arithmetic, elite girls learned dancing, music, and sewing, as well as how to dress and undertake "pious performances."[42] Elite women were expected to know how to run a large household and pass on household management skills to their children.[43] Sarah was now learning how to deal with servants rather than be a servant.

For Jews, being elite also meant language training. Codes of difference and dominance were embedded in the way people spoke. Language and accent were key. Even the wealthiest Jews were tainted by association with the Jewish poor: *Punch* magazine, for example, make the accent of a ragman come out of the mouth of the upwardly mobile Benjamin Disraeli, a convert since childhood.[44] Speaking the *right* way signaled that one was part of the ruling elite, deserving of deference.

Language was equally important for aspiring and upper-class women. As we saw for Hannah, language could make the difference in financial success, but it also impacted social status. For non-Jews, education provided elite young women with a basic knowledge of French, which signified politeness. The goal was primarily pronunciation and accent rather than true fluency.[45] For elite young Jewish women, a rudimentary knowledge of Hebrew was similarly essential. Equally important, Sephardic schools taught students how to *ladinar*—that is, to read the Pentateuch in the elegant baroque Spanish used in many Western Sephardic prayer books. Western Sephardi Jews did not speak Ladino—the Judeo-Spanish used by Eastern Sephardim—but fluency in Spanish and/or Portuguese was considered a meaningful part of Western Sephardic identity, and it was a prerequisite for Jewish educators in London and the colonies.[46] Thus, congregant Rachel de Crasto's eighteenth-century British prayer book was inscribed in Portuguese, even though the book itself was in the elegant, baroque Spanish taught in Western Sephardic schools (fig. 46). For a former slave and former Christian like Sarah, this education would have been almost as imperative to her process of becoming a full member of the Jewish community as her conversion in Suriname. London was the perfect place for Sarah to learn how to become part of upper-class Jewish society, and the lessons she learned there would help her when she came to New York.

Education also gave Sarah Jewish peers she could rely on in times of need and separated her from the poorer Jews attending the Jews' Free School in the East End, an institution whose students and faculty we will hear about in the final chapter of this book. Children from elite Jewish families like the Montefiores and Rothschilds attended Hurwitz's Academy and then Garcia's Sephardic-run school after it opened in 1815.[47] Elite Barbadians from the Barrow and Montefiore clans attended both institutions, as did the later children of Abraham Rodrigues Brandon. Although the records from the era when Sarah was in London are lost, she was probably introduced to Jewish British society through one of these elite schools. School connections would follow her as she moved. Upper-class Jewish families did not limit themselves to London but rather had outposts of their merchant houses across the Atlantic World, including in New York. The children of Barbadian Rachel Montefiore[48] ended up in New York, as most likely did Rachel herself in the final years of Sarah's life. Her uncle, Joshua Vita Montefiore, likewise emigrated to the United States and published a weekly political journal in New York.[49] Connections in London meant social cachet in America.[50]

In addition to the coeducational elite Jewish schools, a Sephardic woman named Hannah Gomes ran a "Ladies School" for Jewish girls in rural Peckham. Here girls learned Jewish values like *tzedakah* as well as engaging in Jewish and secular studies. We know Sarah's much younger half-sisters boarded at Hannah Gomes's school, and in Chanukah of 1841, the girls helped distribute meat and bread to seven poor families in the area.[51] Their work was both generous and the Jewish equivalent of the "pious performances" required of non-Jewish gentlewomen. Sarah most likely also learned about Jewish women's charity while at school. This education would serve her well, as women's role in *tzedakah* was also changing in New York in the years just following Sarah's marriage. In

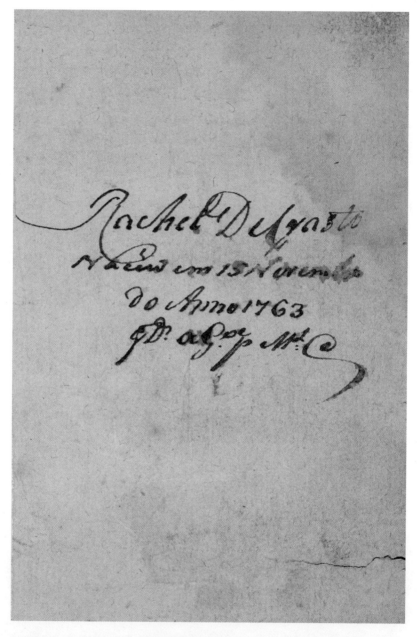

Fig. 46. Inscription for Rachel De Crasto (b. 1763) in Joseph Messias, *Orden de las oraciones cotidianas* [Order of the daily prayers] (London, 1721). Courtesy of the Weisz Western Sephardi Collection, Oxford University.

Philadelphia, Rebecca Gratz began the Female Hebrew Benevolent Society (FHBS) in 1819, which provided "food, fuel, shelter, and later an employment bureau and traveler's aid service."[52] It was exactly the kind of help women like Hannah needed. Moreover, unlike earlier synagogue-centered Jewish charities, it *only* serviced Jewish women and their children, and the organization was female led. In 1820 the women of Congregation Shearith Israel in New York followed suit, establishing a local FHBS expressly "for the relief of indigent females *particularly*."[53] The first director of the society was Richea Levy, Sarah's future sister-in-law.[54] Education helped Sarah become the kind of person who gave rather than received charity.

Like the Sephardic finishing school she attended, the miniature prepared Sarah to become the wife of an Atlantic World Jewish elite. The portrait on ivory is the first—and only—glimpse we have of Sarah, and perhaps it is the most crucial evidence of how she wanted to be seen. Miniatures were a key way Jews and other Europeans and Americans entered the marriage market. Ivory miniatures were frequently commissioned for engagements and weddings,[55] but they also functioned as portable gifts or tools in marriage negotiations.[56] Miniatures could be sent across town or across oceans to help make a match.[57] Portraits mattered, as they required the sitter's approval, and thus on some level they presented the sitter as she or he wished to be understood. They were also deeply intimate: small and portable, they were meant for the eyes of the beloved.[58] In her portrait, Sarah presents herself to her future husband as a fashionable yet modest British heiress, the appropriate bride for a wealthy New York Jew. She is captivating and precious.

The materials and process used to make Sarah's portrait mark her as part of elite London culture and call to mind how far she had travelled since being born enslaved. Sarah's portrait is small—only 2¾ by 2¼ inches—but expensive. The ivory on which it was painted was cut from an elephant's tusk in slices less than a millimeter thick, with attention to where the ivory's grain would run fine.[59] The sheets were so thin, they were transparent, giving the miniature its unique properties. Any scratches left by the saw were scraped off with a knife or piece of glass, and the ivory was then polished smooth with pumice or cuttlefish shell. It would then be bleached using either the sun or a hot iron. This process gave the ivory a "pale warm tint" that mimicked the skin tones of elite Western Europeans.[60] When combined with watercolor, the material gave the sitter's painted skin and clothes an almost magical, translucent glow.

This transparent glow came at an artistic cost, however: the high surface tension of the ivory meant that the paint had to be applied by lightly scratching the surface with scrapers and then hatching with parallel brushstrokes or stippling by layering and overlapping tiny dots of color.[61] These methods allowed for changes in gradation of color without muddying the paint.[62] Charles Fraser's portrait of H. F. Plowden Weston, for example, uses the dot technique (stippling) on his face and hatching (short parallel lines) on the background (figs. 47–49).[63] The Weston miniature also clarifies why new technologies in digital photography have changed the field so dramatically. At 3⅞ inches tall by 3¼ inches wide, this is a very small object. By digitally zooming in on it, we can see the minutiae of the artist's process otherwise invisible to the naked eye. Moreover, unlike a magnifying glass, high-resolution digital photographs can be viewed at a remote distance from the object itself, thereby allowing scholars to place objects side by side virtually in order to compare techniques even though the actual miniatures today may be separated by oceans and be too fragile to travel. This comparative process provides insights into how the miniatures were made.

The materials and skill required to make the details on miniatures meant good ones could cost more than full-size portraits in oil.[64] Despite

Fig. 47. Charles Fraser, *H. F. Plowden Weston*, 1824. Watercolor on ivory; 3⅞ × 3¼ in. Courtesy of the Gibbes Museum of Art, 1974.004.

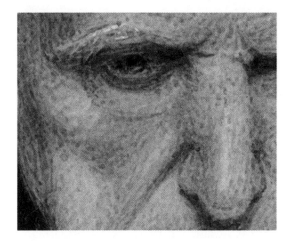

Fig. 48. Detail of stippling on face, Fraser, *H. F. Plowden Weston,* 1824. Courtesy of the Gibbes Museum of Art, 1974.004.

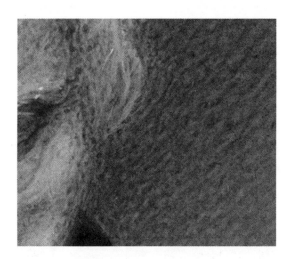

Fig. 49. Detail of hatching on background, Fraser, *H. F. Plowden Weston,* 1824. Courtesy of the Gibbes Museum of Art, 1974.004.

this cost, most Jewish portraits that remain from this era are miniatures.[65] The process for making them was painstaking. With Sarah's education complete and the portrait painter's materials prepared, she was ready to begin the sittings for her miniature.

Sarah's First Sitting: Sketching a Face

Sarah's miniature would have required at least three sittings and therefore necessitated she have access to leisure time, a strange commodity for a woman born enslaved. Although some artists signed miniatures or used a distinctive style, Sarah's portrait is anonymous. Despite this anonymity, I refer to the artist as "him" throughout the chapter. To be sure, there were female miniaturists—including Jewish women. Catherine (Mendes) da Costa (1679–1756), for example, was known for her portraits of family members, including those of her father, Dr. Fernando Mendes, the personal physician to King Charles II of England, and her young son Abraham (fig. 50).[66] Even more unusual is her beguiling self-portrait (fig. 51). That said, Catherine—like many female miniaturists—was an amateur. Chances are good that the artist who made Sarah's miniature was a man.

In the first sitting, the artist would have placed Sarah in a room with both strong light and shade.[67] As the light fell directly on Sarah's face, the portrait maker would have outlined her face in pencil on drawing paper, then placed the paper below the translucent ivory so it could be copied

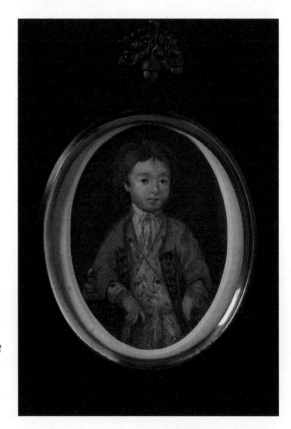

Fig. 50. Catherine Mendes da Costa, *Locket Portrait of Abraham da Costa*, 1714. Courtesy of the London Jewish Museum.

Fig. 51. Catherine Mendes da Costa, *Self-Portrait*, 1720. Courtesy of
Henry R. Lew.

with a delicate brush using short hatches or dots in a "neutral" shade of
watercolor.[68] Typically this pencil would be covered later by paint, and
the drawing paper would be removed from under the ivory. In some instances, however, the underdrawing remained and shows through, such
as the detail of the tie on a dress from a portrait of a girl from the Museo
del Prado (fig. 52).[69]

After outlining Sarah's face in a neutral tint, color would then have
been placed on the ivory to create Sarah's pupils, and light shading in a
neutral color would have been used to mark her chin and neck, keeping
her body's curves "light and clear" (fig. 53).[70] Special attention would
have been given to Sarah's eyes and eyelids. In the portrait, Sarah's large
eyes hold ours, her lips just barely turned up at the corners. Her smile is
as enigmatic as that of a Greek kore. The end result of the first sitting was
a "light pearly flesh," typically outlined in Indian ink and lake, with light
shading using vermillion and indigo.[71]

The pearly color of Sarah's skin in the miniature is no accident:

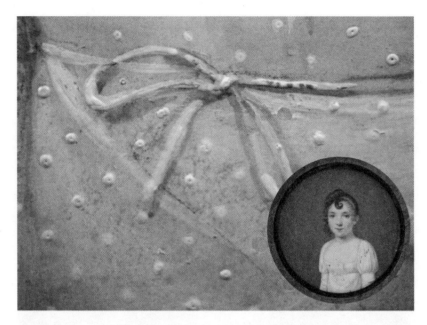

Fig. 52. Detail (with full miniature inset), Le Chevalier de Châ-teau-bourg, *Portrait of a Girl*, 1807. Watercolor on ivory; diam.: 2⅗ in. Courtesy of Museo del Prado, O-675.

Fig. 53. Detail, *Portrait of Sarah Brandon Moses*, ca. 1815–16. Courtesy of AJHS.

watercolor miniatures on ivory are a genre dedicated to whiteness and bespeak a moment in Atlantic World history when race and skin color became increasingly aligned with elite status. The "translucent, whitish tone of the ivory" was used to create flesh tones and served as the base color for the skin, as seen in a detail from the portrait of Sarah's brother Isaac: the forehead, whites of the eyes, and shiny area under the eyes all make use of unpainted ivory to create glowing skin (fig. 54).[72] Sometimes a sheet of silver leaf was even placed behind the portion of the ivory where skin was shown in order to enhance the glow of whiteness.[73] The alignment of whiteness and elite status may also explain why miniatures were so popular among Atlantic World Jews precisely at the moment when their racial status had come into question with claims that Jews were "swarthy" and "black."[74] While early on some artists had tried using oil paints for ivory miniatures, they quickly found that oil paints tended to slip off the base. Even when oil paints could adhere with gum or glue, they obstructed the ivory's translucent luminosity.[75] Watercolors, in contrast, allowed the sitter's skin to appear lustrous and glowing.

The watercolor on ivory technique made it hard for miniaturists to

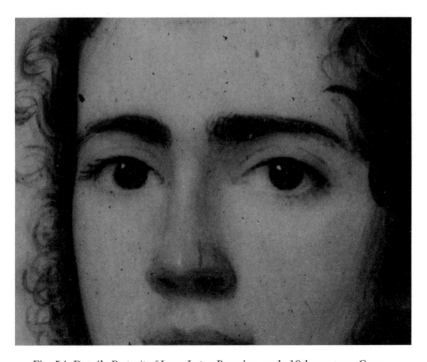

Fig. 54. Detail, *Portrait of Isaac Lopez Brandon*, early 19th century. Courtesy of AJHS.

achieve darker skin tones: applying enough pigment to give the skin a dark tone meant the sitter was commonly left with a scratchy, rough appearance. This visible roughness is evident even in "high quality" portraits of interracial women from Suriname (fig. 55) and from early New York (fig. 56).[76] Although this scratchiness was visible even to the naked eye, details of the brushstrokes highlight the problem. One strategy painters developed for showing darker skin on ivory was to use hatching—short lines of paint, crossed and overlapped to create a gradation in color. This same strategy was used by most miniaturists to get darker paint to adhere to the background of miniatures. While it gave an appealing texture to fabrics, hair, and backdrops, it was rather disastrous for evoking the beauty of uniform skin that did not glow white.

Portrait painters who actively wanted to depict smooth dark skin were more likely to use oil on canvas or pastels on paper (see fig. 63).[77] From the 1840s to 1850s, British miniaturists working among elites in India would perfect techniques for depicting glowing, darker skin using watercolors on ivory.[78] At the time Sarah's portrait was made, however, most artists' attempts at creating darker skin tones on ivory ended up implying the skin itself was flawed.

Fig. 55. Detail of hatching (with full miniature inset), anonymous, *Portrait of Surinamese Girl*, ca. 1805. Watercolor on ivory; 2½ × 2⅓ in. Courtesy of the Rijksmuseum, Amsterdam.

Fig. 56. Detail of hatching (with full miniature in inset), Anthony Meucci, *Mrs. Pierre Toussaint*, ca. 1825. Watercolor on ivory; 3⅓ × 2⅗ in. Courtesy of NYHS.

In ivories from New York and Surinam, such as the *Portrait of a Surinamese Girl* (fig. 55) and *Mrs. Pierre Toussaint* (fig. 56), the skin color of the sitters becomes marked in the language of the miniaturist. According to manuals from the day, although a "scratchy" texture was appropriate in small amounts when painting hair, for skin it was "disagreeable." Dark shading on skin was deemed "masculine" and hence "undesirable" for women.[79] All told, the "axioms of the beautiful" that painters were told to keep in mind were distinctly European. "A short upper lip indicates high breeding," explained one manual writer, and even if the sitter had a *nez retoussé* (upturned nose), the painter should take care that it was not "exaggerated in the picture."[80] Likewise, when women's skin, such as on the lower arm, was naturally darker, manuals advised "cautious discretion" when depicting the tones. Also, if the sitter's skin was "very yellow" (a skin tone increasingly associated with partial African ancestry), the painter was advised to use a "more powerful yellow" nearby "to overpower by contrast this undesirable peculiarity."[81] Although the artist was expected to "observe and imitate" the "peculiarities" of each face he painted, he was also expected to make the sitter "agree" with the "standard of antiquity" regarding what was considered best.[82] Failing to do so suggested that the woman in question did not conform to these standards.

Despite manual makers' suggestion that their biases had been shared since antiquity, the value that they placed on skin color reflects late eighteenth- and early nineteenth-century notions of race.[83] The bias against dark skin, particularly for women, in miniatures is the work of racecraft in which, under the gaze of the painter, certain skin tones take on negative associations. As Karen and Barbara Fields note, "Everyone has a skin color, but not everyone's skin color counts as race."[84] In contrast to contemporary miniatures of women for whom the artists wanted to foreground African ancestry, Sarah Brandon's skin is depicted as pearly and smooth. Indeed, if one were to judge only by the miniatures, both her skin and that of her brother were several shades lighter than that of her European father when he was painted in oil later in life.[85] Either Sarah's skin was light enough not to require the techniques used by the other artists or the painter decided to forgo color for the sake of letting the ivory's natural glow exude through the paint. Regardless, what I would like to accentuate here is that the genre itself idealized whiteness, and Sarah's portrait takes advantage of this reification.

The first sitting would have taken less than an hour to ensure that Sarah would not become fatigued, as her relaxed muscles would cause her image to look dull and languid.[86] With that work completed, Sarah would once again be free, and the artist would move on to the second step, which did not require Sarah's presence at all.

Step Two: Background and Dress

Before the next sitting, the miniaturist would have worked on the sunset-like background, taking special care that the color harmonized with Sarah's dress and "the color of the flesh" of her face.[87] As with the depiction of skin, the fragile ivory gives the portrait's background a translucent, romantic glow. The soft sunset of blues and pinks in the background sets

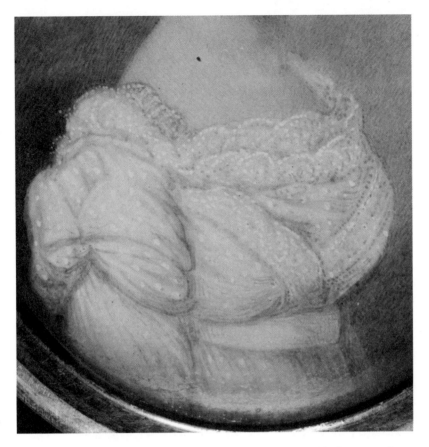

Fig. 57. Detail, *Portrait of Sarah Brandon Moses*, ca. 1815–16. Courtesy of AJHS.

off Sarah's luminous skin and her gown's white folds (see figs. 40 and 57). If the painter followed the sage advice of miniaturist manuals, he would have posed an assistant wearing Sarah's white dress by the same window where he began her portrait, so the clothing could be painted while sparing Sarah the "tediousness" of too many sittings.[88] As the subject of an expensive miniature, Sarah's time was deemed valuable.

The choice of clothing was important. Like the use of ivory and the brushstrokes used to create her skin tones, clothing was imbued with sumptuary codes about "what goes with what and whom."[89] Sumptuary codes in both Europe and the Americas politicized dress either through actual legislation or through the unspoken rules about an individual's identity. While we might be used to thinking about governments' use of clothing to mock or limit Jews, such as by mandating hats or badges, or individual Jews' use of fringes, head coverings, or special coats to proclaim allegiance to Jewish tradition, Jews in the early nineteenth-century Atlantic World often used clothing to address their racial assignment and status within society.[90] Sarah's white dress with its delicate lace drew attention not only to her elegance, style, and purity but also to her literal freedom from labor.

Although Sarah's portrait is undated, the square neckline, high waist, and ruched sleeves suggest her dress dates to about 1815, when Sarah was sixteen years old.[91] If Sarah looks like she leapt from the pages of a Jane Austen novel, that is because she wears a neoclassical "Regency style" white gown, probably made of muslin or silk, fabrics favored for their ability to mimic the marble of classical sculpture.[92] Below the high waist that we see in the miniature, the gown would have had a long, narrow skirt that, combined with the light material, would have draped gracefully over her lower body and "evoked the clinging draperies of antique statues."[93] The vogue of modelling miniatures of women on classical models is exemplified by Lorenzo Theweneti's *Portrait of a Miniaturist* (ca. 1820), in which the lady's hairstyle, bust line, and even the tilt of her head mimic the classical statue to the artist's left (fig. 58). Just behind the marble bust is a small version of the Apollo Belvedere statue that was used by both fashion magazines and early racial scientists to embody the perfect white Saxon male body.[94] Although parallels to antiquity implied, as the miniaturist manual did, that beliefs about beauty were "timeless," by the 1810s, mimicking the classical body through fashion was increasingly about the intersection of race and the "ideal" body.

The neoclassical dress in Sarah's miniature not only positioned her as cultured and idealized her body but also emphasized her freedom. This freedom was both theoretical and practical. In France, the style was first associated with the revolution, and then with Empress Josephine and her husband, Napoleon, the latter of whom was strongly linked in the minds of most Jews at the time with Jewish emancipation, despite his own anti-Semitism.[95] Sarah's future husband had been invited to the coronation of Napoleon the First, and he kept the invitation throughout his life as one of his treasured possessions.[96] Yet in very real ways, the dress also declared Sarah to belong to a class of women who were free not to work. The whiteness and delicate lace of the dress would have been easily tarnished by the physical work it took to clean and run a nineteenth-century household. Thus, wearing it implied Sarah was free from manual labor.

Fig. 58. Lorenzo Theweneti, *Brother of the Artist Painting a Lady*, ca. 1820. The Tansey Miniatures Foundation, Celle. Photograph by Birgitt Schmedding.

The Barbadoes Mulatto Girl.

Fig. 59. Agostino Brunias, *The Barbadoes Mulatto Girl*, after painting by the same (ca. 1764), published in London in 1779. Engraving; 8⅘ × 6⁹⁄₁₀ in. Courtesy of Barbados Museum and Historical Society, Bridgetown.

The dress also gendered Sarah in response to racial messages about Jewish women and women of mixed African descent. When the "Grecian" style first appeared in 1800, its exposure of the body's lines was considered "indelicate" and "shocking."[97] By the time Sarah's portrait was made, however, the style was deemed "chaste, neat, and simple," even though the shape of the breasts was often emphasized and evening versions of the style left a fair amount of the back and bosom revealed.[98]

Sarah's dress also marks her portrait as indebted to West Indian notions of whiteness and how they were encoded in dress. Notably, Sarah's dress is more modest than not only Empress Josephine's but also that of some of her North American Jewish counterparts, like Eliza Myers (1808) or Sally Etting (1808, 1815–18), whose dresses were lower cut, with barer shoulders and shorter sleeves.[99] Sarah's dress also contrasts with seductive depictions of "Creole" women by Lucien Amans, Agostino Brunias, and others (fig. 59; and see fig. 63). Sumptuary laws in the colonies sometimes forbade enslaved women from fully covering their chests in order to emphasize the women's inability to govern their own bodies. Even in places where covering one's chest was not formally forbidden for slaves, laws regarding how much fabric needed to be given to slaves meant enslaved women often did not receive enough cloth "to afford the type of body coverage considered a *sine qua non* for free settlers—and even for indentured servants."[100] In this context, the ability to cover her body signaled greater freedom for Sarah and not less. Sarah's portrait defies West Indian racial stereotypes and demurely covers her body.

Final Sittings: Sarah's Face and Hair

Once the painting of Sarah's clothing was completed, she would have returned for her second in-person sitting, in which all colors would be applied to her face using the small, stippling dots or extremely short lines (fig. 60).[101] The artist followed the recommendation of guides of his day, avoiding gray or dark tints when depicting her face's shading lest they bestow an undesirable "masculine appearance."[102] This specter of "manliness" haunts the portrait made of the young Surinamese woman in the Rijksmuseum (see fig. 55). The gray paint used to hint at darker skin tones cut two ways, as it also implied that somehow her feminine virtues were wanting. Gray paint was seen as more appropriate for men's faces, so much so that some elite Englishwomen refused to have any shadows put on the face of their portraits at all.[103] In contrast with the Surinam-

Fig. 60. Detail, *Portrait of Sarah Brandon Moses,* ca. 1815–16. Courtesy of AJHS.

ese portrait, Sarah's miniature uses lighter tones that emphasize Sarah's femininity, here aligned with whiteness.

In the final sitting, every part of the miniature would be examined and perfected, starting with the hair. In the miniature, Sarah's curly brown hair is pulled back in a Grecian knot. Tendrils delicately frame her face. Notably, her head is bare. She lacks the stylish *tignon* found in *Portrait of a Surinamese Girl, Mrs. Pierre Toussaint,* and numerous other portraits of free women of color (see figs. 55, 56, 59, and 63). In certain colonies, free women of color were required to wear head wraps, but some also co-opted them as signs of cultural pride.[104] Women of color in both Suriname and Barbados wore distinctive styles of head wraps, and the portrait of Mrs. Pierre Toussaint suggests that stylish Afro-Caribbean women in early New York continued this practice. Like Sarah, Mrs. Toussaint (née Marie-Rose Juliette Noel) was born enslaved in the Caribbean (in this case Haiti) but became free and wealthy in the United States.[105] Unlike Sarah, she continued to have strong ties to New York's African American community. In addition to being the wife of a famous hairdresser,[106] she started a school for African American children in the

Fig. 61. Pierre Jacques Benoit, *Cinq femmes esclaves se rendant à leur église un jour de fête* [Five enslaved women going to various places of worship], in *Voyage à Surinam . . . cent dessins pris sur nature par l'auteur* (Brussels: Société des Beaux-Arts, 1839), plate xi, fig. 20. Courtesy of the John Carter Brown Library, Brown University.

city.[107] Sarah's unadorned hair signals her single status in the Jewish religion and adds to her racial ambiguity by not signaling a clear allegiance to styles worn primarily by women of color.[108]

The neatness of Sarah's hair is equally significant. By the early nineteenth century, racial scientists increasingly insisted that Jews' "black, curly hair," along with their "brown skin color," revealed their lingering "Oriental" origins.[109] Indeed, caricatures from this era used out-of-control hair to undermine claims that Jews could govern their bodies and hence take part in politics.[110] For Jewish women, unruly hair took on more-sexual associations. In anti-Semitic works such as Pierre Jacques Benoit's depiction *Five Enslaved Women Going to Various Places of Worship* in his book *Voyage à Surinam*, Jewishness is equated with loose and revealing clothing and unrestrained hair (fig. 61). The women are, from left to right, a Moravian, a Calvinist, a "young Christian going to church on a holiday," a Jew, and a Lutheran.[111] The Jewish woman is the only one whose hair creeps down her back, escaping completely from the *tignon*. Loose hair, licentiousness, and Jewish practice become intertwined in the visual language of the drawing. In contrast, Sarah's neoclassically styled hair emphasizes her virtuous restraint and aligns her with the Greco-Roman tradition increasingly associated with whiteness.

Fig. 62. Pierre Henri, *The Artist's Family*, ca. 1800. Watercolor on ivory;
2¾ × 3⅜ in. Metropolitan Museum of Art, 2000.25. Courtesy of the
Metropolitan Museum of Art.

Hair completed, the painter would have next added white to Sarah's
eyes near the darkest portion of the eyelids, heightening their impact
(see fig. 60). Eyes were vital to the language of miniatures. Often, as in
Sarah's case or in Pierre Henri's *The Artist's Family*, eyes in miniatures
seem neotenic, too large for the face (fig. 62). Like popular miniatures
of lover's eyes, the oversized eyes of Sarah's portrait draw us in with intimacy—but the right kind of intimacy. Sarah's miniature was part of an
exchange through which her husband would come to know a version
of herself. As one art historian puts it, miniatures elaborate an interper-
sonal intimacy that "does not reveal a truth about the self but is a process
of becoming, whereby the subject's wish to know the other's potential
self evolves in sharing a type of being-as-becoming."[112] Sarah's miniature
forms a dialogue between her past and future self.

Sarah's eyes are significant as the portrait reclaims intimacy for marriage. They are also part of the racecraft of the portrait. As Fields and Fields note, a key strategy of racecraft is the gaze. Paintings of interracial women from this era, such as Jacques Lucien Amans's *Creole in a Red Headdress* (fig. 63), tend to be at once voyeuristic and deeply indebted to what Saidiya Hartman refers to as the "discourse of seduction."[113] On the one hand, the young woman with her bare shoulder is all about scopophilia, the love of looking, the "pleasure that is linked to sexual attraction (voyeurism *in extremis*)."[114] The model's submission to the viewer is emphasized by the inward turn of her shoulders and the downward tuck of her chin. Yet unlike in most voyeuristic works in which the object of the gaze does not—and cannot—return the gaze, here the young "Creole" woman looks back over her shoulder, complicit with desire, an interest underscored by her bared throat and tilted head.[115] Hartman refers to this racialized myth of mutual affection as the "discourse of seduction," in which "women were made to seem not the victims but the perpetrators of their own sexual abuse" by ascribing subjectivity and agency to the women "only to the extent that they could be made responsible for their own sexual violence."[116]

The complicity of Amans's model is most noticeable when contrasted with Elizabeth Kleinveld and Epaul Julien's 2012 photographic re-visioning of the painting (fig. 64). Unlike Amans's model, here the woman's chin is parallel with the floor, her shoulders are rolled back, emphasizing her power, and her left thumb is positioned upward.[117] Just as important, the woman in the photo arches her left eye, as if to question and rebuke attempts to fetishize her body.[118] Sarah's portrait also uses the gaze to challenge her body's reception as seductive or seducing. The young Jewess's deep-set, almond-shaped, and larger-than-life eyes gaze back at the beholder, holding the viewer close.[119] Yet here the intimacy was deliberately positioned as innocent rather than knowing. The largeness of Sarah's eyes makes her appear even younger than she actually is, innocent and vulnerable. The delicate intimacy of her gaze is critical to the genre of miniatures and particularly their role in creating marriages.

The portrait was now done. Sarah and her father would not have seen the completed version until it was encased under glass, polishing the final look.[120] Sarah's portrait was ready to find its companion. In 1817, Sarah and her portrait did just that: Sarah met a young Jew, Joshua Moses, who was in London on business. He was the middle son of Reyna Levy and Isaac Moses of New York. Joshua was a man with a portrait of his own (fig. 65). The match would be a success.

Fig. 63. Jacques Guillaume Lucien Amans, *Creole in a Red Headdress,*
ca. 1840. Oil on canvas; 28¾ × 23⅝ in. Courtesy of the Historic New
Orleans Collection, Williams Research Center, New Orleans, LA.

Fig. 64. Elizabeth Kleinveld and Epaul Julien, *Ode to Aman's Creole with a Red Headdress*, 2012. Photograph; 36 × 25½ in. Courtesy of Jonathan Ferrara Gallery, New Orleans, LA.

Fig. 65. Louis Antoine Collas, *Joshua Moses*, 1804. Watercolor on ivory; 2¼ × 1¾ in. Courtesy of AJHS.

Marriage

On March 19, 1817, Sarah found herself underneath the chuppah at London's Portuguese synagogue, Bevis Marks. Acting as Joshua's "father and mother" were Jacob Israel Brandon, the congregation's *presidente*, and his wife. For Sarah, there were Mr. Massiah and Mrs. Lindo, important members of Bevis Marks with connections to Barbados. Whether at school or in the synagogue, there were always fellow Jews nearby who knew of her enslaved past, but unlike in the Caribbean, that past did not hold Sarah back in London.[121] Her father's generosity helped make the past moot. Sarah brought more than a miniature to the marriage: her father provided a £10,000 dowry, roughly $30,000,000 of purchasing power in today's money.[122]

Within a year of the marriage and before her first child was born, Sarah had followed her new husband to New York, where she would spend the final third of her short life. Joshua bought a house near that of his parents on the lower tip of Manhattan, and Sarah settled into New York Jewish life (fig. 66). Sarah benefitted from the new kin network she joined. Like Isaac Moses before him, Sarah's brother-in-law Moses L. Moses was the *parnas* of Congregation Shearith Israel.[123] Joshua soon became a voting member of the congregation, and he made sure his wife

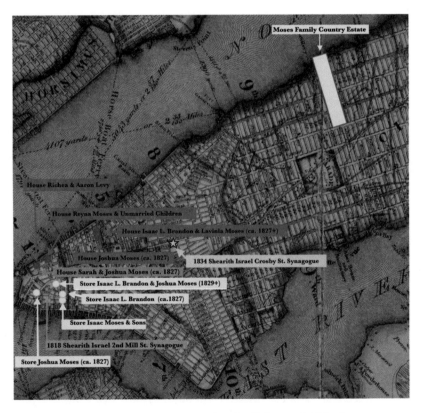

Fig. 66. Map of the Moses and Brandon family homes in Manhattan, 1820–30. From John Randel, *The City of New York as Laid Out by the Commissioners with the Surrounding Country* (New York: P. Maverik sculp., 1821).

had a seat in the balcony to call her own.[124] When Sarah's brother Isaac joined her in New York, the Moses family smoothed his way into Jewish high society. Isaac became Joshua's business partner and married Joshua's sister Lavinia.[125] They bought a house nearby. Once denied voting rights in Barbados because of his African ancestry, Isaac Lopez Brandon was welcomed as a full member of Shearith Israel, with a seat adjacent to the congregation's president.[126]

Records suggest that connections to the Moses clan helped Sarah and her brother be categorized as "white" in New York and U.S. records. In 1820, the census taker classified Sarah and her young children as "white," the default category into which Jews in New York fell at the time.[127] Unlike in Barbados, Suriname, Jamaica, and Curaçao, where censuses and the militia sometimes separated Jews into a category between "whites" and "blacks," Jews in New York faced prejudice but not the same degree of racial uncertainty found in parts of the Caribbean; yet even in the Caribbean, Jews were not considered enslavable unless they had partial African ancestry.[128] Sarah's London marriage also protected her. As the wealthy, fair-skinned wife of a "white" man, Sarah was parsed as white by the census taker. It is also possible Sarah's early years in slavery did not matter as much in New York as they would have in other places. Prior to 1850, criteria for what "race" people belonged to varied by state, and before 1920 there was no "one drop rule" for the census. In 1820s New York, "race" was in the eyes of the census taker, and as such, it was fairly arbitrary for people who were racially ambiguous.[129]

What was not ambiguous, though, was the U.S. law forbidding immigrants with African ancestry from becoming citizens. Yet in 1829, Sarah's brother Isaac petitioned and received citizenship, with God and his brother-in-law, Moses L. Moses, as his witness.[130] Moses's role in this process is intriguing, for the very same census taker who decided all of the inhabitants of Joshua Moses's household were white in 1820 had a different thought when it came to the household of Reyna, Moses L. Moses, and her other unmarried children. Of the eleven people living in the house, two were "free colored people"—an unnamed woman between the ages of fourteen and twenty-five and another unnamed woman over the age of forty-five. Who were these women? Barbadian relatives of Sarah and Isaac? Servants? Former slaves? Were they some of the same four "other free people" that were neither "white" nor "Indian" that had been living in Isaac and Reyna's household according to the 1810 census?[131] The historical record is depressingly mute.

Marrying a Jew from New York changed the destiny that would have awaited Sarah had she returned to Barbados or married a man from other parts of the United States. Even after Sarah's death, "whiteness" was defined in Barbados as the absolute absence of any African ancestor. No matter how wealthy or how pale Sarah and her children might have been, they would have been classified as "colored" or "mulatto" had they still lived on the island.[132] Notably, even after Isaac became "white" in the United States, he would still have been classified as "coloured" when he was in Barbados for business. Likewise, if Sarah had married one of the prominent Jewish men from New Orleans and lived there, she would have faced the same "one drop" rule of race.[133] It was not that early New York was not racist; city officials just defined the color line differently.

Sarah died in 1828, just before she turned thirty and shortly after the birth of her ninth child.[134] Less than a decade later, her husband, Joshua, followed her to the grave. Yet Sarah's children would benefit from the way travel, money, and a match made through portraits had reshaped their mother's world. Sarah's sons would serve in the white militia of the U.S. army in both the Mexican American and Civil Wars,[135] and her son Israel would become the first child of a formerly enslaved person to graduate from the College of Physicians and Surgeons in the City of New York, later Columbia Medical School (fig. 67). Presumably his mother's history was unknown at the time to his teachers, as less than five years later in 1850 another racially ambiguous student—James Parker Barnett—was

Fig. 67. Anonymous, *Israel Moses*, ca. 1845–67. Daguerreotype; 3¾ × 3¼ in. Courtesy of AJHS.

expelled for having parents who were discovered to be "Creole" rather than "Anglo Saxon."[136] Another of Sarah's sons would serve as president of Shearith Israel, and her third to last child, Lionel, would marry Selina, the granddaughter of Rev. Gershom Mendes Seixas.[137]

It was Selina and Lionel's daughter Blanche who in 1936 donated Sarah's miniature to the American Jewish Historical Society. It is not surprising that Blanche knew little about Sarah: even Lionel had barely a chance to know his mother before she died. When Blanche looked at Sarah's miniature, she saw only its glowing ivory whiteness. The role the ivory had played in marking Sarah as white was no longer visible. This result may have been the most powerful work of whiteness and racecraft: the ability to not have one's race count.[138]

Conclusion

In this chapter, I have focused on an object owned by an early Jewess who moved to New York for marriage. As with Reyna's silver beakers, the object that Jewess owned—an ivory portrait—played a role in cementing her to her new kin. This middle chapter about Sarah's marriage to Joshua falls between two previous chapters about Jews who married yoke mates and two subsequent chapters about those who married soul mates. A generation before, Reyna Levy Moses's marriage bound together two merchant houses. Less than ten years after Sarah Brandon Moses died, a distant relative of her husband's—Sarah Ann Hays Mordecai—would openly marry for love. These changes in marriage also brought about changes in kinship, such that women became more connected to their new husband's family than to that of their blood relations. Sarah's story lies somewhere in between these extremes.

On the one hand, like Reyna, Sarah's marriage brought together two major traders—Isaac Moses of New York and Abraham Rodrigues Brandon of Barbados. The match clearly benefitted both Joshua and Isaac Moses and the merchant houses of Isaac Moses & Sons. Although Isaac died shortly after the marriage, the dynasty he had created gained an enduring connection with lucrative southern sugar markets. The match also helped build the Rodrigues-Brandon empire. New York was quickly becoming an influential trade center, and Joshua's father, Isaac Moses, was one of New York's key Jewish merchants.[139] Sarah's phenomenally large dowry reflects her father's desire to use her marriage to guarantee a lineage for himself through a female line. On the other hand, Sarah's marriage reveals something new: the kin she gained through her marriage reshaped who she and her children would be. Superseding her father's overtures and love, it would be the Moses clan that most defined her post-marriage life. Sarah's portrait is part of the new courtship rituals that came into being as romantic love took root. The miniature's intimate gaze attests to the power of the new world of love and the stronger bonds to the family of a woman's husband that came along with it.

While Sarah's portrait speaks to the shifting landscape of marriage, it also teaches us something about race. Most stories of racial shift from this era have been told under the category of passing, that is, when someone categorized as a certain race leaves behind their past and "pretends" to be of another racial group.[140] The verb "to pass" originally meant an overstepping of bounds, a deviation or straying, or, as the *Oxford English Dictionary* puts it, that someone has gone "beyond (one's province, knowledge, etc.)."[141] "Passing" implies someone "is" a certain race and, more particularly, that the original designation was somehow "less." It suggests that Sarah was really "coloured" as her childhood records in Barbados proclaimed and not "white" as she was labelled in the New York census. Sarah Brandon Moses, however, did not pass. Lying about her past was never an option for Sarah nor her brother Isaac. Everywhere the siblings lived, they lived among other Barbadian immigrants aware of their early lives as enslaved people. New York was no different. Sarah's husband, Joshua, and his brothers had been schoolmates with the grandchildren of Sarah's former owner.[142] Sarah was not "pretending" to be white; whiteness itself had changed, and she had changed along with it.

Sarah's portrait reminds us of the role racecraft played in the creation of early American Jewish families. At the opening of the chapter, I noted that racecraft includes ideas about "what and whom . . . how different people must deal with each other . . . where human kinship begins and ends, and how . . . [people] look at themselves and each other."[143] Jewish law—like science—rejects "race" as a real category.[144] A Jew is a Jew, and there is no such thing as "Jewish DNA," despite what DNA genealogy tests seem to suggest.[145] Yet early American Jews found themselves in dialogue with how other people in the colonies constructed race. Stepping back and looking at how objects helped Jews create family stories about whiteness helps underscore the way race was crafted in early America.

Thinking about how racecraft in the past impacted family history can also remind us how we continue to craft race with our own categories and genealogical pursuits. Speaking of Sarah and her mother as "multiracial" or "interracial" suggests that her father, Abraham Rodrigues

Brandon, was not of this category merely because he was accepted as white and all his known ancestors were Sephardic. Yet by the time Abraham's family fled Iberia, it was a rare "New Christian" family that had not married non-Jews at some point in their history.[146] Moreover, if DNA tests reveal anything, they show that various groups of Jews (such as Jews from Iberia, Germany, Russia, etc.) differ from each other because they resemble in part the communities of people they lived among, sharing DNA as a result of conversion, intermarriage, or illicit sexual encounters. Abraham—like all Jews alive today—was just as "interracial" as Sarah was; scholars just choose to believe the story of his being a "pure Sephardi" and opt not to mark him (and perhaps also themselves) in that way.[147] The myth of "pure" races is part of the work of racecraft.

Portraits like Sarah's played an important role in negotiating connections across the oceans. Like the other objects I focus on in this book, there was nothing inherently "Jewish" about ivory miniatures. To be sure, many elites in the Americas and Europe used them as a way to shape how others, particularly intimate others, saw them. Yet in an era of revolution and Jewish emancipation, ivories also took on a different resonance when used *by* Jews. Ivory miniatures helped present Jews as part of the Atlantic World elite to which they aspired, an elite that increasingly insisted upon whiteness. In the next chapter we will see how women's roles in the elite world changed as notions of marriage, love, and education gave Jewish women in New York options unavailable to women a generation earlier.

FOUR

Commonplace Things

Miriam Gratz Mordecai was not present on the hot day in June 1892 when forty-one men met at the Jewish Theological Seminary at 736 Lexington Avenue, but the meeting would prove vital to her family's legacy.[1] Scholar Cyrus Adler had sent out invitations to "prominent Americans" whose credentials in Jewish history derived from their positions as professors, curators, and rabbis.[2] By the end of the day, the gathering had created the American Jewish Historical Society seemingly out of thin air, with Oscar Straus as chairman and Adler as secretary. No women were present, most likely because Adler had not thought to invite any. In retrospect this seems ironic, as today women hold most of the society's key positions, including executive director, senior archivist, and president of the academic council. Adler would eventually remember to reach out across the gender line, speaking to the National Council of Jewish Women in 1897, but even before then women had begun to interject their way into his organization. Of the 178 early members listed in 1893, six were women: Charity S. Cohen, Rose Frank, and Elvira Solis of Philadelphia; Corrine Jackson and Henrietta Szold of Baltimore; and Isabella H. Rosenbach of New York.[3] Like Miriam Gratz Mordecai, most were descendants of early elite Jewish families, and their ancestors would feature prominently in *Publications of the American Jewish Historical Society,* the association's new journal.

While not yet a member, Miriam would become the first woman to publish anything for the society, penning a brief note for the journal's inaugural volume that highlighted the history of her ancestor Joseph Simon and her relationship to him.[4] Her note was a harbinger of things to come. It was not just that by the next issue, Isabella Rosenbach would already appear as the first female coauthor of a full-length article. Miriam's note also emphasized a different way of thinking about how identity travelled. Her genealogy was markedly different from pedigrees of men like Malcolm Stern a couple of generations later, since Miriam traced her connection to Jewish American history through her *maternal* line (fig. 68; appendix 4).[5]

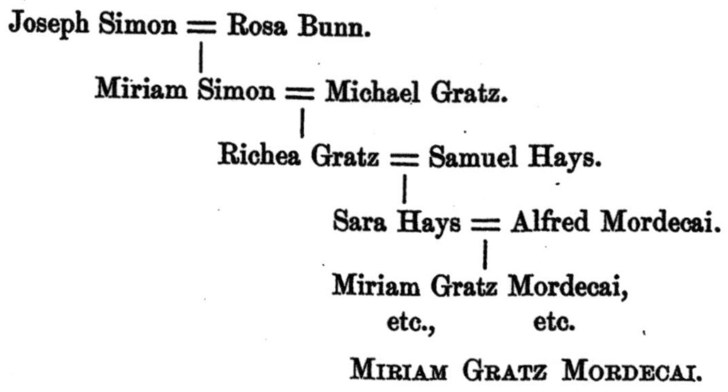

Joseph Simon = Rosa Bunn.
|
Miriam Simon = Michael Gratz.
|
Richea Gratz = Samuel Hays.
|
Sara Hays = Alfred Mordecai.
|
Miriam Gratz Mordecai,
etc.,   etc.

MIRIAM GRATZ MORDECAI.

Fig. 68. Miriam Gratz Mordecai's maternal lineage. From Miriam Gratz Mordecai, "Notes," *Publications of the American Jewish Historical Society* 1 (1893): 122. Courtesy of AJHS.

Yet Miriam had inherited more than her tie to Joseph Simon from her foremothers. Her mother, Sarah Ann Hays Mordecai (1805–94), had bequeathed a love of family, writing, and community as well as an emphasis on female ancestors. Despite being the middle child of ten, Sarah Ann had been the storyteller and record keeper of her generation, writing the first biography of her famous aunt, Rebecca Gratz. Although she wrote Rebecca's biography in 1872, Sarah Ann waited until 1893 to self-publish it, identifying herself solely as "one of her [Rebecca Gratz's] nieces."[6] The same year as Miriam wrote her note, Sarah Ann donated her book to the newly formed American Jewish Historical Society.[7] The biography was, as Sarah Ann herself claimed, "not a memento of statistics, but of *love*," one that emphasized Rebecca's contributions to the larger Jewish community and her extended family as much as her individual excellence.[8] Sarah Ann's focus on women as the carriers of

Jewish history was unusual. Despite women's early role in the society, initially when women published in the journal they—like their male colleagues—tended to write about men. Isabella Rosenbach's 1894 article, for example, was on Aaron Lopez—the man whom Hannah Louzada wrote to in Spanish requesting charity.

Writing about women was decidedly slower to catch on in *Publications of the American Jewish Historical Society*. The first female featured on her own merits (rather than as the wife of someone more famous) was also Rebecca Gratz, Miriam's great-aunt, who headlined in a brief note in 1903. The note, however, was a comment once penned by author Washington Irving, while Sarah Ann's prior insights on the very same subject went ignored.[9] This exclusion was a trend. The first full article spotlighting a woman would have to wait until 1925, when Rebecca's letters were published,[10] and "woman" or "women" as a subject would not appear in a title in the society's journals until 1968 and then only in a book review.[11] A full article centered on women as a subject did not appear until another decade had passed,[12] and gender would not be a featured topic until the second half of the 1990s.[13] This absence obscures how even early on the style and form of Jewish family writing was gendered differently between men and women. Sarah Ann's biography of Rebecca had not appeared out of nowhere. Writing had been a lifelong passion for Miriam's mother, but it was not only her female-focused subject that was unconventional. Sarah Ann had favored genres that emphasized community and embraced what were increasingly understood at the time as the feminine rather than masculine modes of discourse.

Miriam's role in the fledgling historical society owes a debt to the work of her mother. Sarah Ann's distinctive understanding of authorship, lineage, and self was epitomized in a book that occupied the center of her life for nearly all of her adult existence. When she was only eighteen, Sarah Ann Hays had opened a blank book bound in red leather and begun her life's work, a collage of drawings and poems (figs. 69 and 70). While that might seem a young age to begin so auspicious a project, she was almost the same age her mother, Richea Gratz, had been when she wed fellow Jew Samuel Hays in 1793.[14] Unlike the biography of her famous aunt, the book Sarah Ann began in 1823 would never be published, but it remained one of her prized possessions and a constant companion. She continued to annotate it for over fifty-five years.

Although someone recognized the red-leather-bound book's significance and donated it to the historical society, scholars have largely neglected it ever since.[15] Yet the exact reasons why the book failed to gain

Fig. 69. George Todd, *Miss Sarah Hays*, n.d. Silhouette. Courtesy of the Boston Athenaeum.

attention, I argue, highlight why it *should* interest us deeply, particularly if we want to know more about Jewish women or Jewish families in early America. In the previous chapters, I have examined three objects owned by early Jewish women who lived at least a portion of their lives in New York: Hannah Louzada's letter, Reyna Levy's silver beakers, and Sarah Rodrigues Brandon's ivory miniature. Sarah Ann's book shows how far women had come since the 1750s in writing their own destinies. Women

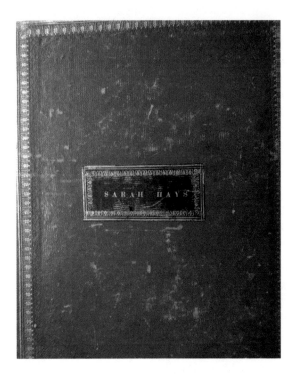

Fig. 70. Sarah Ann Hays
[Mordecai], common-
place book, 1823–94.
Courtesy of AJHS.

had more choice in whom they married and more choice in what they
could do in society. Moreover, men had started to recognize women's
contribution to both Jewish and secular life. Sarah Ann's book reveals
three key ways that her life—and those of Jewish women of her era—had
changed: the intellectual paths Jewish women travelled, the emotional
paths Jewish women took, and women's role in the preservation of Jewish
families. These three paths would change how the Jewish family was understood. Given the book's significance, it seems all the more troubling
that her work has been ignored, so let me first offer an explanation of why
Sarah Ann's red-leather book has been so neglected and misunderstood.

Gendered Neglect

At first glance, it seems impossible that so few scholars have read or
relied on Sarah Ann's book in their scholarship on Jewish American
women. We have so few objects made by women themselves from the
early era. Why would both historians and literary critics ignore her book?

Most likely this oversight is due to the fact that her book is not a type of work we value today. Rather, it is an archetypal early American genre, the commonplace book. Like yearbooks, social media, scrapbooks, Pinterest, or vision boards in the late twentieth and early twenty-first centuries, nineteenth-century commonplace books were interactive, communal, and, above all, gendered. Although not used solely by women, they were an imaginative space where primarily women could create conceptions of themselves that were interwoven with the "central ribbon of family life," pasted together to create pastiches over time.[16] While that communal interactivity has made them less valued as "literature," commonplace books are critical for understanding how women constructed their multifaceted identities. Like the matriarchal genealogy of her daughter, Miriam, Sarah Ann's book can help illuminate a female-centered way of thinking about self, writing, and history.

If you have never seen or read a commonplace book, you are not alone. While commonplace books were, well, commonplace from antiquity up through the eighteenth century, they fell out of fashion toward the end of the nineteenth century.[17] At their most basic, commonplace books are collections of quotes, images, and ideas valued by an individual.[18] Ancient commonplace books reflected the Roman understanding of reading as *legere*, a Latin verb used not only for reading but also gathering or collecting, such as the Roman practice of selecting bones from cremated remains.[19] Hence reading was "an inherently active, discriminating, and selective exercise."[20] Early on, men used commonplace books for collecting philosophical or theological quotes, but by the late eighteenth century, young women turned to the genre to navigate the new turbulent waters of romance.[21]

By Sarah Ann's lifetime, both Jewish and non-Jewish women felt the pressure to marry for love.[22] How, though, could a woman determine a young man's emotions so she could respond appropriately? Like high school yearbooks in the second half of the twentieth century, in which students asked both friends and potential beaus to write notes that were at once personal and public, commonplace books were a socially acceptable way nineteenth-century women could solicit and exchange romantic gestures. Yet just as in high school yearbooks from later eras, nineteenth-century emotional gestures were not solely voiced by men. Women used commonplace books to build and establish friendships and place other women at the center of their emotional lives.

Women's commonplace books were highly social. In this sense, commonplace books parallel social media platforms today like Facebook and

Snapchat, as the items "posted" and shared were meant to be seen by reading communities. The ideas quoted in transcribed passages were important, but just as crucial was the commonplace-book keeper's ability to decode what was meant when a *certain someone* dedicated a particular poem or quotation to her. Such a scene occurs in Jane Austen's *Emma* (1815), when Emma and her friend Harriet desperately try to interpret the "charade" written by the bumbling Mr. Elton in order to better understand his intentions.[23] As in Austen's novel, the decoding of commonplace entries was a social event: it was not just that friends might glance at previous entries in one's book before writing down their own ideas, but that certain entries required the book's owner to seek advice about how to understand and interpret what was intended by the words. Commonplace books creatively bound together writers and owner as well as owner and readers. To be sure, commonplace books tell us *what* women read, but they also reveal *how* women read. And how women read can help us better understand changes in individuals and the family.

If nineteenth-century women's commonplace books were exceptionally good at creating a community of writers and readers, scholars have found them less intriguing in terms of literary or artistic merit. It is not only Sarah Ann's commonplace book that scholars have ignored. As one critic put it, today "the commonplace book has been a subject of little research and less debate."[24] Commonplace books do not fit today's definition of literary or artistic genii: they are multiauthored and deliberately imitative; they float happily between prose, poetry, and image, giving equal weight to all genres. Any lack of originality we perceive today reflects old slander against the genre. Back in antiquity, the Roman philosopher Seneca justified the art of commonplaces through the allegory of the honey bee. In his *Epistulae morales,* Seneca suggests that writers of commonplace books should "copy the bees, and sift whatever we have gathered from a varied course of reading . . . then by applying the supervising care which our nature has endowed us . . . we could so blend those several favors into one delicious compound that, even though it betrays its origin, yet it nevertheless is clearly a different thing from that where it came."[25] That is, for Seneca, the genius of the keeper of the commonplace book lay in the way he collected "pollen" from various sources and made something new and richer from it—the "honey" that was his book.

The idea of a commonplace-book compiler as a bee who collects pollen from her sources is a metaphor that Sarah Ann herself seems to have had in the back of her mind. Most of her own illustrations in the book are of flowers (fig. 71), and many of the quotes include either references

Fig. 71. Sarah Ann Hays [Mordecai], *Flower Basket*, in her common-place book. Courtesy of AJHS.

to flowers or are taken from flower dictionaries, such as the 1830 *Flora's Dictionary* we know she owned.[26] Flowers were central to nineteenth-century women's education because botany was an acceptable form of women's science tutelage and because—like commonplace books—flowers were thought to meld the world of the intellect and the emotions.[27]

Sarah Ann's commonplace book is the closest thing she wrote to an autobiography; yet it makes for a very strange autobiography. Similar to women's scrapbooks today, her book was imitative yet individual, communal yet personal, intellectual yet emotional. Rather than writing everything in its pages, Sarah Ann collected items she valued for their connections to others as well as for their intrinsic merit. Autobiography literally means "self-life-writing" and Sarah Ann's commonplace book reveals what kind of "self" she had been taught to value. Literary forms dedicated to self-scrutiny proliferated in the early nineteenth century, only one strand of which spawned the kind of memoirs we associate with standard autobiographies today.[28] The self who was scrutinized in Sarah

Ann's work is of a type Seneca and his honey bee analogy did not anticipate. To be sure, the genius of nineteenth-century women's commonplaces was still the act of compiling (making honey from bits of pollen), but their compiling was more communal than that executed by Seneca's lone bee. For nineteenth-century women like Sarah Ann, the paths and connections women made while collecting their quotes (the pollen) were just as meaningful as the honey itself. This change is strangely fitting. Scientists have mapped the journeys of real honey bees, and they reveal complex and intricate networks of relations between the bees and their crop (fig. 72).[29] The paths and networks created by Sarah Ann as she compiled her commonplace book were as intricate and important as the items she and her friends collected. Sarah Ann's book reenvisions the art of the bee.

Of the five women I discuss, Sarah Ann is the only one who, we know for certain, married for love. She married without a dowry and got engaged without first seeking the permission of her parents.[30] Her

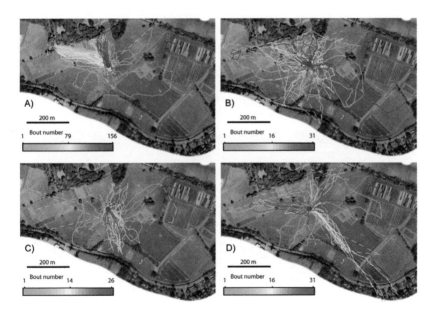

Fig. 72. "Every flight path taken over the course of four bees' lives. The blue dot indicates the site of the nest." Joseph L. Woodgate, Stephen C. Pratt, James C. Makinson, Ka S. Lim, Andrew M. Reynolds, and Lars Chittka, "Life-Long Radar Tracking of Bumblebees," *PLOS ONE* 11, no. 8 (2016): https://doi.org/10.1371/journal.pone.0160333.

commonplace book provides us with a unique vantage point on the shifts in Jewish women's lives that made her choices possible. Sarah Ann also married much later than either Reyna Levy or Sarah Brandon Moses, both of whom married when they were only seventeen. Sarah Ann, in contrast, married when she was thirty-one.[31] In the years before, she was busy—like a bee—creating a series of networks and relationships that would last her a lifetime. In later years, when her marriage bore an almost unbearable stress, those networks proved to be a safety net.

Sarah Ann needed those networks. Like more and more Jewish women of her era, Sarah Ann's marriage took her away from the large Jewish community she had known and into small town New York life. To be sure, as a member of the Hays family, Sarah Ann had important ties both to New York City and to Shearith Israel: her father, Samuel Hays, had been born in the city and apprenticed under Haym Salomon,[32] whom he followed to Philadelphia. Born in Philadelphia, Sarah Ann had lived near Mikveh Israel, the spiritual home not only of her father's but also her mother's family, the Gratzes (fig. 73).[33]

Yet after Sarah Ann married Alfred Mordecai, a rising star in the U.S. military, she found herself repeatedly displaced and finally living in Watervliet, New York, where her husband oversaw the U.S. Army's arsenal (fig. 74). Watervliet (sometimes known as "West Troy") was an army town north of Albany,[34] along the Hudson River. Sarah Ann was 160 miles

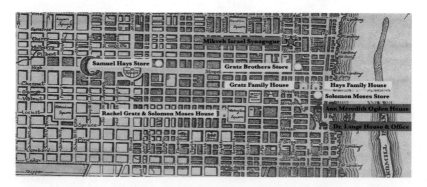

Fig. 73. Sarah Ann Hays's Philadelphia. From F. Drayton, *Plan of the City of Philadelphia from the Actual Surveys* (Philadelphia: R. H. Filbert, 1824). Locations based on *Robinson's Original Annual Directory for 1817* (Whitehall, PA: James Robinson, 1824); E. Whiteley's *The Philadelphia Directory and Register for 1820* (Philadelphia: M'Carty and Davis, 1820); and Robert Desilver, *The Philadelphia Index, or Directory, for 1823* (Philadelphia, 1823).

Fig. 74. William James Bennett, *Troy. Taken from the West Bank of the Hudson, in Front of the United States Arsenal [in Watervliet]*, 1838. Hand-colored aquatint; 19½ × 27¹³⁄₁₆ in. Courtesy National Gallery of Art, Washington, DC, 1985.64.132.

north of Manhattan. In living outside of the city, she was like many Jews of the era for whom New York City was a place to visit rather than a permanent residence. Compared to either New York City or Philadelphia, Watervliet offered little in the way of organized Jewish life. Even Troy, the larger city across the river, was limited in its Jewish population. The first Jew to arrive—Emanuel Marks—had not settled there until 1843.[35] Despite the organization of a synagogue in the 1850s, infighting often left the congregation without a minyan.[36] The community was also a far cry from the Jewish high society to which Sarah Ann was accustomed: most members of Troy's synagogue were recent immigrants and either peddlers or small-time merchants.[37] The highest praise given of Troy's few Jews by locals was that they "paid their bills promptly" and were "inoffensive."[38] Although only across the river, even Troy's few Jews were a world away from the Mordecais.

When Sarah Ann was under stress, she reached out not to the poor Jews of Troy but back to her commonplace book's networks—networks that connected her to the elite and well-developed Jewish communities of which she was now only a distant satellite. That network supported her as she struggled to raise Jewish children in a town where her husband was often more interested in being an American military leader than in maintaining Jewish ties. Sarah Ann's commonplace book both constructed kinship and rethought women's role in maintaining Jewish family lines. These paths were so important to Sarah Ann that later in life she annotated her book, marking next to unsigned entries and cryptic initials the identity of various contributors.

She traced three paths while collecting her entries: intellectual paths, emotional paths, and paths that tied her to her family and other Jews, a network I am calling the "Jewish family romance." These paths reveal three key ways her life—and that of Jewish women of her era—had changed since the 1750s when Reyna Levy was born and Hannah Louzada's husband had died. While Reyna Levy and Sarah Rodrigues Brandon had married Northern merchants with strong synagogue ties, Sarah Ann's husband was different. Alfred Mordecai was a career military man raised in the South but trained and serving in the North. The Civil War separated his family not only from his wife's but also from the army family he had dutifully trained and served. As we will see, the paths his wife had laid out in her book would prove his salvation as the war tore his world apart.

The Bee's First Path: Women and Intellect

The first path that defines Sarah Ann's book is an intellectual one. Unlike Seneca or later Enlightenment-era commonplace collectors like John Locke, Sarah Ann did not tend to collect philosophical quotes. Instead, she used her book to display her talents and tastes in poetry and art. As Sarah Ann herself noted in her biography of her aunt Rebecca Gratz, being a well-educated nineteenth-century American woman meant knowing classics like John Milton and Alexander Pope as well as contemporary Romantic authors like Sir Walter Scott.

If you look at a map of all the works quoted in Sarah Ann's commonplace book (fig. 75), it becomes clear that she favored Romantic-era writers (rendered in pink), which comprise about 40 percent of the works quoted. Another 40 percent were classics such as Renaissance writers like Shakespeare (purple), Cavalier poets (green), Augustan-age giants like Pope (teal), and explicitly Christian writers like Milton and More (yellow). Only about 20 percent of the book was original work (orange).

As Sarah Ann herself explains in her biography of Rebecca, a well-read woman should be able to offer "beautiful snatches of poetry" from a wide variety of sources to fit any occasion.[39] Sarah Ann's commonplace book interweaves her own voice with the popular literature of her day, displaying a similar desire to appear elegantly educated.

Women's and men's magazines from England and the early United States are the source of these "beautiful snatches" and quotable quotes. Illustrations likewise tended to be modelled on drawing manuals. It did not matter that the quotes and drawings were recycled. On the contrary, Sarah's quotation map displays her knowledge not only of the original authors but also of the literary magazines themselves, works that served as a sort of virtual museum for what was truly valuable. Magazines displayed what people of taste were known to revere and created a "transatlantic pool of tropes, images," and symbols.[40]

Like those magazines, Sarah Ann's museum-like display of good taste reflects a new understanding of what the commonplace was. Early nineteenth-century Americans, such as Sarah Ann and her circle of friends, learned how to write "modern" commonplace books from a variety of

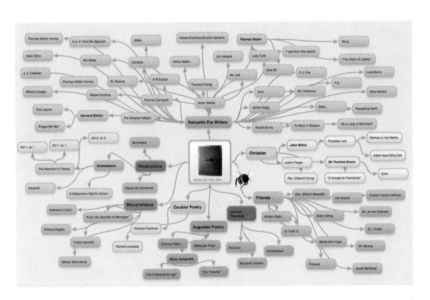

Fig. 75. Schema of works included in Hays [Mordecai]'s commonplace book, by era and type. Romantic era (pink), Shakespeare (purple), Cavalier poets (green), Augustan age (teal), Christian writers (yellow), and original work (orange). Courtesy of author.

places: in addition to popular magazines, advice manuals and published commonplaces provided guidance.[41] The form of Sarah Ann's book reflects all these influences.

The very first page of Sarah Ann's book reveals her indebtedness to guides on commonplace writing (fig. 76). Family friend Dr. John Lange appears to have penned Sarah Ann's cover page.[42] While intricate, the title page is hardly original. As I have already noted, originality was not the point. Rather, the title page mimics John Bell's extremely popular *Commonplace Book Form'd Generally upon the Principles Recommended and Practised by Mr. Locke* (London, 1770) (fig. 77).

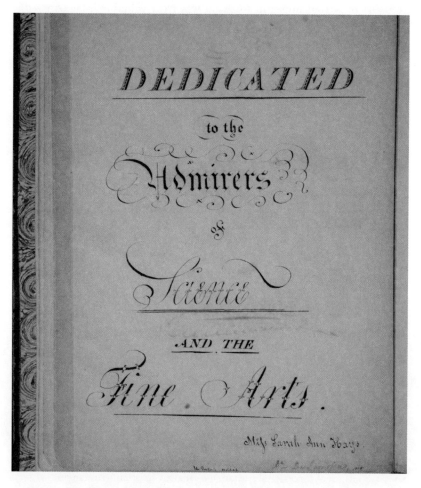

Fig. 76. John Lange, frontispiece to Hays [Mordecai]'s commonplace book. Courtesy of AJHS.

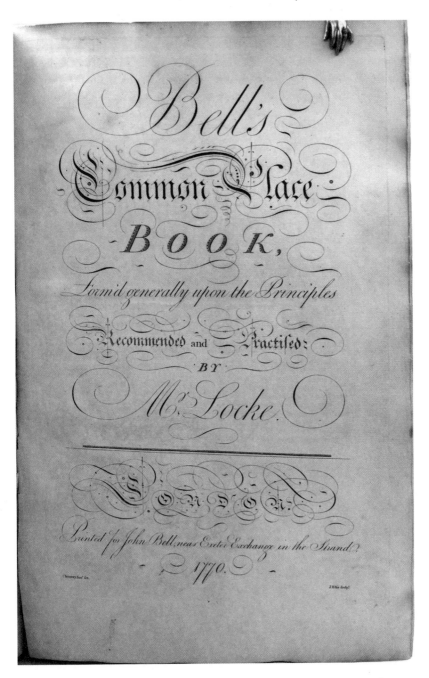

Fig. 77. Title page for Bell's *Commonplace Book Form'd Generally upon the Principles Recommended and Practised by Mr. Locke* (London, 1770). Courtesy of Antipodeon Books.

It is easy to dismiss both title pages as a typesetter's nightmare: each line is a bizarre mishmash of styles and fonts pointing the reader in different directions. Designer Carlos Segura argues, "Some fonts are so decorative . . . they tell a story beyond the words."[43] Yet if scripts and fonts tell a story, the story told by the frontispiece Lange created for Sarah Ann

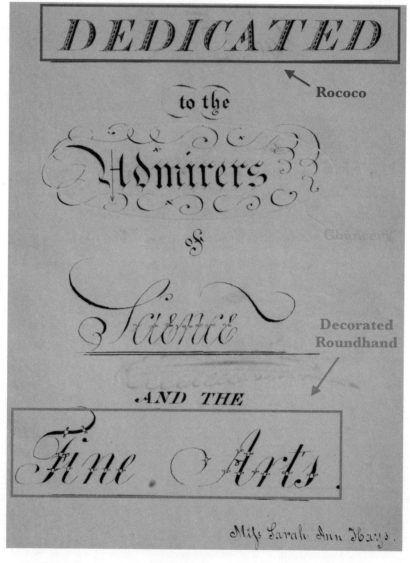

Fig. 78. Fonts used in the frontispiece to Hays [Mordecai]'s common-place book. Courtesy of AJHS.

seems confused. The lettering moves between rococo, a style popular in France between 1720 and 1770 and associated with elegance, the upper classes, and privilege;[44] chancery, a variant of the gothic script associated with the medieval era and "anti-Enlightenment libertine darkness";[45] and decorated roundhand, a script that was originally the basis for all business penmanship training (fig. 78).[46] It is as if Lange cannot decide if the protagonist of Sarah Ann's story is an aristocrat, a medieval throwback, or a businessman. This hodgepodge, however, is essential.

Brought together, this mishmash of scripts does double duty. First, it illustrates the very nature of the commonplace book that follows: a collection of a wide range of ideas and emotions, each with their separate histories, united in a single volume. Second, in the case of Lange's frontispiece, it establishes the virtuosity of the elements Sarah Ann's commonplace book will contain. Sarah Ann's book is indebted to ornamental penmanship both in the handwriting itself and in the inclusion of "flourishings" taught by penmanship manuals, such as drawings of a bird, an angel, and a pen (fig. 79). In nineteenth-century America, ornamental penmanship was considered one of the "fine arts," with the same cachet as portrait or landscape painting. Ornamental penmanship was also moral, as advocates argued it "elevated the mind and might even purify the debauched."[47] This purification was akin to the work of the commonplace book itself: by collecting "sublime passages and elevated sentiments,"[48] the collector ideally would elevate the mind above the mundane to a higher truth, crystallized like sweet honey.

The images in Sarah Ann's book similarly display a good education in art. The image across from Lange's title page is by Sarah Ann's friend Ann Meredith Ogden, who grew up less than two blocks away in Philadelphia (fig. 80).[49] Like the title page, Ogden's drawing places the book in dialogue with other art of the era and showcases the creator's talent. Drawing was one of the primary accomplishments girls of a certain class were expected to learn, and it was regularly taught at schools for "young ladies."[50] At such schools, women learned not only needlepoint and penmanship but a variety of techniques for drawing, including watercolors and painting furniture.[51]

One of the most common ways that young women learned to draw and paint was by copying pattern books and drawing manuals such as *Hints to Young Practitioners in the Study of Landscape Painting* (1810) or *A Series of Progressive Lessons Intended to Elucidate the Art of Flower Painting in Water Colours* (Philadelphia, 1818).[52] Ogden's drawing of the bouquet of flowers—like flower illustrations by Sarah Ann herself—displays her mastery of exercises on how to shade, outline, and tint leaves and how

Fig. 79. Sample flourishing of bird, in Hays [Mordecai]'s commonplace book. Courtesy of AJHS.

to create a variety of different types of flowers, one the most difficult of which was the moss rose, a favorite throughout the book.[53] The composition and motifs illustrated in Sarah Ann's book resemble the stock pastoral and romantic scenes practiced in other "schoolgirl art" of the era (figs. 81–83). Pasting drawings into one's own or other people's commonplace books was an elegant way to share and show off these skills in a socially acceptable manner.

Fig. 80. Ann Meredith Ogden, *Flowers*, in Hays [Mordecai]'s common-place book. Courtesy of AJHS.

Fig. 81. Workbox with floral spray motif, ca. 1810–30. Courtesy of Betsy Krieg Salm.

Fig. 82. Top of Elizabeth Perkins's work table. Courtesy of the Historical Society of Old Newbury and the Cushing House Museum.

Fig. 83. Ann Meredith Ogden, *Pastoral Scene*, in Hays [Mordecai]'s commonplace book. Courtesy of AJHS.

In addition to showcasing their knowledge of the commonplace genre and elite women's education, entries in Sarah Ann's book pay homage to popular literary magazines, including their publication of items explicitly intended for inclusion in commonplace books themselves. Sarah Ann's first entry, for example, appeared originally in the *London Magazine*, a leading publisher of Romantic poetry, with the instruction that it was meant to be "Written in the First Leaf of a Friend's Album."[54] Including excerpts from such magazines marked Sarah Ann and her friends as people of taste—that is, as people who read literature that was popular and lauded in its own day.

Sarah Ann's book also echoes the structure of such fashionable literary magazines. Periodicals like the *London Magazine* aimed to provide "readers with a field of possibilities" and thus left it in large part up "to them to decide what approach to take or what conclusions to take away."[55] Particularly as compared to novels, literary magazines did little to enforce a "prescribed order" in which to read entries.[56] Sarah Ann's commonplace book employs the same reading principle: entries do not appear in chronological order nor in the alphabetical order suggested by Enlightenment commonplace manuals such as the earlier popular one by Locke.[57] This structure marks a change in the genre of commonplace books, which now aspired to the model of Romantic-era literary magazines, with their open form and emphasis on readers' participation.

Unlike Reyna Moses's beakers or Sarah Rodrigues Brandon's portrait, Sarah Ann's commonplace book established its owner as part of an intellectual world by creating a series of relationships between her and writers and artists of her era as well as famous writers of the past. Jewish women's letters from the day show that women found reading classics "elevating" and "refining"; moreover, when shared with non-Jewish friends, passages from Shakespeare provided "a secular source of shared spiritual and moral values."[58] Sarah Ann's reading network not only illustrates what nineteenth-century Jewish women read and saw but also elucidates the type of education they valued: a schooling that was "classical" and yet modern, cerebral yet emotional. This intellectual world is important for understanding individuals like Sarah Ann but also a new generation of Jewish American women who played an increasingly large role in educating Jewish children in both secular and religious subjects, a role actively encouraged by Orthodox rabbis like Isaac Leeser and Samuel Myer Isaacs.[59]

A generation earlier, Jewish American congregations had hired men, typically ones trained in Europe or Caribbean *yeshivot*, to educate Jewish American children. But by the 1820s, women became more vital to Jewish education, founding both secular schools and Hebrew Sunday schools.

For some wealthy women like Sarah Ann's aunt Rebecca Gratz, Jewish education was an act of charity. For others, educating children was one of the few socially acceptable jobs open to women of status. In times of financial trouble, women in both Sarah Ann's and Alfred's families turned to running schools to support themselves and their male kin.[60] When Sarah Ann first married Alfred, she could rely on her husband's military career, but when the war interrupted his career trajectory, Sarah Ann and her daughters kept the family financially afloat by opening a school.[61]

One reason Jewish women like Sarah Ann were able to take their place in education was that women's relationship to morality had changed. While once American culture had deemed women more sinful than men,[62] by the first half of the nineteenth century the cult of sentiment changed their moral status. Women's culture suddenly seemed more significant and ethical. Sarah Ann's commonplace book was part of that moralistic, female-centered culture. Even as Sarah Ann's book displayed her learning, it reveled in an emotional life—and it is to this path that I now turn.

The Bee's Second Path: Emotional Bonds

Just as Sarah Ann's book places her in an intellectual network, so too it uses emotions to connect her and her peers. The entries embrace sentimentalism—that is, "the expression of unwarranted emotion in decorative, florid language."[63] While sentimentality sometimes presents an obstacle for modern readers "who are more comfortable with spare language and checked feelings,"[64] the overflow of emotions did important social and ethical work in nineteenth-century America. American female proponents of sentimental fiction, such as Harriet Beecher Stowe, followed the belief of Scottish common-sense philosophers that sensual indulgence, particularly in the fine arts, could be profoundly moral. Certain emotions, particularly "emotions of taste," were a "powerful goad to moral improvement" and "coax[ed] human beings to God."[65] These emotions were also gendered, as they aimed to stir in the audience the "'feminine' qualities of 'Humility, Timidity, Sensibility, and Kindness.'"[66] Much like landscape gardening, botany, or drawing flowers, literature was meant to overwhelm the emotions and uplift the senses.[67] Reading commonplace books gives us a small window onto the rich emotional lives of early American Jewish women as they collected pieces to spur them to feel correctly.

The poems in Sarah Ann's book used emotions to lift up readers into a realm where people disconnected by space, time, or loss could reconnect with each other or the divine. Extreme punctuation such as dashes and exclamation points aimed to supercharge the language, while the rhyme and meter of ballad stanzas encouraged readers to associate the ideas in the poems with the uplift found in familiar religious hymns and sentimental popular songs. A sample entry provides a sense of the typical style included in Sarah Ann's book:

> The poet, too, who, borne along
> In thought to distant time,
> Pours forth his inmost soul in song,
> Holds fast this hope sublime!
> He would a glorious name bequeath,
> Oblivion shall not blot,
> And round that name his thoughts enwreath
> The words—"Forget me not!"[68]

While such poetry may seem trite today, the "decorative, florid language" and gushing sentiments expressed in many of the entries in Sarah Ann's book sought to forge connections between people and, through those connections, the attainment of a truer, elevated self. This hope was one key reason why Sarah Ann's biography of her aunt was a memoir of love, not of statistics.

Emotions were central to friendships during the era in which Sarah Ann lived, and Jews were no exception. Letters exchanged between women in her family are rife with chaotic and extreme emotions. When Rachel Gratz wrote to her sister Rebecca in 1806, she said she would "expose my whole heart to you, that heart which is now agitated by a thousand feelings, but in each is love, affection, and gratitude for you. . . . Friend Oh! God how will you approve of its change I fear I tremble doubt yet hope you will not quite disapprove."[69] Extreme emotions bound the sisters to each other and to the divine. Rachel was not alone in her range of feeling. Literary scholar Lucia McMahon notes:

> As individualism and the "culture of sensibility" took hold in early nineteenth-century America, new emotional standards for intimate relationships were enacted. Individualism asserted that one's "true" or "inner" self was unique, private, and concealed from the outer world. But to assert and validate one's individuality, it was

perhaps necessary—and desirable—to realize a sense of connection with other individuals. A key goal of nineteenth-century relationships, then, was the achievement of shared selfhood through sincere and candid communication.[70]

Like letters, commonplace books provided a space to reveal, share, and even create that selfhood. Romantic love allowed people to disclose their "true selves" by "strengthening, and sometimes even creating . . . the 'romantic self.'"[71] Emotions were paramount to the "immersion of one's self with another,"[72] and this immersion accomplished ethical work. According to eighteenth-century Scottish philosopher David Hume, emotions like sympathy bridged "the gaps of cultural and racial difference," thereby allowing people to connect despite different experiences.[73]

This desire to spark moral action may help us understand why some entries in Sarah Ann's book revel in "negative" emotions, such as sadness and loss. Ideally the emotional bridge healed ruptures in the real world. "Fellow-feeling," sentimental writers believed, could "motivate the public to relieve oppression and pain."[74] Hence, while romance, friendship, and happiness were some of the most common themes, inscribers also spoke of melancholia—a pain Sarah Ann knew all too well. Within three years of starting the commonplace book, Sarah's Ann's older sister, Miriam, died on July 2, 1826. While eventually Sarah Ann would name one of her daughters after her beloved sister, at the time Sarah Ann and her mother were plunged into sorrow. Rebecca Gratz noted in a letter to a friend that Miriam's loss "threatened to break down all their strength. . . . Sister & Sarah Ann seemed ready to sink & I was afraid I would lose their health."[75]

The commonplace book was a space where Sarah Ann could share and explore the depth of her sorrow. It was also a Jewish space. To be sure, Christian commonplace books from this era are also increasingly filled with discussions of death and mourning, but they more consistently fall back on the consolations provided by the afterlife, resurrection, and the tradition of "Christian relics."[76] In contrast, the entries about loss and despair in Sarah Ann's book surrounded her like a minyan during the kaddish, many voices working together to form a chant of laments and praise that would eventually heal.

Sorrow and pain, however, were not merely things to be moved past. Nineteenth-century women understood the strength of emotions differently than we do today because the sublime power of "negative" emotions was considered imperative to the "romantic self." As Susan Sontag notes about tuberculosis in the early nineteenth century, "melancholy . . . was the artist's disease, according to the theory of the four humors. The melancholy character—or the tubercular—was a superior one: sensitive, creative, a being apart."[77] Lord Byron famously said, "I should like . . . to die from consumption."[78] Others suggested that suffering correlated with a certain superiority. It was believed, for example, that the poet John Keats "fell victim to tuberculosis because his sensitive nature had been unable to withstand contact with a crude world."[79] Nineteenth-century Americans were certainly aware of the horrible suffering that accompanied tuberculosis, but they also thought the disease "spiritualize[d] the self, as the fever burns away the body to expose the spirit within."[80] In the age in which Sarah Ann lived, suffering was not only unavoidable but also helped one achieve a better, truer self. Sharing one's pain with others, then, was a gift.[81]

For nineteenth-century Americans, emotions were linked to a new ideal of kinship. Philosophers and theologians agreed: "People who shared 'sentiments'—meaning both feelings and opinions—could form 'families' linked by common sentiments, if not blood."[82] Many early nineteenth-century women's novels emphasize that "family" could "designate something chosen, rather than a given set of biological or legal relations."[83] That is, instead "of proposing that one should love one's family," the novels assert instead that "one's family will be whatever one loves."[84] Crucially, this new family was not solely between Sarah Ann and the men who courted her. Contemporary writers argued that "'true' friendship . . . existed between equals, [people who] exhibited mutuality of thoughts, emotions, and sentiments, and depended upon confidence, sincerity, and candor in communications." True friendship was "an affectionate union of two persons," who ideally were close in age, with similar dispositions, and of the same sex.[85] The high-pitched and romantic emotions exchanged between female friends wove a new network of kinship.

Consequently, of the sixty-eight entries in Sarah Ann's commonplace book by people other than Sarah Ann for whom the gender is discernible, exactly half were by women. Moreover, women's entries were some of the most intimate and original. This preeminence was not unusual. New ideas about sexual difference led women to craft a "female world of love and ritual" that provided an "intimacy and emotional fulfillment that seemed nearly impossible to obtain in male-female relationships."[86] Thus, female intimacies were not only essential but also cherished. To be sure, the elevation of romantic love as an ideal for marriage paralleled the idea that emotional connections with others could help people achieve their "best" and "truest" selves. Yet for young women like Sarah Ann, the emotional bonds that helped her build her "true" self were as much with other women as with male potential romantic partners. This theory is borne out in Sarah Ann's commonplace book, in which exchanges with women were key to the development of Sarah Ann's own voice as a writer and artist.

Sarah Ann was not alone in valuing female friendships. In 1800, her famous Aunt Rebecca wrote that "the bitterest moments of pain in my existence" occurred when she found herself estranged from a newly married friend.[87] Likewise, Sarah Ann notes in her biography of her aunt, when one of Rebecca's non-Jewish friends died of a fever, Rebecca, "to show her grief and affection, wished to wear the garb of mourning" typically worn by blood relatives.[88] Despite her mother's disapproval, Rebecca wore mourning for a full year. It was a rare moment of disobedience. Female members of the Gratz family (whom Sarah Ann was tied to through blood) and the Mordecai family (to whom Sarah Ann would be tied through marriage) were incredible letter writers.[89] Like Sarah Ann's commonplace book, their letters reveal Jewish women's critical roles in building families through the language of emotion, affection, and friendship.

The Bee's Third Path: Jewish Family Romance

If Sarah Ann's commonplace book allowed her to forge new paths of friendship, it also gave her an opportunity to practice romance. Significantly, her family was there to guide her and to reinforce the role Judaism should play in her love life. As intermarriage rates increased and men disproportionately married out, women were increasingly pressured to maintain Jewish families.[90] Sarah Ann also needed assistance because emotions were increasingly scrutinized as women shifted from marriages based on social and economic motives to the ideal of romantic love. The fear that there would be no one to help in finding a proper loving relationship was expounded upon in plays and literature of Sarah Ann's day, including fellow Jew Mordecai Manuel Noah's *She Would Be a Soldier*, which was performed in Philadelphia to wide acclaim in June of 1819, when Sarah Ann was thirteen.[91] As early as 1791, when Susanna Rowson published *Charlotte Temple*, "novels in America show[ed] the risks of trusting emotions that turn out to be passions, not moral sentiments."[92] Many a young heroine found that her "wild swings of feeling" were leading her into seduction, not moral enlightenment.[93]

Sarah Ann's commonplace book includes warnings about the perils of romance between men and women, perhaps most evocatively on a page that features a butterfly drawn by Sarah Ann herself, emphasizing the value of friendship over romance (fig. 84). The original poem is by "P.H." and was included in journals such as the *New Monthly Magazine* (1821) and the *Cincinnati Literary Gazette* (1824). It opens as follows:

Love, like the butterfly, takes wing,
    He courts the rose but to forsake;
Ah! then beware his treacherous sting,
    Which leaves the fester'd heart to break!

But friendship has the ivy's truth,
    And closer twines when tempests lour:
It takes its root in early youth,
    And blossoms in life's latest hour.

Here we find the warning that romance leaves young women open to pain and abandonment but that friendship can save them. It does not take too much imagination to read the male butterfly, who has a "treacherous sting" that may leave his victim with a "fester'd heart," in sexual terms. Both the butterfly and poem bespeak the interwoven world of convention and individualism that formed part of a "transatlantic pool of tropes, images, and symbol[s]" to which warnings about emotions and sex belonged.[94] Just as the poem parroted British seduction literature, the way the butterfly was drawn echoed English models.[95] While neither the poem nor the drawing was particularly unique, by claiming them for her book and herself Sarah Ann placed her personal quandary in the midst of a whirlpool of discussions about how women should best deal with the perplexing new world of the heart.

Family members, most notably Sarah Ann's oldest brother, Dr. Isaac Hays, chimed in about the perils of romance. Isaac's first entry for Sarah Ann was an excerpt from Richard Lovelace's "The Scrutiny," in which the main speaker is a rake—that is, a libertine who acts out of lust, not love, and aims to seduce women. The poem warns of men's infidelity and the danger of being taken in by admirers. In making this warning, Isaac updated the role his uncle had played to the siblings' mother years earlier. When Richea Gratz became engaged to Samuel Hays, her brother Simon wrote to her, "Take our mother as an exemplar: please your husband and observe God's commandments."[96] Unlike his uncle, Isaac cautions his sister on feelings as much as behavior.

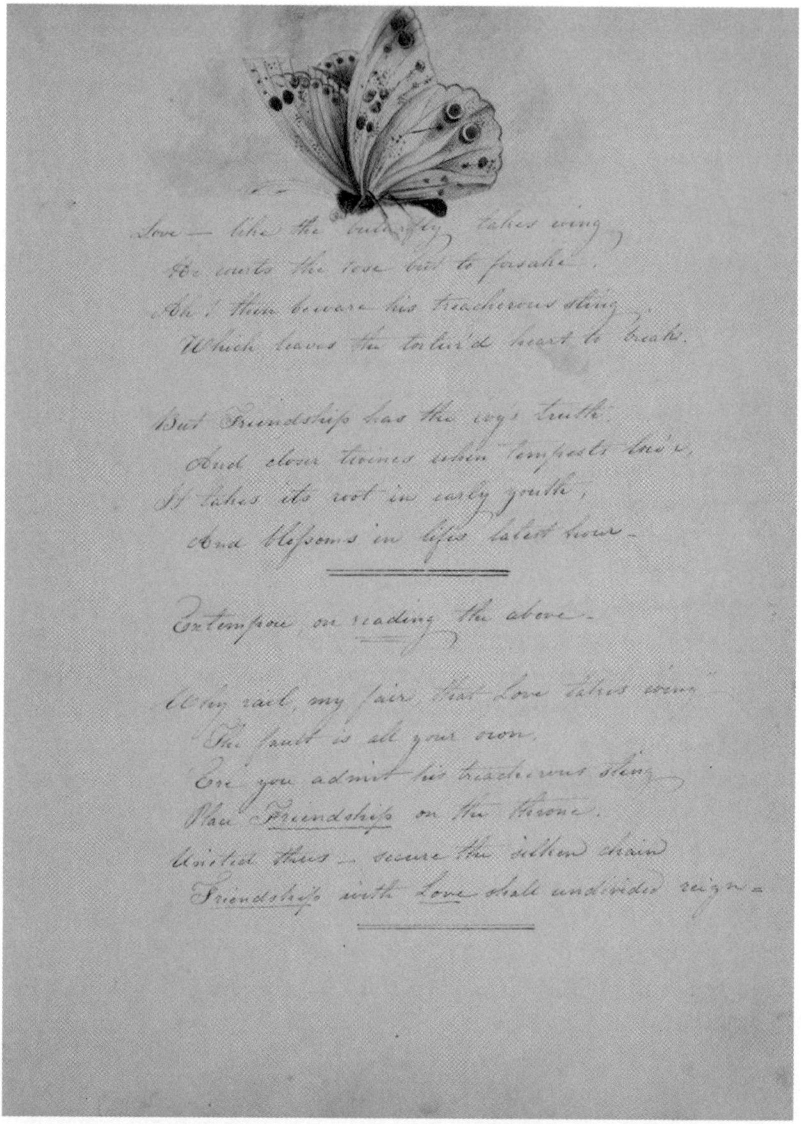

Love — like the butterfly takes wing
So courts the rose but to forsake.
Ah! then beware his treacherous sting
Which leaves the tortur'd heart to break.

But Friendship has the ivy's truth,
And closer twines when tempests lour,
It takes its root in early youth,
And blossoms in life's latest hour —

Extempore on reading the above —

Why rail, my fair, that Love takes wing
The fault is all your own.
Ere you admit his treacherous sting
Place Friendship on the throne.
United thus — secure the silken chain
Friendship with Love shall undivided reign —

Fig. 84. Sarah Ann Hays [Mordecai], *Butterfly*, in her commonplace book. Courtesy of AJHS.

In addition to her brother, other men in Sarah Ann's family provided guidance on how to feel or practiced romantic gestures with her. Of the Jewish men who included signed entries in her book, three were relations: Isaac Hays and two cousins, Gratz and Benjamin Etting. Five other Jewish men added to her book: David Cohen, Gustav Meyer, Myer Levy, Jack Seixas, and Sarah Ann's future father-in-law, Jacob Mordecai. While some—such as Jacob Mordecai—rather drearily quoted scripture, others dealt with the problem of Jewish assimilation. Gustav Meyer, for example, quoted from young Benjamin Disraeli's extremely popular first novel, *Vivian Grey*, published in 1826. The hero of *Vivian Grey* is a precocious Jewish dandy who, despite his personal charm, is thwarted in his pursuit of a political career because of anti-Semitism. In the excerpt in Sarah Ann's commonplace book, Vivian Grey laments the folly of youth: "For what is youth but a sketch—a brief hour of principles unsettled, passions unrestrained, powers undeveloped and purposes unexecuted."[97] These unrestrained passions are Vivian's undoing, and the novel ends with him falling to the ground "senseless" after an "unfortunate" love affair.[98]

Female relations chimed in regarding the need to channel emotions productively toward Judaism. One example comes from Sarah Ann's first cousin, Miriam Gratz Moses, the daughter of Rachel Gratz and Solomon Moses, whose courtship was discussed in chapter 2.[99] Miriam quotes a poem by Dutch Jew Isaac da Costa that actively encourages Jewish pride and identity. It opens thus:

Yes! bear—confide—be patient ever
    My brethren of the chosen race!
Whose name oblivion blighted never,
    Whose glories time shall ne'er efface;
Vanquish the Atheist's desperate boldness,
    Shame the presumptuous threats of hell!
The age's apathy and coldness—
    Ye are the race of Israel.

Unlike Disraeli's novel, which desires assimilation even as reveals it to be impossible, da Costa's poem was written as a rebuke of attempts to "cleanse" Jews of their Jewishness by French emancipationists. The excerpt in Sarah Ann's commonplace book explicitly styles Jews as "us" versus an anti-Semitic (and misguided) "them." To be Jewish, da Costa claims, is to be part of something grand, emotionally rich, and spiritually uplifting, even though by 1820 da Costa had himself converted to Christianity.[100]

Fig. 85. Thomas Sully, *Alfred Mordecai*, ca. 1830s. Courtesy of the Jacob
Rader Marcus Center of American Jewish Archives, Cincinnati.

The gestures toward Jewishness and concern regarding rakes and
unbridled emotions stand in contrast to the vast majority of romantic
inclusions in Sarah Ann's book, which tend to be from non-Jews.[101] This
was hardly surprising: gentiles outnumbered Jews in Philadelphia, and
the beautiful women in Sarah Ann's family had long been courted by
non-Jews.[102] It is hard to know how seriously the scribes or Sarah Ann

took their words, as most are written in the syrupy style of the day. Yet some, like Juan Antonio Rousseau, inscribed Sarah Ann's book repeatedly, with "thoughts of Love . . . Express'd with all the poet's power."[103] Did her heart flutter as she read the lines? Regardless of how this courting was received, friends and family seem to have noticed. Non-Jewish men may sing Sarah Ann's praises as an object of romantic interest, but their entries form an odd dialogue with warnings of romantic peril and the insistence on upholding the faith by kin and Jewish men.

Despite attention that she received from non-Jewish men, Sarah Ann eventually accepted the hand of a Jewish man from the South, Alfred Mordecai (fig. 85). He was dashing, and she was ready. Even before she met her husband, the commonplace book gave her a space to practice the art of courtship, to learn how to receive admiration and to know when to check it. After her marriage, these early attempts to bolster Sarah's sense of Jewish distinctiveness would prove more important than she might have thought.

Marriage

Sarah Ann's marriage to Alfred was hugely successful, though like many good marriages, it was not without its struggles. Although it is not clear if Alfred ever wrote in Sarah Ann's book,[104] his father, Jacob, left several shaky entries. Jacob, along with Isaac Leeser, had been an important resource for Sarah Ann's Aunt Rebecca, who relied on Leeser and Mordecai for Jewish books and works-in-progress.[105] Yet Jacob's writings were deceptive at best for the future that life among the Mordecais offered. Although Alfred's father held a firm line religiously, Alfred had lived nearly all his life at a distance from any formal Jewish congregation in Warrenton, North Carolina.[106] Moreover, during his years as a cadet and later an assistant professor at West Point, he had grown further estranged from his family. Biological kin had been augmented by his military family (fig. 86).[107]

Displaced to Watervliet, New York, Sarah Ann found herself in tension with the demands of her husband's military family. First, there was the distance: letters show Sarah Ann longed to be closer to the Gratzes, the Hayses, and the Jewish community that revolved around the synagogue, but Alfred's military career and secular inclinations pulled her in the other direction. Upon their marriage, Alfred noted to a friend that, unlike himself, "my wife is of a strict Jewish family."[108] They had made a bargain: Sarah Ann could instruct the children in the Jewish religion until they

Fig. 86. Anonymous, *U.S. Military Commission to Crimea,* ca. 1855.
From left to right: Alfred Mordecai Sr., Lt. Colonel Obrescoff, Rich-
ard Delafield, and George B. McClellan. Whole-plate daguerreotype.
Courtesy of the Library of Congress Prints and Photographs Division,
LC-USZ62-54737.

"reached an age at which they could decide for themselves."[109] Yet when
the time came, Alfred refused to allow his sons to be circumcised,[110] and
without this rite, technically they would be marginal Jews who could not
even be buried in a Jewish cemetery.[111] It must have been a bitter betrayal
for Sarah Ann. When tragedy struck, such as the death of one of Sarah
Ann's young children, she fell back on her old network of kin and friends,
whose letters provided "soothing words to comfort me," "with affection
in one hand and religion in the other."[112] When she grew "sick of chills
at the Arsenal," she and her children sought comfort in the bosom of
close friends, renting "country accommodations for the summer" at spas
favored by the Gratzes so she could once again be surrounded by family.[113]

The beginning of the Civil War brought the conflict between family and military life to a head. Alfred ran the ordnance department at
the Watervliet Arsenal.[114] As a major, he had attained more authority in

the U.S. Army than any Jew up to that point.[115] Yet as tensions between the North and South escalated, the governor of North Carolina begged Alfred to quit his post and help the South prepare for war.[116] Jefferson Davis likewise offered Alfred command of the Confederate Corps of Artillery.[117] After the fall of Fort Sumter, all of Alfred's brothers found themselves officially behind Confederate lines, and his sisters began to sew shirts for Confederate soldiers' uniforms.[118]

Would Alfred fight as a Northerner or a Southerner? If he fought as a Northerner, he would have to fight against his biological brothers and other blood relations. Yet if he fought as a Southerner, he would fight against the Northern men who had comprised his military family for decades. Alfred's first solution was to defer: he pleaded with his superiors to be transferred from the Watervliet Arsenal to some "out of the way place, perhaps California, where, he hoped, the war would not reach."[119] Meanwhile angry letters arrived from his brothers. "All eyes . . . are turned towards you," his brother George wrote.[120] If he would not fight with the South, George warned, "[Alfred] will be regarded with jealousy and superstition," threatening that he would be marooned "among a people with whom you can have no sympathy."[121] When the request for transfer was denied, Alfred resigned. One friend noted, "Poor Maj Mordicai [sic] looks miserable."[122] His military career was over at the very moment when it might have rocketed forward.

The Southern Mordecais were devastated. "And thus . . . you sink into obscurity instead of attaining the position and honors to which you are entitled," nagged Alfred's sister.[123] Sarah Ann and Alfred's son Alfred Jr. was also dismayed. A graduate of West Point like his father, Alfred Mordecai Jr. joined the Union Army of Northeast Virginia and would go on to become a Civil War hero. By the end of his career, Alfred Jr. was promoted to brigadier general.[124] Alfred Sr. was not completely without allies, however. Even though the family was forced to leave Watervliet "under cover of darkness," Sarah Ann and their daughters had given Alfred Sr. their "warm support" for his decision.[125]

When Alfred Sr. decided to resign from his position in the military, it was Sarah Ann's safety net of intellectual, emotional, and Jewish bonds that caught the family. Alfred's resignation left him isolated from the military family he had built over the years and at odds with his Southern kin, who could not understand why he failed to fight on behalf of the Confederacy.[126] Once the most powerful Jew in the military, Alfred was now blasted as an "unprincipled coward and traitor" by both the Northern press and his Southern relations.[127]

Alfred and his family abandoned New York. Forced to re-create himself in a new career, Alfred began anew among his wife's kin and acquain-
tances in Philadelphia. Even before they left Watervliet, letters between
Sarah Ann and her friends and family laid the groundwork for his fresh
start. His wife and daughters—including the young Miriam—opened a
school to support the family. Despite his misgivings about religion during his life, Alfred was laid to rest in a Jewish cemetery, nestled among
many of the early inscribers of Sarah Ann's book.[128]

Conclusion

Looking at how and why Sarah Ann wrote her commonplace book underscores how works created by Jewish women in the 1820s to 1850s rethought the bonds between themselves and others. Between 1750 and
1850, the New York Jewish community changed dramatically. It was not
just that the city grew from a small town to a large metropolis, although
it did. Jews had also begun to live in surrounding areas and to immerse
themselves in non-Jewish life, including life in the army and at West
Point. Jewish women were impacted by larger changes in American culture, including the push for women to create unique identities and rich
emotional lives with strong bonds to other women and family members.

Between the marriages of Reyna Levy and Sarah Ann Hays, Jewish
women went from having their marriages arranged for them to choosing whom they married for love. The simplest version of this story is that
women had been "emancipated" from the bonds of their blood kin. Yet
the shift toward romantic love impacted single women as much as married ones. As women took on roles as educators in the Jewish community, the development of their intellects took on new meanings. Women's
emotional lives were understood to be connected to their virtue, and the
strong emotional bonds they forged with other women—and sometimes
men—reinforced the ethical role they played in Jewish and American
life. Finally, as women's relationships to the family shifted, letters and
works like Sarah Ann's commonplace book helped women figure out
and navigate the new roles and paths they would take.

Like many other women during this era, none of Sarah Ann and Alfred's daughters chose to marry. In 1893, when Miriam Gratz Mordecai
included her maternal line in the story of Joseph Simon, she wrote "etc.,
etc." after her own name. But as far as we know, there was no "etc.," as
Miriam had no children. By the time she published her "Note," she was

already fifty, and she must have known the possibility of future offspring was unlikely.[129] The war that had devastated her father's career was partially to blame. Over 2 million men from the North and 880,000 men from the South fought in the Civil War—nearly 10 percent of the country's *entire* population.[130] Many, including some of Sarah Ann's cousins, never made it back.[131] Other Jewish families, like Isaac and Angelique Levy of Augusta's family, lost half their sons.[132] The Mordecais were unusually lucky: Alfred Jr. made it home, and Augustus and Gratz were too young to fight. All three boys would marry, though none would pass Judaism on to the next generation.[133] For Sarah Ann's daughter Miriam, writing the Jewish past was a way of preserving it for the future, and she was among the women who played a primary role in keeping that tradition alive.

When Miriam began to write for the American Jewish Historical Society in the 1890s, she told her family story through a female line. In emphasizing women's roles in maintaining family, Miriam echoed her mother's own writing. According to Sarah Ann, a Jewish woman's deeds, memory, and love carried more weight than marriage or motherhood when it came to perpetuating tradition. Not once but three times in her biography of her aunt, Sarah Ann refers to Rebecca using the language of Proverbs 31: Rebecca is the "virtuous woman" (*eshet chayil*), "whose price is far above rubies," who gives "the fruit of her hands," and whose "own works praise her at the gates."[134] This allusion is intriguing, as the *eshet* of *eshet chayil* is commonly translated throughout the song as "wife" and not as "woman," since the poem is often read as a formula for what a man should look for in a spouse. Yet neither marriage nor biological motherhood was central to Rebecca's legacy.

Women's writings would carry on the family line. When Sarah Ann sat down to write Rebecca's biography, she realized with "almost horror" that her grandchildren "might never know that such a person" as her aunt had existed.[135] Once, Rebecca had been not only elegant, beautiful, and worldly but a "ministering angel," loved by those whose lives she touched.[136] By writing about her aunt, Sarah Ann passed on that legacy to "our families and their descendants; for my children and their children forever."[137] The intellectual paths and emotional paths Jewish women took did not conflict with familial duties but rather established the route for the family's preservation.

FIVE

Family Silhouettes

While the trials of ship travel cost many Jews, like Judith de Mereda, their possessions if not their lives, occasionally objects created for early Jewish women in New York have only survived *because* of shipwrecks. Almost two hundred years after Judith placed her shaky foot on New York soil, the greatest and most prolific silhouette artist ever to set up shop in New York was making his way back across the ocean to Europe. Auguste Amant Constant Fidèle Edouart had spent ten years cutting some of the finest silhouettes ever seen in North America before he boarded the ship *Oneida* back to Europe with twenty-five other passengers in 1849. His European return should have been triumphant. Nestled in with the baggage were Edouart's European and American reference folios containing duplicates of his best work for over two decades, including portraits of nobility, kings, and world leaders. But just before they reached safe shores, the brig hit a storm, and the *Oneida* was wrecked off Guernsey Island in the English Channel. Miraculously, all the passengers survived and some baggage floated ashore, including a few of Edouart's beloved books and folios. A family on the island—the Lukises—took in the beleaguered artist, and when Edouart left, he gifted them the precious folios. He never made silhouettes again.[1]

Much of what we know about Edouart's work derives from the rescued folios he gave to the Lukis family. After being passed down through the islander family for years, the silhouettes were eventually sold and made their way into museums, galleries, and publications.[2] Women played an influential role in making them public. In particular, Mrs. E.

Fig. 87. Augustin Amant Constant Fidèle Edouart, *Full-Length Silhouette of Jacob Isaacs, Jane Isaacs, and Mr. and Mrs. Samuel Myer Isaacs with Samuel Jr.*, 1845. 8⅖ × 11 in. Courtesy of AJHS.

Nevill Jackson catalogued the American portraits in 1921, and Hannah London collated the catalogue's Jewish American silhouettes with those in East Coast archives and museums in 1941.[3] Recently the American Jewish Historical Society and the Loeb Jewish Portrait Database updated London's list. They discovered that silhouettes were remarkably popular among antebellum American Jews. The portraits were much cheaper than the ivory miniatures made for Sarah Rodrigues Brandon and her future husband, and a wide range of Jews in the United States turned to silhouettists to capture a moment in their lives. By the time Edouart headed back for Europe, the form was already beginning to be eclipsed by daguerreotypes, but for the 1840s, the craft of silhouettes provides a unique window onto Jewish American life.

So it was that on April 5, 1845, one such Jewish family found themselves posing for Edouart. Jane Symons Isaacs and her young brood were fortunate enough to sit for the world's most famous silhouette maker as they fulfilled this rite of passage for stylish Americans of the 1840s (fig. 87). Although family groups could be "attended at their own residences,"[4] most New Yorkers chose to have their likeness cut at Edouart's fashionable lounge at 285 Broadway Street, near the Granite Buildings, at the corner with Chambers Street, an intersection which today marks City Hall Park's northwest corner, just across from where the almshouse had once stood (fig. 88).[5] There, potential sitters could peruse various trinkets displaying Edouart's connections with high society, including a gold, bejeweled snuff box from the emperor of Austria and a valuable diamond ring given to him by France's Charles X.[6] Even more enticing was Edouart's exhibition, *Likenesses of Distinguished Characters, in the Church, State, Navy, Army, Literature, Science, and Art.*[7] There was a lot to see in the years before most of the collection ended up at the bottom of the sea: 25,000 silhouettes in the American collection, 125,000 more from Europe, all with autographs appended.[8] Every sitter had the thrill of knowing they would join this collection, as Edouart always cut his portraits in duplicate. One copy went to the patron; the other was placed in Edouart's celebrated scrapbooks, annotated with the patron's signature and date.[9]

The collection received rave reviews: "One could hardly imagine," one visitor gushed, "that shadow likenesses could be so accurate, and so full of character and expression."[10] Poses revealed people's "characteristic attitudes and employments," whether a "husband and wife quarrelling," people playing chess, or "John telling his story to Mary the cook." All those portrayed seemed "absolutely alive" and "admirably perfect."[11] When the Isaacs family posed for Edouart, they too hoped their fundamental essence as a family would be revealed.

Despite the excitement of Edouart's fashionable lounge, Jane and her brood most likely would have posed after hours at their home in a three-story building at 94 Elm Street (see fig. 88).[12] April fifth was a Saturday, and Jane's husband, Rev. Samuel Myer Isaacs, was one of the Jewish Sabbath's most fastidious champions. As the silhouette's marginalia indicates, Samuel had been Congregation B'nai Jeshurun's "rabbi" at the Old Elm Street Synagogue from 1839 to 1844. Although not officially ordained, Samuel was more learned than most Jewish American congregational leaders of his day.[13] From 1845 onwards, he led the newly formed congregation Shaaray Tefila, whose first synagogue would be built on Wooster Street in 1847, less than two blocks from the Isaacses' second home at 176 Prince Street. While both B'nai Jeshurun and Shaaray Tefila would eventually be known as Conservative or Reform congregations, in the 1840s they were "bulwarks of orthodox traditional Judaism."[14] The Isaacses were an important part of that defense. For Samuel, "orthodox traditional Judaism" was timeless: Jewish ritual and liturgy should not be changed by "adding or diminishing, abrogating or altering our

Fig. 88. Map of Jane Symon Isaacs's New York, 1830s–50s. "Plan von New-York, 1844" (Hildburghausen, Germany: Verlag des Bibliographischen Instituts, 1844). Courtesy of New York Public Library Digital Collections.

form of prayers, handed down to us from the Men of the Great Synod, אנשי כנסת הגדולה and other saints of a later date."[15] The Isaacs family portrait displayed the values the family held dear: mitzvot and women's role in Jewish traditions.

Although Samuel and others of his generation would claim that the traditionalism they preached reflected the ways of their forefathers,[16] their Judaism was actually astonishingly modern in many ways, including the roles women were expected to play in it. Yet unlike the Reform movement, which—at least according to Samuel and Leeser—sought to override women's voices,[17] traditionalists expanded women's roles while emphasizing female difference. Just as Jane stands at her silhouette's center, so too women in traditional synagogues in New York began to play more public roles as nurturers of the Jewish family writ large. Jane's early life as a London orphan prepared her for this role. Women's "moral and spiritual influence" infused nineteenth-century homes, and American Orthodoxy analogized women's role in Judaism with this domestic model.[18] The family silhouette reflects women's new importance in Samuel's congregation and home.

Although the Isaacses' family portrait was made by a popular artist in a fashionable genre, the silhouette differs from other early American Jewish silhouettes. The atypical arrangement and props reenvision Jewish gender and family structure. The Isaacses' silhouette also distinctively restyles the Jewish head. Anti-Semites caricatured Jewish facial physiognomy, and the Reform movement responded by deemphasizing Jewish difference by allowing Jews to pray bareheaded like Christians. In contrast, the Isaacs family silhouette highlights the positive role of the Jewish head in maintaining Judaism and Jewish distinction. While headgear still signals Orthodox Jewish identity today, scholars have generally ignored how this symbol came into being. The Isaacs family's hats were not stylish but rather centered Jewish difference on mitzvot. In sharp contrast with previous women featured in this book who attended Western Sephardic congregations, Jane's customs were also explicitly Ashkenazi. Taken in sum, the Isaacses' silhouette reveals the monumental transformations in Jewish life in New York in the 1840s.

The Birth of Orthodox Judaism in New York

The Isaacs family's Judaism emerged from the thunderous changes shaking New York Jewish life in the 1840s. Immigration had already dramatically increased the city's size throughout the 1820s, but from 1830 to 1860, the city quadrupled from two hundred thousand to over eight hundred thousand people. Over a million lived in the larger metropolitan area.[19] Like Jane and her husband, many new New Yorkers were foreign born. By 1855, over half the city was composed of immigrants, with 176,000 from Ireland and 98,000 from Germany alone.[20] While Irish refugees were predominantly Catholic, many of the Germans were Jewish. These immigrants, along with other Jews from the Netherlands, England, and the Caribbean, remade New York into the largest Jewish city in the Americas.

When Sarah Brandon Moses arrived in New York in 1818, the city had not seemed so different from half a dozen other middling Jewish communities in the Americas. Jews comprised less than half a percent of New York's urban population. Indeed, before 1824, the city had only needed one small synagogue, Shearith Israel, which used the Western Sephardic rite but welcomed all Jews. Then, when the population exploded, the synagogues started multiplying: B'nai Jeshurun broke away from Shearith Israel in 1825, and in its wake several other Ashkenazi congregations were founded.[21] Certainly national origins and traditions played a role in the divisions, but so did the Reform movement and the surge in the city's Jewish population: seven thousand by 1840 and sixteen thousand by 1850.[22] As early as the mid-1840s, a quarter of all American Jews called New York home.[23]

This foreign influx would also change how Judaism was practiced in the city, and the Isaacses met those changes head on. By 1850 most Jews in New York City did not belong to a synagogue at all, though some purchased seats for the high holiday services.[24] One counter to secularism was the rise of the city's Jewish Reform movement, which emphasized progressive rather than ceremonial acts and Talmudic law.

Isaac Mayer Wise, who arrived from Bavaria in 1846, was one of the movement's important innovators, as were Leo Merzbacher and Samuel Adler of Temple Emanu-El. What began as a discussion society in the 1830s had transformed into a full-fledged Reform congregation on the corner of Grand and Clinton Streets by 1845. It was popular. Temple Emanu-El grew so quickly that by 1847 the congregation had bought a new building for $12,000. By 1868, they could afford to pay $650,000 for an elaborate Moorish revival building on 5th Avenue. At first, Emanu-El's changes seemed minimal: prayers were reduced and a choir was added, but seating remained separated by gender, and men still wore hats and prayer shawls. Over the next two decades, the innovations became more pronounced, and for traditional New York Jews, more alarming. Seating became mixed, organs played in the synagogue, requirements for *b'nai mitzvah* shrunk, and prayer shawls disappeared.[25] By 1859, hats were also gone. The innovations did not go unnoticed. While Temple Emanu-El's leader felt they were modernizing "in order to strengthen, not diminish, Judaism," not everyone saw it that way. Other congregations defined themselves against the changes, and Samuel Myer Isaacs played a key role in the new Orthodox traditionalism that was part of the backlash.[26]

And Orthodoxy *was* new. Although now as in the 1840s, Orthodox Judaism "maintains that basic Judaism is not subject to change,"[27] the Isaacses' lives were not stuck in the Middle Ages nor were they identical to their forefathers' lives. Rather, like most fundamentalist religions, nineteenth-century American Orthodox Judaism was led by traditionalists who felt liberalism threatened their core identity. They responded not only with scripturalism and "the centering of the mythic past in the present" but also with *selective* modernization.[28] Like Philadelphia's Isaac Leeser and Rebecca Gratz, Jane and her husband used innovations to mobilize Jews toward tradition. Jewish newspapers built up Orthodox community and identity, Jewish education changed to include female teachers, and women created female benevolent societies.

For both Leeser and Samuel Meyer Isaacs, Orthodoxy's emphasis on women contrasted starkly with the Reform movement. Although reformers in Frankfurt and London claimed "to promote concord and the happiness of families," traditionalists accused them of hurling "the burning torch of discord in[to] the holy life of the family, to separate children from parents, husbands from wives, brothers from brothers."[29] None suffered more than women, whom Leeser and others felt were naturally inclined to Orthodoxy, as women had "not found in the coldness of philosophy and the whirling and turmoil of enjoyments any compensation for the soft emotions of religious feelings, to which the female mind leans so preeminently, which were to be sacrificed to their husbands' modes of life."[30] By enlarging women's roles, Samuel counteracted reformers' supposed denigration of Jewish women's voices and addressed immigration's devastating impact on the Jewish family.

For even as the city offered opportunities, immigration tore apart Jewish family life. Most of the nearly ten thousand Jewish immigrants arriving in New York City between 1830 and 1850 were poor. Manufacturing lured them to the urban crucible. Sugar refining, tanning and leather processing, tobacco milling, and printing were among the city's most popular industries. Shipbuilding was paramount, as was the construction of barrels, kegs, and casks for shipping wares around the world.[31] Yet the same poverty drawing Jews across the ocean disrupted Jewish family structure. Even when German Jewish immigrants liquidated everything they owned, their possessions would "rarely bring enough cash to move a whole family" to the Americas.[32] While the Isaacses arrived as a married couple, most Jews arrived unattached. Families often sent an oldest son, oldest daughter, or a brother-sister pair. Sometimes promises lured single women onto ships: they married either during the voyage or immediately after arrival.[33] The Isaacses quickly learned that, if "traditional" Judaism were to survive, its ministers would need to repair Jewish family life broken in transit.

Jane and Samuel communicated their new Orthodox ideal via the family silhouette because their new Orthodoxy centered on family.[34] As Samuel explained in 1844, "Wherever a Jewish family take up their residence, it is a safe guarantee that they become good neighbours, excellent citizens, and deeply anxious for the prosperity of the land they adopt."[35] Although often presenting individuals, silhouettes were the perfect genre for enshrining the family's role in tradition. Silhouettes were fashionable in part because they proudly displayed family lineage in a domestic setting. They also served as signposts for filial remembrance.[36] To be sure, the ivory miniatures used a generation or two before the Isaacses arrived also displayed lineage and helped convey memory. Yet, unlike miniatures, the Isaacses' silhouette centers that memorial on the family.

Through the silhouette, the Isaacses presented their family ideal to a larger audience. Silhouettes were much more performative than miniatures, whose size and fragility made viewing deeply intimate. In contrast, the Isaacs family silhouette is "letter size" (8¼ × 11¾ inches) and more durable. Moreover, while the Isaacses would receive their copy to be displayed privately in their house at 94 Elm Street, they understood that a duplicate would go on display in Edouart's fashionable lounge, constantly available for public perusal, with the family's names and the date penciled underneath.

Both at home and in the lounge near City Hall Park, the Isaacses' silhouette showcased a new and unique understanding of Jewish families. Although many other American and New York Jews had Edouart cut their portraits, none so clearly gestured toward Orthodoxy's values. The Isaacses' portrait could not have been made—or made sense—ten years earlier. Although Jane became Orthodoxy's female face, her childhood friends probably would not have predicted her ascent. Her story from rags to respectability would echo that of many other immigrants. In the 1880s German Jews were seen as elites, amidst a sea of newer Eastern

European immigrants. When they had arrived, however, many had been poor and struggling. Jane's early education positioned her to become the face of women's role in the Jewish communal family.

Jane Isaacs Among the Immigrants

When she stepped off the brig *Emery* in New York harbor on September 10, 1839, Jane Isaacs was newly married. The city would remain Jane's home until her death in 1884. Her youth and newlywed status was a pattern other Jewish women arriving in the city would understand. Mere days before the brig had embarked, Jane (Shana) Symons had wed Samuel Myer Isaacs at No. 66 Leman Street in London. She had just turned sixteen. The honeymoon could hardly be described as pleasant. Jane was forced to get acquainted with her new husband in crowded quarters surrounded by twenty-six other passengers. And the trip was long and hard. For nearly sixty-five days, the weather fluctuated between calm seas and violent storms. Samuel would later remember, "We had been at sea a few days, . . . becoming tired of the monotonous life we were leading, making no headway, but constantly becalmed."[37] Hours later the travellers found themselves in grave danger from an approaching storm. Even the arrival in New York was frustrating, as they reached the harbor midday Rosh Hashanah. In his sermons, Samuel would devote himself to "the defense of pure religion undefiled, calling the faithful to observe the full Mosaic law, the Levitical dietary rules and purification rites, and especially to keep the Sabbath."[38] It would have taken a deep faith in Providence not to dwell on having just missed celebrating the new year of their new life on solid ground with a minyan.[39]

The newlyweds' personal incongruence also likely complicated the trip. Although they had both grown up in Jewish London, the thirty-five-year-old Samuel was over twice Jane's age. The couple appear to have been self-conscious about their age difference, as the shipmaster recorded Jane's age as twenty-one, a generous year older than many married women on board.[40] In truth, Jane would not be twenty-one until five years later, nearly the time when the silhouette was cut. Although under Edouart's scissors Jane appears middle-aged, with a slightly hunched back and double chin, these appearances are deceptive. The double chin is a ribbon from the bonnet hiding her hair, and her hunched shoulders are a shawl disguising her pregnancy. Barely twenty-two when the silhouette was made, she was carrying her fourth child.[41]

More than years separated husband and wife. Samuel's lineage brought learning and respectability. Jane's did not. Like many British Jews migrating to America in the 1830s and 1840s, Jane came from the Shoreditch neighborhood in London, the same neighborhood where Sarah Rodrigues Brandon and Joshua Moses would meet and marry a few years before Jane's birth on March 9, 1823. Unlike Sarah and Joshua but like most neighborhood residents, Jane was probably humbly poor. An Ashkenazi Jew, her world revolved around the Duke's Place Synagogue, also known as the Great Synagogue. Although just around the corner from the Sephardic synagogue Bevis Marks, it was a world away (fig. 89).

When Jane was born, most of London's eighteen thousand Jews were Ashkenazi.[42] Many, like Jane's family, were immigrants from Germany, with a few from Holland and Poland. Most new arrivals were destitute.[43] These were lean years for the London synagogues, which fought to keep the poor from Christian missionaries' soup kitchens. Spiritual and physical needs intertwined, as the synagogues ordered extra flour to make

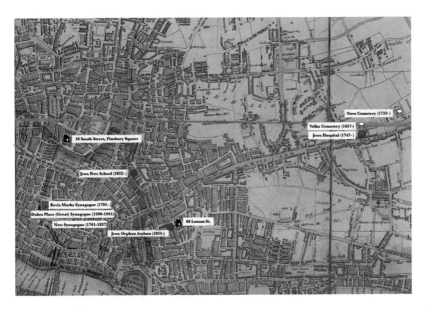

Fig. 89. Map of Jane Symons's Jewish London, 1820s–30s. "Laurie and Whittle's New Map of London with Its Environs, &c. Including the Recent Improvements," Lionel Pincus and Princess Firyal Map Division, New York Public Library. Courtesy of New York Public Library Digital Collections.

matzah for poor Jewish immigrants' Passover. Burial costs for needy Jews due to the "great influx of poor from different parts abroad" also drained synagogue coffers.[44]

Jane's male relatives do not appear in any early London trade directories, suggesting they were lower-class laborers rather than business owners. Some of London's poor Jews worked as artisans making pencils, embroidery, glass, or watches, or even cutting diamonds; others became criminals or prostitutes. The majority eked out a few pennies as hawkers, often selling secondhand clothes and rags.[45] Like most poor Jews, they were unwelcome in the British capital. Peddlers were disparaged by Jews and non-Jews alike. One reviewer in the *Gentleman's Magazine* in 1830 pointed out, for Englishmen, it was hard "to separate the idea of Jews from peddlers who cry 'old clothes,' hawk sealing wax, and have a peculiar physiognomical character" (fig. 90).[46] To denigrate Jews, people called

Fig. 90. George Woodward (?), *A Jew Pedlar*, ca. 1795. Hand-colored aquatint; height: 10⅗ in. Courtesy of the Library of the Jewish Theological Seminary, JTS PNT E12.32b 43.

them "old clothes," "bad shillings," or "oranges and lemons."[47] Poor Jews had become depersonalized, equated with the wares they hawked.

Jane's life began amidst this poverty and anti-Semitism. One of her earliest lessons would be how easily Jewish identity could be molded by, and reduced to, clothing choices. Jewish peddlers became a national symbol of the con man, tricking people into thinking that a change in appearance would make them something—or someone—else.[48] The *Gentleman's Magazine*'s notion of Jews' "peculiar physiognomical character" reflected the belief that Jews—particularly poor Jews—could never change their essence. The drive to prove these Englishmen wrong was strong, as was the lure of assimilation. When Jane and her husband eventually migrated to New York, they fought to inculcate a pride in Jewish appearance.

Stereotypes of poor Jews remind us how rarely what we know about early nineteenth-century London's Jewish poor comes from sources they themselves created. Poor voices were rarely recorded at the time. Even "begging letters" have "disappeared almost without trace and were not quoted."[49] The absence of this perspective owes much to the poor's lack of English, inadequate access to the Jewish press, and their need to work long, hard hours in sweatshops.[50]

Jane's early years reflect this paucity of evidence. Although her parents and grandparents attended the Great Synagogue at Duke's Place, the family appears in the synagogue records only for marriages and the occasional birth. Apparently they lacked the money to be synagogue leaders and honorees. Jane's parents, Jacob Symons and Mary (Miriam) Marks, married on August 23, 1815. Although her mother used the last name Marks, Jane's grandfather's surname was Kekenbeker, or "cake baker," suggesting he may have been a baker from German-speaking lands.[51] Notably, Tebi Tsevi Hirsh Kekenbeker's three known children did not retain the surname, preferring the more British-sounding name Marks (appendix 5).[52] Their first names also reflected the family's transition from immigrants to English Jews. Although they all had Hebrew names, they apparently preferred their Anglicized first names: Jacob, Simon, and Mary.

The Markses' relative absence from synagogue records and their new "British" names probably do not indicate, however, that they were reformers. Although Georgian London (1714–1830) is generally known for rapid Jewish assimilation, these changes affected the Jewish poor less than their wealthier coreligionists.[53] As historian Todd Endelman notes, "The staunchest supporters of traditionalism—those who continued to fill the synagogues or purchase kosher meat, for example—were overwhelmingly from the lower class."[54]

Whatever her parents' religious views had been, Jane and her younger sister Catherine had to make their own way as orphans.[55] Orphans had mixed prospects. Most children in poor Jewish families worked from an early age, with even eight- and nine-year-olds helping support their families. Any spare money families had tended to go toward educating boys, who first learned the liturgy and Torah for use in synagogue.[56] Yet, as an orphan—like other destitute Jewish children—Jane had access to education at the Jews' Free School, which had opened in 1817. Formerly the Ashkenazi Jews' Hospital at Mile End, the Jews' Free School provided poor children with both a limited general education (arithmetic, religious education, English) and training in trades (fig. 91). Not only could girls attend the school, they were singled out for this new education. A wealthy Jewish woman explained in an 1818 manual that while at the school, girls would learn "thrift, gratitude, subservience, and industry."[57] This training would help the graduates learn their place in society. To be admitted to the school, Jane would have had to prove her family was "respectable" or "worthy" poor, a status bolstered by her parents' and uncles' marriages in the synagogue.[58] Once she turned thirteen or fourteen, Jane would have been placed with a wealthier Jewish family as a servant. Before then, the school provided not only a home but also food and clothing, courtesy of the Baroness de Rothschild.

Unlike Jane, Samuel was born into a well-to-do Jewish family in 1804 in Leeuwarden, Holland. Although not as large as London, beautiful Leeuwarden was hardly a backwater: the city housed the Netherlands' largest northern Jewish community. A year after Samuel's birth, the town built a new synagogue—a grand red-brick edifice with high-arching windows and seating for six hundred Jews.[59] Samuel's father, Myer Samuel Isaacs, was a distinguished merchant-banker who was also devout: four of his five sons would become prominent rabbis. When the Napoleonic wars cut the family off from their trading partners, Myer fell into debt. The family moved to London in 1814, fleeing the invading French forces. There they too settled near the Great Synagogue. In 1818, Myer opened a private Hebrew school and educated his son in the Torah and Talmud. Religion would guide the Isaacses' new life. Myer eventually became the burial minister and Sabbath lecturer at the New Synagogue on Leadenhall Street.[60] Samuel benefitted from his father's learning and emigration. Although fluent in Yiddish, Samuel also spoke English without an accent. Once in New York, his dual fluency would help position him where tradition and modernity intersected. By the time he married Jane, Samuel was a "professor of Hebrew" at the Jewish Orphanage and

Fig. 91. Anonymous, *Jews' Hospital in Mile End, Old Town*, ca. 1816.
Engraving. Courtesy of AJHS.

had become connected with not only Solomon Hirschell, the Great Synagogue's chief rabbi, but also Sir Moses Montefiore, the famous Anglo-
Jewish banker and philanthropist.[61]

While we do not know how the couple met, we have clues. When they
married, Jane was living at 10 South Street, Finsbury Square—presumably as a servant—and Samuel lived at the Jews' Hospital and Orphanage
Home in Mile End, Old Town.[62] Since Jane was an orphan, had they
met initially while teacher and pupil?[63] The orphanage appears to have
played a role in where they married: the ceremony took place at No. 66
Leman Street, just across from the new Jews' Orphan Asylum, which had
opened in 1831 at 69 Leman Street.[64]

Jane's marriage represented a sea change in her young life: she rapidly transitioned from a poor British orphan to an affluent, married
American mother. We have little indication of what the change was like.
Samuel regularly printed his "Diary as a Minister" in his newspaper, *The
Jewish Messenger* (1857–78), but he rarely mentions his marriage's early
years. Likewise, despite the fact that Jane and Samuel's son Myer S. Isaacs
kept a personal diary from 1861 to 1868, he seldom mentions his parents
and provides no insight into their early life. Edouart's portrait of Jane
as a young mother fills in some details of these early years and expands
Stern's 1960 genealogy. Jewish children's lives were precarious in the
1840s, causing mothers emotional turmoil. In April 1845, Jane was also

two months pregnant with the couple's fourth child, Isaac Samuel Isaacs. In 1865, the couple had eight children, not including the children Jane lost over the years. Of the three children Edouart depicts, only Samuel Jr. (known later as Myer Samuel Isaacs) would survive.

Jane's early personal loss paralleled her husband's theological battles. Within a year of his arrival, Samuel instigated a bid to exclude non-observing Jews from membership in B'nai Jeshurun's Old Elm Street Synagogue.[65] Kashruth (dietary laws) became more closely regulated, and congregants who kept their stores open on the Sabbath and *yom tov* (holy days) found themselves censored. Samuel also secured the place of women in Judaism. He strongly supported female-centered practices, particularly women's ritual immersions.[66] Safeguards solidified Jewish women's role in the family. An Ashkenazi *mikveh* had been built in 1833, allowing female immersions prior to marriage and following menstruation and childbirth. Likewise, close regulation of marriage ceremonies helped prevent inter-marriage.[67] These bulwarks were important, since as Samuel explained in 1844, "the marriage of a Jew and Jewess becomes the harbinger of bliss. . . . Our children become the counterpart of ourselves."[68]

Not all traditionalist decisions were popular. Many sparked awkward encounters. After one board meeting, a committee told a congregant that his niece, whom he had raised since she was three weeks old, was not a Jew. Her recent marriage was thus invalid, and any future children "resulting from such marriage would in our Holy Religion be deemed 'mamzarim.'"[69] Another controversy arose when a congregant tricked the *mikveh* attendant into completing a conversion forbidden by the board.[70] The altercations took their toll. The B'nai Jeshurun congregation grew under Samuel's leadership, but Polish congregants seceded to form Ansche Chesed in 1839, followed by a German breakaway in 1843. In June 1845, another schism occurred, with the English and Dutch Jews separating to form Shaaray Tefila (Gates of Prayer). This time, they took Samuel and his family with them.[71] In 1847 Shaaray Tefila built a synagogue at 110–112 Wooster, between Spring and Prince Streets (see fig. 88).[72]

The Isaacses' family silhouette was created amidst Jewish familial controversies. Their portrait is distinctive in several ways, particularly for centering women in the Jewish family and using everyday objects—such as head coverings—to signal ritual's significance in Orthodox life. Ironically, Orthodoxy's new hallmarks also reflected modernizations. Unlike reformers aiming to change Jewish law, Orthodox innovations helped mobilize traditional practice. The Isaacses' silhouette advertised the new "traditional" family life their congregation promoted.

Women's New Role

When patrons asked Edouart to take their likeness, they had choices to make. Who would be in the silhouette? Who would sit, and who would stand? How would the people be arranged? What was their characteristic activity? American Romanticism flourished in the 1840s, a time associated with a narcissistic fascination with the self. Edouart fed that craze by his promise to reveal his sitters' essential selves through the objects or poses they held. Edouart made thousands of silhouettes, but each one is slightly different, underscoring the sitters' individuality. In isolation, the Isaacses' family portrait may appear banal. When compared with Edouart's other silhouettes, however, its distinctive message emerges. The way the Isaacs family answered the questions of who, how, and what to include in their cutting highlights women's centrality to Jewish families and reenvisions Jewish gender.

Edouart's prolificness provides a unique opportunity to compare the Isaacs family silhouette with Jewish and non-Jewish Americans' self-presentation from the 1840s. From 1839 to 1849, Edouart made three to four thousand silhouettes in the United States, many in New York. Because Edouart always cut his portraits in duplicate, a shockingly large number survive today. There are several dozen early Jewish American silhouettes from the 1830s and 1840s, with examples from most major families. When compared with these other silhouettes, the Isaacs family portrait's distinctiveness emerges.

First, the Isaacses' silhouette includes their whole nuclear family, reflecting the role of families—rather than individuals—in the new Jewish Orthodoxy. Most early American Jews had solo silhouettes cut, perhaps imitating the use of miniatures by earlier generations. Samuel himself had favored this style in 1839, mere months after he arrived in New York City (fig. 92).

Even when early American Jews asked for a fancier silhouette featuring a group, it was not typically a nuclear family. Senator and Mrs. Haym Asher, for example, chose to be portrayed with their young granddaughter Rachel (1840), and Mrs. Rachel Cohen decided to include her dog as well as her granddaughter Jessie (1840). Other Jews, such as the Tobiases, similarly included pets (1844). Some Jews favored multigenerational extended family portraits. As a case in point, grandparents John and Rebecca (Lyons) Moss had their silhouette made in 1844 when their son Samuel Lyons Moss was visiting from New Orleans with his child (1844). The same year, Samuel Lyons Moss posed for Edouart with his

Fig. 92. Anonymous, *Silhouette of Samuel Myer Isaacs*, 1839. Courtesy of the Jewish Museum, New York.

wife, Isabel Harris, two of their children, either his parents or in-laws, an enslaved boy, and his horse.[73] When Jane and Samuel Isaacs had their silhouette cut, however, no enslaved people or pets appeared in the scene. This decision was not just because Samuel lived in the North and was a staunch abolitionist; he envisioned family life fundamentally differently.

Like most immigrants, the Isaacses lacked an extended American family: both their fathers were dead, Jane's mother was dead, and Jane's sister Catherine did not arrive in New York until 1846.[74] The new traditional family would be a nuclear one, separate from revered ancestors.

The second distinctive choice the Isaacs family made was to have Jane stand alongside her husband, while her daughter Jane stood among her brothers, thereby underscoring women's more active role in the family. Women standing in silhouettes was unusual and always an active choice made by patrons, since full-length sitting portraits were more expensive: $1.75 for an adult, versus only $1.25 for a full-length standing portrait.[75] Although not outrageous, the difference was significant. In 1850, Mrs. Hendricks of KKSI bought an entire pink merino dress for $1.75, and fifty cents was enough to get trimmings and lace added to your favorite gown.[76] Despite the cost, however, most adult Jewish women sat when in a multiperson silhouette, while their husbands stood. Sitting in silhouettes also carried symbolic weight, and the gendered poses reflected established hierarchies in American families. Since the late eighteenth century, portraits marked children's gender by showing brothers standing while sisters sat.[77] Sitting tended to emphasize relative passivity; thus, Jewish men almost never sat when facing female family members in silhouettes. Jane's and her daughter's active stances in the silhouette differ from contemporary Jewish examples.

Third, the Isaacses' portrait arranged the family atypically: Jane stands beside her husband and is visually paralleled by her daughter. Arrangements in portraits tended to be gendered, and the five Isaacses are arranged unusually for Edouart's Jewish clientele. In nearly all Jewish silhouettes, women face their husbands, with the children assembled between the male and female adults. This positioning reflects a larger trend in nineteenth-century portraiture in which family groups are dominated by men, with women "often depicted deferentially."[78] In contrast to both of these norms, Jane and her husband stand together in solidarity at the far right. Jacob and daughter Jane face each other on the far left, with Samuel Jr. at the family's center, facing his mother. Samuel Jr.'s placement highlights his status as eldest son, something otherwise obscured by his size. As in other early American portraits, size did not always accurately predict children's age.[79] While Myer Samuel (here called "Samuel Jr.") was just shy of four, his younger brother Jacob was only two.[80] The daughter, Jane, did not survive, and her birth date is unknown, but given that Samuel Jr. was born on May 8, 1841, she was either his twin or possibly older than he by between nine and fourteen months, as slightly less than two years separated his birth and his parents' marriage on June 26, 1839. The Isaacs clan's unusual arrangement underscores Jane's role as her husband's second-in-command and creates an echo between Jane and her eldest daughter, who faces the smallest child and functions as a little mother.

These changes reflect the new family program modelled by the Isaacses. Samuel's innovative leadership highlighted the role women performed in the Jewish family. Samuel, along with his counterparts Leeser (of Mikveh Israel) and Lyons (of Shearith Israel), sought to make women's roles in perpetuating Jewish families more public by encouraging women to teach in Jewish schools and by galvanizing elite women to oversee charity to orphans, widows, and the poor. Jane played an important role in showcasing the new ideal woman's role as "a most perfect helpmate": not only did she literally stand by her husband during public functions, she officiated in Shaaray Tefila's Ladies Benevolent Society (1857–67) and New York State's Ladies Mt. Vernon Association of the Union (1857). During the Civil War she acted as Shaaray Tefila Ladies Relief Association's treasurer, aiding sick and wounded soldiers.[81] This emphasis on women as emotionally rich nurturers was a Jewish equivalent of the "cult of true womanhood" prominent in larger antebellum American society. Yet unlike Christians, who often saw the domestic sphere as a "counterpoint to the competitive . . . marketplace, making the home a private refuge from the hustle and bustle of public life,"[82] Jews increasingly extended domestic values into Jewish communal space.

Jane's early education in London prepared her for the new role Jewish women were expected to play in educating American Jewish communities' children. Although a generation earlier men were the primary educators in official Jewish schools, women now became essential players. Whereas once women only operated "dame schools" in their homes, by the 1840s the traditional synagogues began not only to allow but also to encourage Jewish women to educate children in the congregational schools.[83] Shortly after his arrival in New York, Samuel shored up B'nai Jeshurun's school by creating an all-day English and Hebrew school called the New York Talmud Torah and Hebrew Institute.[84] Samuel valued educating Jewish girls and women religiously. He explained that it might be "laudable to train our daughters for the best society," but it was even more critical to remember "there is another society to which they will sooner or later be destined to join [in the world-to-come]." Much of the endeavor's success in Jewish education, he believed, lay "upon the mother," hence "it becomes our duty to train our daughters to comprehend that faith in which they are in here and hereafter, that creed in which they are to influence their future husbands, their sons and daughters."[85] In addition to making Jewish education available to girls, Samuel used the *Jewish Messenger* to guide women on how to transmit Judaism to their children. This newspaper was a "tradition" he borrowed from Leeser's *The Occident*, which had similarly encouraged female Jewish educators by venerating the "talented and deserving ladies" of Miss Palache's Academy and providing inspirational examples from sister congregations, such as the Sunday school Shanare Limud in Bridgetown, Barbados, run by the female superintendent, Mrs. Finzi, in 1844.[86]

The fourth major decision the Isaacs family made regarding their silhouette was what they held, and their choices also reflect changes to women's roles in the larger Jewish family. Edouart's call to fame was his ability to cut people in a characteristic pose, often including props. As in contemporary painted portraits, these objects were typically gendered. Brothers (especially older ones) were commonly depicted holding hats or "male authority sticks," such as whips and canes. Sisters, in contrast, were marked with fans or "female fertility icons," such as fruits and flowers, symbolizing a "passive embodiment of purity, a quality defined by a lack of agency."[87] Books and animals were considered gender neutral and could be held by either sex. This trend can be seen in Edouart's silhouettes of Jewish children like Fanny and Haym Asher (1840), Josiah Moses (1840), Rachel Cohen (1840), and "Baby" Moss (1844), in which boys hold sticks and hats while girls hold flowers.[88]

The Isaacs family's choice of objects rethinks gender in the new Orthodox family. The family portrait differs from typical silhouettes (Jewish and otherwise) in that while the women hold objects gendered female, the males hold either gender-neutral or feminine objects. The female family members fit within common trends. Jane holds a flower appropriate for a progenitor. As one eminent clergyman of the day noted, "It is the greatness of woman that she is so much like the great powers of nature, behind the noise and clatter of the world's affairs, tempering all things with her benign influence only the more certainly because of her presence."[89] Her daughter, Jane, holds a handkerchief, a possession associated with women's self-expression.[90] Handkerchiefs were "for show, not blow." Carrying one in the hand "accented the bearer's physical grace and served as an important element of sentimental fashion"; it was fitting for girls.[91] The males in the Isaacs family steer away from the "male authority stick": Samuel holds a book, highlighting his learning and role as a clergyman, while the sons hold flowers. Perhaps here we can see an early predictor of what Daniel Boyarin would identify as Orthodoxy's "gentler" manhood.[92]

By presenting a nuclear family in which Jane stands next to—rather than opposite—her husband, the Isaacses' silhouette rethinks family structure, giving women a more active role. At the same time, the new Orthodox family highlighted a learned Jewish manhood, with male children as a promise of future fertility.

The Jewish Head

If the Isaacses' silhouette structures and genders the family differently than typical early American Jewish silhouettes, it also distinctively marks Jewishness through head adornments. While on occasion Jewish men, women, or children wear hats and bonnets in Edouart's silhouettes, the Isaacs family is unique in that *everyone* covers their head. They do so because constant headgear was central to the new Orthodoxy in both domestic and ritual settings. Using the head to signal a positive Orthodox identity countered innovations by the Reform movement that eliminated ritual head coverings as well as anti-Semitic art that increasingly used Jewish heads as metonyms for Jews' allegedly distinctive and disorderly physiognomy. Here, for the first time in early Jewish portraits from New York, we see hats referencing not fashion but Jewish practice. Samuel's hat was also explicitly Ashkenazi and thus signaled an important divergence of the new wave of Orthodoxy from Sephardic Americans. The trend would stick: today Orthodox American Jews commonly identify themselves not only as Orthodox but as a specific Orthodox subgroup via head coverings.

In contrast to most contemporaneous American Jews, the entire Isaacs family wears some sort of head covering: Samuel Sr. wears a soft velvet cap, mother Jane wears a bonnet, the boys wear caps, and daughter Jane appears to wear a snood. The mother's head adornment is the most typical. Of the eighteen Jewish American silhouettes in the AJHS and Loeb collections depicting women, thirteen clearly wear hats, bonnets, or caps, and the remaining five wear more ornamental headdresses with ribbons. Likewise, of the nine silhouettes with Jewish girls, five wear bonnets or snoods, one decorates her hair with ribbons, and two wear their hair unadorned. In contrast, the adult Jewish men in the same collections are less consistent in their headgear: one wears a stovepipe hat, one wears a beret, three wear top hats, two (including Samuel Sr.)

wear a slouch cap, and seventeen keep their heads uncovered. Men with more than one silhouette sometimes wore a hat in one portrait but not another.[93] Wearing hats selectively suggests that certain hats—such as top hats—were in accordance with fashion and American hat etiquette rather than religious requirements.

Of the nine Jewish boys depicted in American silhouettes, only the Isaacses' sons cover their heads. Edouart indicates the Isaacs boys are wearing caps through their irregularly shaped heads and the lack of hair sticking up at regular intervals, as is typical in his silhouettes of hatless boys.[94] The Isaacses' portrait is the only multigenerational Jewish American silhouette where all individuals cover their hair.

The Isaacs family's headgear laid claim to Jewish tradition, yet in a distinctly modern way. The new Ashkenazi Orthodox movement's interest in covering the head even when not studying or performing rituals owes something to the Reform movement. As late as the "sixteenth century, when the Shulhan arukh (Jewish law code) accepted by all Jewish communities was written, men's head covering was not yet compulsory. The code stated that covering the head signaled a God-fearing Jew and was especially important during study and prayer (*Orakh hayyim* 2:6; 151:6)."[95] Yet in the nineteenth century when Reformers innovated bareheaded prayer, Ashkenazi traditionalists responded by expanding men's customs of head covering. When there was only one synagogue in New York, constant head covering was not a tradition. Although in his 1813 silhouette Rev. Gershom Mendes Seixas wears a "clerical" hat, most painted portraits depict him bareheaded.[96] Likewise, Samuel's contemporary at Shearith Israel, Lyons, was typically depicted in portraits bareheaded, suggesting he did not consider continually wearing a hat essential to his identity as a Sephardic minister. Yet by the 1840s, covering the head at all times had become a way "Orthodox" Ashkenazi New Yorkers signaled their commitment to mitzvot.[97]

In New York, the controversy over whether Jewish men could worship with their heads uncovered would eventually end up being fought out in court. Judge Richard Larremore ruled for the religious reformers. The *New York Herald's* non-Jewish editors seemed confused as to why hats should matter so much, noting:

> If there is nothing more substantial in Judaism than these traditionary customs, it would be as good a time now as ever to bury it out of sight. . . . There is a Judaism, as there is a Christianity, that is founded in the heart and not in the hat, that worships God in the

spirit without much regard to form or ritual. That is worth preserving; the other is not. Men do not honor God any more by taking off than by putting on hats. They may honor Him by both acts.[98]

Samuel disagreed. For him, the hat symbolized what separated his Judaism from Reform and Western Sephardic *minhag* (customs). Head coverings also set him apart from Christian ministers in New York. James Alexander Patten compiled two hundred illustrated biographies of clergymen in New York and Brooklyn in 1874; only Samuel wears a hat.

Hats took center stage in American Jewish controversies because men's headgear mattered: "Since men represented their families in public space, men's hats, rather than women's, were used to indicate the status of the family."[99] Moreover, at the time the Isaacses' silhouette was made, hat etiquette had become a distinctly male concern. From the 1830s onwards, advice manuals educated men on hat rules. This conduct was as much about when to remove one's hat as when and what kind of hat to wear.[100] Leaving one's hat on when it was meant to be off was an ethical lapse. As one advice manual explained, if a man wore the wrong thing, he would also "probably *do* the wrong thing . . . and *be* the wrong thing."[101] Thus British travellers in Alabama in the 1830s noted with horror when Southerners claiming to be gentlemen neglected to take off their hats upon entering the boat's cabin and "sat with their hats on, during every part of the day, except at meals."[102] Christians in England and nineteenth-century America were expected to remove their hats upon entering a church during services. Only infirmity would excuse a lapse, and then a nightcap might be worn.[103] Likewise, men removed their hats in schools, theaters, concert halls, private offices, auction rooms, art galleries, libraries, and in the presence of ladies. Failing to do so was disrespectful and gave one a negative social reputation.[104] Thus the new Orthodox insistence on continually covering the head put men at odds with gentlemanly conduct in larger American society.

Samuel's headgear also violated nineteenth-century fashion norms. This violation marked an important tenet of Ashkenazi practice, echoing how in the sixteenth century, Rabbi Moses Isserles had adapted Sephardi Jew Joseph Karo's Shulhan arukh, claiming that it was insufficient to simply not wear clothes "unique" to gentiles. For Isserles, Jews should explicitly differentiate themselves "in dress and other practices" by avoiding fashions favored by gentiles.[105] Thus, the soft velvet cap Samuel wore in the silhouette differed from the top hats and stovepipe hats worn by Jewish American men "of style."[106] Even the 1839 silhouette of Samuel alone depicts him "wearing a large soft *cap* and holding a book, two elements that characterize him as a learned, observant Jew" (see fig. 92).[107] The soft cap would come to symbolize the new Ashkenazi Orthodox style of the 1840s. Sephardic *hazzanim* and Samuel's own mentor, Solomon Hirschell (chief rabbi of Great Britain), wore tricornes.[108] In contrast, Samuel's hat resembled the velvet cap of Hirschell's successor, Nathan Marcus Adler (1803–90), who led the Duke's Place Synagogue and London Jewry from 1845 until his death.[109] Elite Orthodox British Jews such as Sir Moses Montefiore (1784–1885) and German Rabbi Samson Raphael Hirsch also favored the distinctive new "unfashionable" style. Today Hirsch is best remembered for the new Frankfurter Orthodoxy, but in 1844 he was the runner-up for chief rabbi in England. At the time Leeser's *Occident* praised Hirsch's "deep thought and being in the spirit of the old orthodox school."[110] Samuel's cap thus positions him as part of the new guard of the "old orthodox school."

His cap publicized the Orthodoxy shaping the lives of his young wife and children. Prior to this era, Jewish boys did not typically cover their heads outside of synagogue. As the Talmud notes, "Men walk in the street with bared or covered head, as they please; women with covered head only; children always bareheaded."[111] The Isaacs boys' hat style was also unfashionable. American boys commonly wore "wide-brimmed, shallow-crowned hats" typically made of straw. After twelve, boys' hats were merely smaller versions of men's ones.[112] Young Jacob and Samuel Jr., however, wear soft caps that mimic their father's.

Jane's headgear similarly distinguishes her from contemporary American women. On the one hand, in the 1840s married women tended to wear a cap at all times, even when indoors, though the style and decoration varied by time of day and occasion.[113] Indeed, most Jewish women in Edouart's silhouettes cover their hair partially. What distinguishes Jane is her bonnet's style and the amount of hair it covers. Most Jewish women in silhouettes wore stylish lawn or muslin caps that rested high at the back of the head.[114] In contrast, Jane's stiffer bonnet rests closer to the front of her head and covers more hair. As such, her hat is passé, resembling styles from a decade earlier.[115]

Jane's hair covering distinguishes her from contemporary fashions and reflects concerns about how "modernity" impacted modesty in Jewish coiffures. The tendency for Jewish women to let regulations about hair covering slide began in the colonies in the late eighteenth century. In 1786, for example, Ashkenazi leaders in Paramaribo asked Amsterdam's High German Jewish congregation to please send a "clear description, with quotation of the laws and the authors which states that it is strictly prohibited to married women to go about with their hair coiffured," so that they could more easily police Jewish women uncovering their hair in the colony.[116] Changes in European practice were blamed. The controversy erupted when a widow, Mrs. Mendoza, discovered "most married women in Europe, among the Portuguese as well as among our congregation, go about coiffured."[117] This revelation "opened the eyes of the evil doers" in Suriname and led to a similar break from tradition. The desire to wear hair "coiffured" reflected pressure on Jewish women to conform to the fashions of the 1780s and 1790s, when hair was worn "wide and frizzed" and then later "swept back from the face with a wide ribbon or gathered into a loose bun or curls."[118] In 1845, it was similarly fashionable to wear hair in ringlets on the side of the face, with the rest in a coronet decorated by "feathers, flowers, lace, artificial grapes," and other ornaments.[119] Jane's more fully covered hair resisted these fashionable trends. Her modest approach also placed her on Jewish New York's theological map. Covering the hair was a point of honor in Orthodox New York. In fact, the rabbi at Ansche Chesed and Rodeph Shalom was fired by his congregants in 1844 for advocating "the uncovering of hair by women."[120] His dismissal instigated reform-minded Jews to form Temple Emanu-El with him as minister.[121] Jane, in contrast, held firm.

Jane's head covering also distinguishes her from non-Jewish representations of Jewish women's unruly and highly visible hair. George Weeden satirized Mordecai Manuel Noah's wife, Rebecca, in 1828 by showing voluminous curls shrouding her face, their wildness accentuated by her billowing head covering.[122] Similarly, when anti-Semitic artist Pierre Jacques Benoit drew five Surinamese slaves from different religions, he used long, wavy hair tumbling down a bare back to mark one slave as Jewish and to underscore her sexuality and supposed immodesty (see fig. 61).

The same artists used men's heads to underscore Jewish men's deviance and disorderliness. From the 1820s to 1840s, artists increasingly mocked Jewish men's noses and hair. Weeden, for example, uses a profile to highlight Noah's "Jewish" physiognomy, particularly his nose and spiraling hair, attributes that early nineteenth-century racial scientists increasingly associated with Jews' "Oriental" lineage.[123] Benoit underscores Jewish shopkeeper Isak Abraham Levy Aron's physiognomy with a similar strategy (fig. 93). Like Noah, Aron is also shown in profile, a strategy that accentuates his hooked nose and leering mouth. Unlike bareheaded Noah, Benoit's Jew wears an oddly folded cap, which strongly resembles an *angisa*, the headscarf women with African ancestry wore in Suriname (fig. 94). The way an *angisa* was folded conveyed information ranging from the wearer's mood to her religion.[124] Indeed, in Benoit's drawing of five enslaved women, each woman wears a differently styled *angisa* (see fig. 61), with the storekeeper's hat most closely resembling that of the Jewish slave.[125] Enslaved women were the least likely people to achieve suffrage, and when Benoit both feminizes and racializes Jewish men's heads, he accentuates their unfitness as full citizens at exactly the moment when the question of Jews' right to vote culminated in the Netherlands.

By accenting the Jewish head, the Isaacses' silhouette responds both to the Reform movement and to new embodied messages about Judaism that arose amidst Jewish emancipation debates. When Jews commissioned portraits, they often refuted the stereotype of the disorderly Jew through

Fig. 93. Detail of Jewish shopkeeper, Pierre Jacques Benoit, *A gauche, la boutique d'un vette-warier ou détaillant; à droite, la boutique d'un snerie ou tailleur; au milieu, un nègre nu se faisant prendre mesure d'un vêtement* [On the left, the shop of a *vette-warier*, or petty grocer; on the right, the shop of a *snerie*, or tailor; in the middle, a naked black slave having his measurements taken for some clothes], ca. 1831, in *Voyage à Surinam . . . cent dessins pris sur nature par l'auteur* (Brussels: Société des Beaux-Arts), plate xvi, fig. 32. Courtesy of John Carter Brown Library, Brown University.

Fig. 94. Cotton Surinamese creole headscarf (*angisa*), before 1960. Courtesy Collection Nationaal Museum van Wereldculturen, Amsterdam, TM-2884-10.

exquisitely tailored suits and stiffly starched neckties. The Isaacses' silhouette uniquely focuses, however, on the Jewish head. By covering their heads so differently from non-Jews, the new Orthodox family allied their bodies with the divine. The family's headgear moved men's head coverings from the synagogue into daily life. The Haskalah (Jewish Enlightenment)[126] had supported efforts in France, Germany, and the Netherlands to emancipate Jews who expunged Jewish difference. The Isaacses' silhouette undoes that erasure.

Despite claims that such traditions go back to antiquity, the Isaacs family's rebranding of the Jewish head responds to the Reform movement and to changes in anti-Semitism. While other innovations of the new Orthodoxy, such as creating female benevolent societies and starting Jewish newspapers, were echoed in traditional Western Sephardic congregations, Samuel's slouch hat referenced other Ashkenazi Orthodox congregations in Europe and the Jewish diaspora. Every head in the Isaacs clan announces itself not just as Jewish but as a particular kind of Jewish. They were neither physically marred as anti-Semites would have it nor the same as Christians. Rather, the family's heads reveal a Jewishness that announces its dedication to the Torah even in a private, domestic space.

Conclusion

Although the Edouart silhouette is the first and only known portrait of Jane, she lived a rich, long life in New York. When she died in May 1884, she was the matriarch of a large family. Four of her children had reached adulthood and married. She had ten grandchildren (appendix 5). Her obituary in the *Jewish Messenger* highlighted her role as an *eshet chayil* (woman of valor). Unlike when Sarah Ann Hays Mordecai invoked the *eshet chayil* in her biography of Rebecca Gratz, Jane was a woman of valor defined via marriage. The newspaper explains:

> A wife and mother should be judged by the household she presides over, the home she provides, the family she rears,—and well may Jane Isaacs have been proud of her husband, her home, and her children.
> How truly it may be said of her,
> "Her children arise up, and call her blessed; her husband also, and he praiseth her.
> Many daughters have done virtuously, but thou excellest them all."[127]

Whereas Rebecca Gratz's niece had used Proverbs 31 to emphasize a womanhood beyond affinal kinship, Jane's eulogist selectively quoted from the same poem to emphasize women's relationship to their husbands and offspring. The verses on the valorous woman's role in earning a living were excluded, favoring instead her domestic role. This domesticity was fitting, as Jane's husband had enlarged women's "public" role by expanding women's maternal roles into the synagogue's sphere. If women were to be public, it was not as earners but as charitable mothers. Notably, this model of extended influence was thus only truly available to an elite sphere of Jewish women who did not need to work to survive.

Before his death in 1878, Samuel continued to solidify what American Orthodoxy meant as the spiritual leader of one of the nation's leading congregations. For forty-five years, Jane lived at the center of that new Orthodoxy, first as a wife and then as the mother of a new generation of Jewish leaders. After their parents' deaths, her sons would continue Samuel's work, including editing the *Jewish Messenger*, New York's first Jewish newspaper.

Jane's role in this family marked the long road Jewish women had travelled since the 1750s when Hannah Louzada had begged Shearith Israel to give her money to make it through the cold northeastern winter. Like Hannah, Jane was an immigrant. Both women had known excruciating poverty. But the New York that Jane encountered when she arrived in 1839 was a far cry from the small town Hannah knew nearly a hundred years earlier. Not only had the city's population skyrocketed, but the Jewish community was also over twenty-three times larger. Moreover, women's roles in that community had changed dramatically. Poor widows like Hannah no longer relied on men on the Mahamad to decide their fates, as female-run organizations like the Ladies Benevolent Society looked out for their own. The silences Hannah's lack of English education created had also been remedied: not only had free and "public" schools made education more readily available even to poor, female children in the city; synagogues also increasingly relied on women to teach and run Jewish educational institutions. Yet the deep inequalities within New York's Jewish community remained: the vast majority of the new arrivals were poor, struggling to survive as Hannah once had. Jane's rags-to-riches story offered a model of the dream many would be unable to achieve.

At least, however, the secular laws that had so hindered Jewish women like Hannah a century earlier had begun to change. In April 1848, the state legislature legalized married women's control over their own property and set the stage for the Seneca Falls Convention that summer.[128]

Bills came before the legislature in the 1840s attempting to enlarge the widow's share so that women like Hannah would not become "a potential drain on the resources of the community."[129] In 1860, widows gained the same rights as men whose spouses died intestate.[130]

Taken together, these changes not only ensured that Jewish women in New York in the 1840s lived more public and independent lives than women a century earlier but also changed their roles in their families. Jewish women's roles in creating and maintaining family life were increasingly recognized. Silhouettes were part of a family's inheritance, displaying the family's lineage, and the Isaacses' paper portrait showcased the roles of women within those genealogies. When Jane hung her silhouette in her three-story home on Elm Street, she did so with the knowledge that she had taken her place among the ancestors.

Conclusion

Nearly 170 years after Judith de Mereda disembarked in New Amsterdam from Recife, another Jewish woman from the Caribbean made her way across the city on a cold and unforgiving day. Sarah Brandon Moses was three months pregnant with her sixth child, a boy who would one day serve in the 23rd Independent Battery of the New York Light Artillery, dying a mere month before the Civil War ended.[1] Sarah, however, knew nothing of that future loss or heroism. She was wrapped in her current sorrow. Her mother, Esther, had just passed but could not be buried. As the extended kin of the synagogue's *parnas*, M. L. Moses, her mother had not had her Jewishness questioned, even though at least some must have known that she had been born to non-Jewish parents and never officially converted. Yet God—or at least the weather—seemed to be against Esther Rodrigues Brandon's final rest. A freak March snowstorm had blanketed the city, freezing the ground and delaying the funerary entourage. When the simple coffin finally made its way to Shearith Israel's second burial ground on Eleventh Street, Esther lay deprived of her possessions, as Judith had once been, wrapped only in the thin white shroud as required by Jewish law.

Today, no stone marks Esther's burial place, though most likely one did in the 1820s. In general, cemeteries are the most egalitarian of archives, at least in terms of who lies there.[2] Although burial markers range from hand-etched wood to magnificent mausoleums, all members of the Jewish community are buried within the cemetery's walls, unless they died abroad or substantially violated communal norms.[3] The remains of rich and poor, old and young, male and female lie adjacent to one another, each marked with memorials meant to withstand the test of time.

Yet the city's constant growth and evolution have destroyed the regularity of New York's earliest necropoleis. In 1830, seven years after Esther's death, Eleventh Street was widened and opened through Broadway to the Bowery. The "improved" street gobbled up most of the synagogue's second burial ground, reducing it to a small triangle (fig. 95). In making these plans, the city ignored the congregation's "insuperable objections to disturbing the dead,"[4] forcing the living to relocate the graves, crowding the dead into the new, much smaller plot. Adding insult to injury, the remaining lot was raised to meet the newly graded street. This necessitated the removal of *all* of the stones and their replacement, often in new locations that were tidy but bore little resemblance to where the dead actually lay.

The new display belied the sheer number of dead packed into the small yard. Many stones were lost or buried in the condensing process, and the stones chosen for display above ground were not random. The triangle housed the remains of "the poor and friendless" as well as some

Fig. 95. Post-1830 triangle of Shearith Israel's Eleventh Street cemetery. Photo courtesy Esther Crain / Ephemeral New York.

of the congregation's most illustrious members, many of whose stones are featured today along the western wall. Family also played a role in the reorganization, taking part in synagogue discussions and writing petitions. Yet Esther's common-law husband, Abraham Rodrigues Brandon, was noticeably silent during the upheaval, perhaps because he had set up house with a new, younger woman, miles away in tropical Barbados.[5] Nor did Sarah speak up for her mother, though for a different reason. In 1828, Esther's daughter Sarah and her youngest grandchild, Ariel, had already followed Esther into the burial ground. Joshua Moses wrote urgently in 1830 to ensure that "the precious remains of my Wife & Child" would be reinterred in a new cemetery, so that one day he and his wife could once again "rest side by side."[6] Today the couple lie together with their son Ariel in the Twenty-First Street Burial Ground. Other kin lie nearby.[7] Esther, however, was left behind in the condensed second cemetery.[8] Her memorial was either lost in the renovations or did not make the cut of who were deemed to merit commemoration above ground.

In *The Art of the Jewish Family*, I have argued that the stories that have been told about Jewish women in early America are limited by the records later generations have deemed worth preserving. Most of the records we have are disproportionately those of the wealthy few, who were more likely to have the education and cachet that made them likely to create records others wanted to collect. The vast majority of Jewish women in early New York—like elsewhere in the Americas—were astonishingly poor. The lives of these women, women like Hannah Louzada who had to rely on communal assistance for food, shelter, and fuel, were incredibly precarious.

Recent attention to charity records held by early congregations has helped round out our understanding of structural inequality in early Jewish life, as has the digitization of over four hundred handwritten volumes from New York's early almshouses, workhouses, lunatic asylums, and hospitals. These accounts are what one scholar has referred to as "insanity's archive," grim reminders of the way in which vulnerable people were socially constructed as marginal, deviant, and criminal, often largely for the sin of being poor.[9] The records reveal not only the families that were "fractured and damaged by the experience of mental breakdown" but also the very fractured nature of record keeping itself.[10] While the earliest of these records from New York dates to 1758, it was not until long after Hannah Louzada's death that records became more systematic. Even then, these reports often only hint at people. In September of 1813, Agnes Lousada, age twenty-four, born in New Jersey, together with her two New York–born sons, Adam (three years) and Jacob (sixteen months), arrived in the almshouse.[11] Were they relatives of Hannah or her son, Jacob?

One of the most frustrating things about working on Hannah Louzada was how elusive her genealogy was either moving forward or backward in time (appendix 1). Louzada (also spelled Lousada) is a common and important name throughout the early American colonies, particularly in the Caribbean, but it has been difficult to connect the branch of Hannah's husband to that of other, better-reconstructed genealogies. Although evidence indicates that Moses Louzada was born in London around 1700 and came to New York around 1717, Hannah's *ketubah* has never resurfaced, quite possibly because the earliest marriage records from some of the most obvious locations in the colonies where she might have gotten married—New York and Barbados—are missing.[12] Hence, no information is known about her before her husband's death in 1750, including her maiden name, where and when she was born, and her parents' names. We do not even know when she died, just that she stopped asking for money in 1770 and appears among the *escava* list in 1773/74.[13] My solution to this problem was to use the records that do remain to make educated guesses about Hannah's background, including where she was born and her education, based on her writing style and linguistic abilities. Hannah's fall from lower-middle-class slave owner is a good reminder about the importance of intersectionality for understanding Jewish women in early America. As bell hooks and others have noted, gender is not the sole—or even primary—factor in determining a woman's fate.[14] It is equally crucial to note that early Jewish women who experienced structural inequality often benefitted from the systematic oppression of other women.

Unlike Hannah Louzada, Reyna Levy Moses rarely had to worry about money. Despite owning numerous silver cups, Reyna almost certainly never had to polish them.[15] Like the Louzadas before Moses's death, Reyna and her husband owned slaves, and their labor—along with that of paid servants—helped maintain the family's house. Stories about Jews and slavery have tended to focus on the southern United States or the Caribbean, but slavery was as old as New Amsterdam. Gradual abolition did not come to New York until 1799, and those already enslaved were not freed until July 4, 1827, over three years after Reyna's death.[16] Databases such as the New York Slavery Records Index, which records enslaved persons and slaveholders in New York from 1625 though the Civil War, have helped tell part of this story, but the personal records of the

Moses family remind us that Jews who do not appear in this database were not always neutral on the subject of slaveholding in the North.

Reyna's genealogy was already more solidly researched, thanks in part to the eagerness of nineteenth-century descendants like Blanche Moses who wanted their ancestors recorded in the early libraries of the American Jewish Historical Society. Marks made on the cups themselves and the research of David Barquist and curators at the Met have ensured we know something about the transmission of the cups through the family line. My argument would not be possible without their prior scholarship. Yet, as with Hannah, there are discouraging gaps in Reyna's story and the history of her silver. For example, because the records of Myer Myers's stores have been lost, it is not clear if the beakers were a gift from Myers or if they were bought by the couple themselves. Silver was essential during this era for both gift giving and commemorating unions. Likewise, it is possible that the marriage between Reyna and Isaac was a love match as well as one that benefitted the men and their businesses. If so, unlike their son, Solomon, and his wife, Rachel, they did not feel a need to keep records of any affection that passed between Reyna and her husband, and this difference is itself telling. In dealing with these uncertainties, I have let trends during the era tip the scale. Most Jewish marriages of Reyna's day were still arranged, but future archival finds may prove me wrong.

Perhaps what is most enigmatic about Reyna is that despite being a former slave owner, she welcomed a former slave as kin. Sarah Brandon Moses's transformation from an enslaved woman of color to a white, elite Jew points to the value placed on Portuguese Jewish ancestry. As a member of the *nação* both through her father and via her conversion, Sarah had ancestral cachet that trumped that of her Ashkenazi husband, Joshua Moses. "Whiteness" was complex in early Jewish New York and was interwoven with class, education, and lineage. Material possessions such as Sarah's ivory miniature helped solidify her social standing. While members of New York's early Jewish community were certainly known for discriminating against people with African ancestry, other factors—including Jewishness—played important roles in racial assignment. Mordecai Manuel Noah, editor of the *National Advocate* newspaper and an important member of Shearith Israel, would later openly complain about "Africans" in New York,[17] but nothing in Noah's personal writings or the synagogue records suggests he saw Sarah as an "African," "person of color," or "black." Moreover, when Sarah's brother Isaac applied to become a member of Shearith Israel in 1823, Noah did not object, even though as a voting member he could easily have done so.[18] The story of women and their objects helps shed light on the larger role of how the "Jewish family" writ large was understood during this tumultuous era.

In her groundbreaking article "Venus in Two Acts," Saidiya Hartman poignantly notes that the history of slavery and oppression has ensured that we know little about the millions of women enslaved in the Americas. By and large, "the stories that exist are not about them, but rather about the violence, excess, mendacity, and reason that seized hold of their lives, transformed them into commodities and corpses, and identified them with names tossed-off as insults and crass jokes. The archive is . . . a death sentence, a tomb, a display of the violated body."[19] Sarah is the exception to this rule, but it is worth noting that the money and mobility that made her story possible was not available to the vast majority of women of partial Jewish ancestry living enslaved in Barbados, Suriname, and other countries around the Atlantic World. Her ability to marry in a synagogue and produce legitimate Jewish heirs was not an option offered to most of the multiracial women who gave birth to Jewish men's children.

Slavery violently disrupted families. By separating individuals from their kin during the Middle Passage and refusing to recognize biological ties as "legitimate or binding" once people were enslaved in the Americas, slavery created what Orlando Patterson calls a "genealogical isolate."[20] Destroying kinship contributed to the social death of enslaved peoples. The lack of information about Sarah's own mother, Esther; grandmother, Jemima; and great-grandmother, Deborah, highlights the violence of the archive as it silenced the past and destroyed futures (appendix 3).

Even amidst all we know about Sarah and her miniature, there is much that remains mysterious. In Hasia Diner's response to my lecture at Bard Graduate Center, she asked many questions about Sarah's agency that I was unable to answer. Did her father or Sarah herself choose the miniaturist? Did they look for someone known for whitening? Did Sarah like the miniature? Could she have rejected it if her father approved? Although it is nearly impossible to know for certain, Sarah's father most likely loomed large in most of the decisions that affected her before marriage. Surely even after being freed, Sarah would have been made to feel she owed a debt to her father that she was unable to ever repay.

As Marcel Mauss notes in *The Gift*, "Each gift is part of a system of reciprocity in which the honour of the giver and recipient are engaged. . . . The system is quite simple; just the rule that every gift has to be returned in some specified way sets up a perpetual cycle of exchanges within and between generations."[21] When Abraham Rodrigues Brandon

stood before the vestrymen of St. Michael's Church in 1801 and manu-
mitted his daughter, she in turn symbolically handed him ten shillings.[22]
This payment hardly evened the debt, however. As one of my colleagues
sagely put it, "Gifts from one's family are never truly free." How much
more so must this have been the case when the parent has not only given
one life but freedom and an enormous dowry? In many ways Sarah's children with their good marriages, righteous actions, and religious dedication were her down payment on Abraham's investment, particularly
Sarah's son Abraham Rodriguez Brandon Moses (1820–82), who like his
namesake would one day be the *parnas* of his congregation.[23]

By the time of her death in 1828, the precarious agency experienced
by Sarah Brandon Moses had shifted. A new generation of women were
raised to be Jewish educators and to value Jewish women's lives outside
of marriage. Although Sarah Ann Hays Mordecai eventually decided to
marry, she married a soul mate rather than a yoke mate. Moreover, both
her biographical and autobiographical works suggest Sarah Ann was in-
fluenced by a new cult of "single blessedness," which deemed unmarried
women not as a dead end to family lines but as important conveyers
of a spiritual tradition. In 1820, the women of Shearith Israel formed
their own benevolent society, which cared for poor Jewish women and
raised funds for the poor through balls, dinners, and synagogue offer-
ings. In 1838, women of the same congregation began a Sunday school
and offered education to poor Jews. Whereas a generation earlier, Jewish
women's places were primarily in the home, taking care of children, by
the 1820s they had started to take on roles that helped care for American
Jews more generally and shape public religious life. Sarah Ann's commonplace book reveals the fundamental role intellectual and emotional
paths played in the lives of Jewish women during an era of monumental
changes in what it meant to be female.

Yet, as Barbara Mann pointed out to me, there is something very
American about this shift:[24] while American Jewish women's European
counterparts held salons as early as the 1780s to showcase and develop
their literary intellects, it was not until 1895 that Rosa Sonneschein
started the *American Jewess*, a literary magazine directly aimed at American Jewish women.[25] Like salons, the *American Jewess* fostered a sense of
intellectual community that bridged public and personal spheres and a
culture of educated Jewish women's voices. Both salons and the *American
Jewess* encouraged women's "self-betterment" and intellectual growth,
seeing female work as playing an essential part in "human progress."[26]
Yet unlike European salons, the *American Jewess* and earlier American

commonplace books were more democratic, something taken up by the middle classes, as well as by "aristocratic" Jews. For Sarah Ann and her contemporaries, commonplace books provided an opportunity to share ideas, sentiments, and literary tastes. Her book complemented her later work as a schoolteacher rather than being an elite form of leisure.

Sarah Ann's commonplace book reminds us of the variety of ways that Jewish American women created kin. Unmarried women were the primary creators of Jewish women's cultural production in the first three quarters of the nineteenth century, playing key roles in Jewish education, literary production, and charities. Jewish women perpetuated legacies through their emotion, intellect, and ability to nurture ties beyond blood kin. Raising other women's biological children, whether in orphanages or schoolrooms or by taking them into their own homes, had its parallel in the commonplace book form. Both were a "cooperative means of production."[27]

Single women were valued. Much has been made of the twenty-first-century "crisis" in which Orthodox women find themselves unable to marry. One chronicler of the modern predicament lamented that while in the late twentieth century, it was normal for Orthodox girls to be engaged or married by the end of high school, in 2014, of the seventy-two girls graduating from a well-respected, girls-only Orthodox school in a "major American city," only thirteen were engaged or already married by the time of graduation.[28] A popular *shadchan* (matchmaker) nervously estimated recently that "a girl in the yeshivah world who is over the age of twenty-five has less than a 15 percent chance of ever getting married."[29] Yet back in the first part of the nineteenth century, Jewish women like Rebecca Gratz saw their lives as blessed by privilege. Their creativity inspired others, and they used the opportunities given to them to help Jews who had fewer resources. Moreover, because they had time to develop their inner and truest selves, women who waited to marry were "worth the wait" (fig. 96).[30] While some like Louisa Hart may have disagreed,[31] at least a percentage of Jewish women found that marrying late or not at all was an opportunity rather than a curse.

While Sarah Ann's commonplace book points toward the larger role women played in creating Jewish American culture in the antebellum era, the Isaacs family's silhouette underscores how the expansion of women's and domestic space into the "public" spaces of Judaism was important in both the Reform and Orthodox segments of New York Jewish society. While typically changes in religious practice are seen through a male lens, from 1840 to 1860 women in New York radically changed the

Fig. 96. Advertisement, *Mishpacha Magazine*, Aug. 6, 2014, 521. Courtesy of Baron Herzog Winery and *Mishpacha Magazine*.

way Judaism was understood. Gender and the Jewish family were battle-grounds for theological debates, and women were active players in the changes being proposed. Both Rev. Jacques Judah Lyons and Samuel Myer Isaacs married women who would not only support them emotionally at home but who actively participated in synagogue life. Even before they married, Grace Nathan Lyons was one of the founders of Shearith Israel's new female-led synagogue school. Jane Symons Isaacs likewise came to her marriage with the education necessary for helping with Shaaray Tefila's school and for playing leading roles in the synagogue and the city's charitable organizations.

The theological battles of the 1840s to 1860s regendered Jewish bodies and the family in response to rising anti-Semitism and sectarian disputes. Prior to this era, the Western Sephardic rite and customs dominated synagogues in the United States in general and New York in particular. Western Sephardim generally favored clothing that was similar to the fashions of their gentile neighbors, with the exception of clergy, who—at least during services—tended to wear hats that were deliberately out of fashion, such as the tricorn. Portraits suggest, however, that even clergy tended to dress according to the general fashion in everyday life. The influx of Ashkenazi Jews and debates about "proper" Judaism changed that tradition. The body and head became important sites to mark Jewish difference for both men and women, in ways that still resonate today in certain boroughs of New York. Jews who choose to emphasize "sameness," whether in religious gender roles or by dressing just like other New Yorkers, now found that some believed their choices ideologically aligned them with reformers. New York Judaism had fractured, and ideas of gender had splintered along with it.

Throughout this book, I have argued that the lack of a detailed history of women in early America is due in part to the types of evidence scholars have been willing to use as well as the way archives were built. Yet, as Marisa Fuentes notes, "the very call to 'find more sources' about people who left few if any of their own reproduces the same erasures and silences they experienced . . . by demanding the impossible."[32] Instead of reproducing these erasures, I have sought to use the fragments that do exist to think about the very active process of creating an absence of early Jewish women's lives in the historical record and the structural factors that silenced certain Jewish women in early New York, particularly the work of poverty, secular laws, poor social services for the mentally ill, slavery, racism, and unequal access to education.

Yet thinking about archives can also provide a glint of optimism. The archives of ten years ago are not the same as the archives of today, as digital media have radically altered the way we preserve, store, and present data. These archival changes have in many ways made this study possible. Scholars like Arthur Kroker suggest that we are in a moment of "archival drift" in which "the *form* and *content* of the cultural archive have been literally blown apart by the violence of digital technology. . . . Archive drift, therefore, always has a doubled meaning; namely that the actual *content* of the digital archive is literally at drift—unbounded, animated, deeply relational—in the universe of social media, and that the *form* of the archive patterns itself on the waves of code drift within which it finds itself and, on behalf of which, the form of the digital archive increasingly comes to represent the key trajectory of technological society."[33]

One of the great joys of working on this project has been to stumble upon new evidence—such as the miniature of Abraham Rodrigues Brandon, Sarah Rodrigues Brandon's father, in chapter 3—which was posted by descendants on the new "democratic" archives of genealogy services and then promoted through social media. Where once such objects remained hidden in family attics, now they are unbound from the very real physical limitations of what a historical society can hold. These artifacts remain deeply relational, bound to oral family traditions passed down through generations that may conflict with or challenge the variants of those stories found in the archives. Moreover, they are infinitely sharable; descendants who never met can reconnect via online posts and share photos, heirlooms, and stories that were once the prized possession of only a single descendant. Digital technology not only allows us to see differently by, for example, zooming in on a miniature, but it also widens our view to include things previously hidden. To be sure, there is a strange democracy afoot, in which one piece of misleading information can be repeated and magnified as it spreads from website to website, until it almost seems true. Yet family trees and legacies are at the heart of the stories told here, and in this new age, lines of connection that once seemed irreparably broken can be reforged in unexpected ways.

Investigating American Jewish history through the lens of women does more than restore gender balance to our understanding of the past. Ideally, thinking through gender allows us to see how the very evidence that scholars have relied on to construct the past has been filtered through a gendered bias. Between 1750 and 1850, men were most often able to create the types of evidence historians have tended to value, and the gatekeepers of early archives in synagogues and historical societies were predominantly male and tended to prioritize ways of being Jewish that favored men. This early predisposition has continued to obscure the histories of poor, elderly, non-European, nonbinary, and physically marginalized Jews. Moreover, this emphasis on men and men's writings has encouraged Jews in our own era not only to identify with male heroes[34] but also to construct a vision of Jewish womanhood that is passive and at the margins of historical narratives. The era from 1750 to 1850 is typically understood as the time of revolution and Jewish emancipation, culminating in Jews attaining full American citizenship and particularly the right to vote. Such a narrative ignores that in 1850 the vast majority of American Jews were still denied full rights either because of their gender, age, or lack of property.

Even when the story of American Jews between 1750 and 1850 has focused on migration or theological change, these stories—with the exception of works that explicitly focus on gender—have often centered on elite male actors, with little attention to how biases in the past limit stories and people in the present. Shifting our gaze to women allows us to think more critically about important developments in Jewish life, particularly how family and kinship were changing. Shifting our gaze also allows us to think critically about how women's speech has been understood as "unreliable, thwarted, or acquiescent" and hence expunged from the archive.[35]

The objects I chose for this book reflect my desire to rethink what makes something useful. In each instance, I selected the objects first, and then let those objects lead me to the women. For people who work primarily with art or material culture, this will seem like an obvious approach: when telling an object-driven story, one should start with the best objects available. What in the world makes an object the best, though? In the context of museum collecting, "best" often means things that are beautiful, well-crafted, precious, made of expensive materials, and paragons of their genre. While at least some of the items I used clearly fall into this category (Reyna's cups, for example), others, like Hannah's letter, do not. For me, the "best" has meant that the objects have a certain depth and tension about them. They are objects that surprised me, challenging what I thought I knew. They are far from perfect: instead their tears and scratches revealed how they—and their owners—have been marred by time and circumstance. They are objects that seem to deliberately thwart easy answers and instead shift and shimmer in different ways each time I look at or listen to them. They are personal and individual, irreducible to a type. They are as complex as the women who owned them.

I have tried to honor the women's and their objects' distinctiveness.

As much as I am interested in the relationships women had and the larger changes in which they participated, throughout this book I have used women's first names to emphasize their personhood and to separate their identities from patronymics. While in the nineteenth and early twentieth centuries women were diminished in scholarship by calling them Miss or Mrs., I have invoked the personal to underscore the fullness of women's lives outside of men. Focusing on women's voices and experiences exposes how certain forms of expression—such as begging letters, commonplace books, everyday objects, and portraits—were used strategically by women to construct a kind of self that other types of evidence often obscured. Over the course of the hundred years I cover, this self was increasingly relational, bound to others through affection and intellectual ties. The quotidian objects I focus on in this book have rarely been deemed "Jewish enough" by scholars for constructing an American Jewish history. I have aimed to show that their Jewishness is in how they were used rather than in the genres themselves, and between 1750 and 1850, quotidian objects played a central role in creating Jewish selves and families.

The stories of these families are significant for how we understand not only the past but also the present. Stories are more than just words. Studies of stereotyping have shown that extensive exposure to biases in print and visual media perpetuates myths that contribute to people's understanding of themselves and others. As Geneva Gay points out, "Members of both minority and majority groups are negatively affected by these images and representations."[36] Cultural displays of heroes and heroines, whether in social media, museums, books, or the classroom, convey important information about what the Jewish community today values, as well as who and what is (and is not) important. Gay argues that over time we take in these messages and "come to expect certain images, value what is present, and devalue what is absent."[37]

Throughout this book, I have suggested that one way to respond to the lack of primary documents by early Jewish American women is to think beyond the boundaries of the print archive. By turning to objects women owned, I ask us to rethink that history of silence. It is my hope that the biographies I have related here will be the start of discussions about the vibrant roles Jewish women played in the past and continue to play in the present—and will play in the future.

Appendices

TABLE 1

Hannah Louzada Family Tree

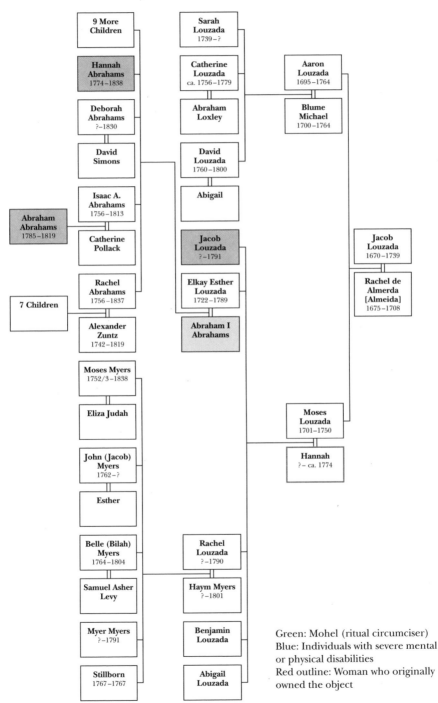

Green: Mohel (ritual circumciser)
Blue: Individuals with severe mental or physical disabilities
Red outline: Woman who originally owned the object

TABLE 2
Reyna Levy Moses Family Tree

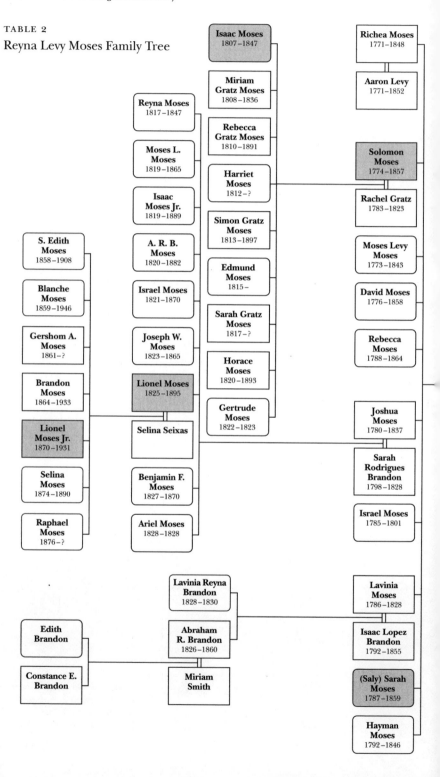

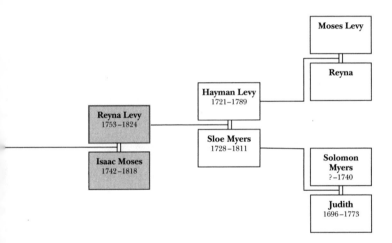

Rounded box: Unmarried
Gray: Owned silver beakers
Red outline: Woman who originally
owned the object

TABLE 3

Sarah Brandon Moses Family Tree

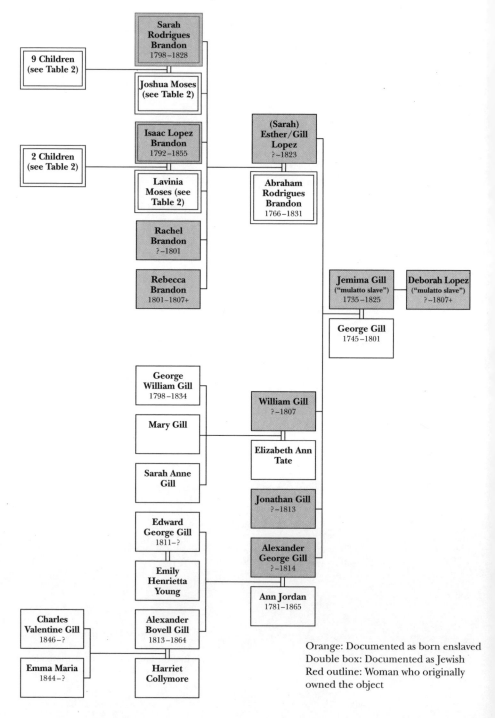

Orange: Documented as born enslaved
Double box: Documented as Jewish
Red outline: Woman who originally
owned the object

TABLE 4

Sara Ann Hays Mordecai Family Tree

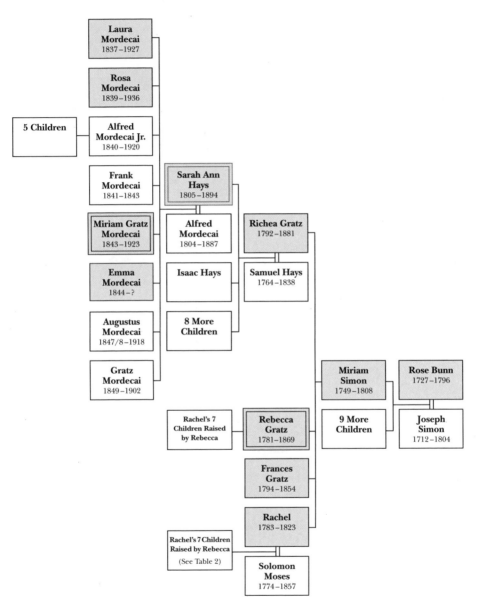

Yellow: Miriam Gratz Mordecai's female relations
Double box: Women who emphasized women as conveyors of Jewish identity
Red outline: Woman who originally owned the object

TABLE 5

Jane Symons Isaacs Family Tree

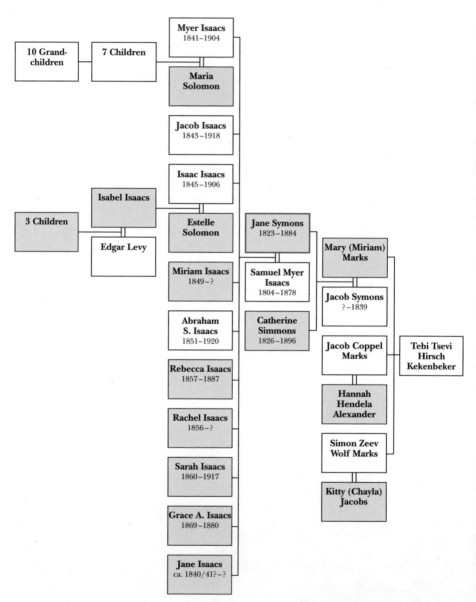

Yellow: Jane Symons's female relations
Red outline: Woman who originally
owned the object

TABLE 6

Table of Judaica Types by Gender, 1750–1840

	Object Type	Common Materials	Where Typically Collected Art Museums, Historical Museums, Libraries, Synagogues	Primary Gender Using Object 1750–1840 in America Male, Female, Ungendered
Klay Kodesh	Torah scroll	Parchment	HM, L, S	M
	Mezuza scroll	Parchment, Ink	HM, L, S	UG
	Haggadah	Paper, Ink, Leather	HM, L, S	UG
	T'fillin scroll	Parchment, Ink	HM, L	M
	Purim megillah	Parchment, Paint, Ink	HM, L, S	M
Tashmishey Kedusha	Mezuza case	Variable	AM, HM, S	UG
	Torah breast plate	Silver	AM, HM, S	M
	Torah covers	Cloth, Silver, Wood	AM, HM, S	M
	Rimonim	Silver	AM, HM, S	M
	Tallit	Cloth	HM	M
Tashmishey Mitzvah	Sabbath candelabrum	Silver, Metals	AM, HM	F
	Kiddush cup	Silver, Metals, Wood	AM, HM	M
	Chanukah menorah	Silver, Metals	AM, HM, S	M
	Passover seder plate	Ceramic, Metals	HM	UG
	Shofar	Horn	HM	M
R'shoot	Ornamental wedding ring	Silver, Gold, Enamel	AM, HM	F
	Spice box	Silver, Metals, Wood	AM, HM	M
	Etrog box	Silver, Metals, Wood	AM, HM	M
Quotidian	Begging letters	Paper, Ink	HM, L	UG
	Beakers	Silver, Metals	AM, HM	UG
	Ivory miniatures	Ivory, Watercolor	AM, HM	UG
	Commonplace books	Paper, Ink, Leather	HM, L	UG
	Silhouettes	Paper	AM, HM	UG
	Teacups	Ceramic, Porcelain	AM, HM	UG
	Portraits	Paint, Canvas	AM, HM, L, S	UG
	Photographs	Daguerreotype	AM, HM, L, S	UG

Glossary

affinal kinship: related through marriage

Akedah: the binding of Isaac

angisa: the headscarf that women with African ancestry wore in Surinam

chanukiahs: Chanukah lamps

chuppah: the marriage canopy

consanguineal: related through blood

eshet chayil: a virtuous woman

escava: literally, laying to rest. The Sephardic term for the memorial prayer said at the graveside, on Yom Kippur, and on the anniversary of the dead. The text used today by Western Sephardic communities appears on De Sola Pool, *Book of Prayer*, 206–7.

Great Migration: the wave of Jewish migration to the United States largely between 1880 and 1920, primarily of Ashkenazi Jews from Eastern Europe escaping pogroms and Sephardic Jews from the (former) Ottoman Empire

hatching: the use of short parallel lines to apply paint

Haskalah: literally, wisdom. The term refers to the Jewish Enlightenment that emphasized both Jewish uniqueness and Jewish integration.

hazzan (*hazzanim*, pl.): a synagogue official who, between 1750 and 1850, typically conducted services or led the chanting but did not have the educational background or standing of a rabbi or *hocham*. In New York, the *hazzan* was referred to as "reverend" by the end of this era.

hevrot: organizations

hocham: wise or learned man, usually a Talmudic scholar. The title
  given to the religious leader of synagogues in the early Jewish Atlantic World who had positions similar to a rabbi today.

kashruth: dietary laws

ketubah (*ketubot*, pl.): the Jewish marriage contract

kiddush: the blessing made over the wine as part of the ritual meal held
  on the Sabbath and during Jewish festivals. A special kiddush cup
  was often used solely for this ritual.

klay kodesh: Jewish ritual objects that are "endowed with inherent sanctity and must, according to Jewish law, be treated with the greatest
  care and circumspection and handled only in specific ways"
  (Zenner, *Persistence and Flexibility*, 263).

kohen (*kohanim*, pl.): a Jew who is a direct patrilineal descendant of
  Aaron and hence a member of the priestly caste

Mahamad: the synagogue governance board in Western Sephardic
  congregations

mikveh (*mikva'ot*, pl.): a ritual bath; a *mikveh* attendant is the person
  who oversees ritual immersions at the bath to ensure safety and
  that the immersion conforms to ritual standards. Between 1750 and
  1850, women oversaw female immersions and men oversaw male
  immersions.

minhag: an accepted tradition or custom, often considered binding

minyan: the ten men (and later sometimes women) over the age of
  thirteen required for parts of traditional Jewish service

mitzvah: an obligation or good deed

mitzvot: the 613 commandments derived from the Hebrew Bible and
  explained in the Mishnah, Talmud, and rabbinical commentaries

nação: Jews of the Portuguese nation or, as they are commonly known
  today, Western Sephardim. As Daviken Studnicki-Gizbert notes,
  this term was also used at times to include *conversos* and non-Jewish
  Portuguese people living in the Americas (*Nation upon the Ocean Sea*,
  70–71).

parnas (*parnassim*, pl.): president of the Mahamad; sometimes called
  parnas presidente

pidyon haben: the redemption of the firstborn

Old Christian: people in Iberia without any Jewish or Muslim ancestors
  and their descendants

New Christian: Iberian Jews and Muslims who converted to Catholicism

rimonim: Torah finials

r'shoot: quasi-sacred Judaica that have "some association with Jewish

religious and ritual life but have according to Jewish law no sanctity
nor are they absolutely required for the fulfillment of that act"
(Zenner, *Persistence and Flexibility*, 264).

rúbrica: a flourish. An essential part of official signatures in Iberia and
the Spanish colonies, such that a signature without a *rúbrica* was
deemed less authentic than a *rúbrica* alone.

Sephardic (adj.), **Sephardim** (n.): Jews whose ancestors lived in Spain
or Portugal

shadchan: matchmaker

shamash: warden

shochet: ritual slaughterer

Shulhan arukh: the code of Jewish law written in 1563 in Tsfat by the
Sephardic rabbi Joseph Caro

slichot: Jewish penitential poems and prayers

stippling: a painting technique that involves placing small dots of paint

sumptuary laws and codes: laws meant to regulate consumption that
restricted extravagance to certain groups. These laws are typically
about food, furniture, apparel, and other luxury items.

tashmishey kedusha: Judaica that is treated as constantly holy, even
though technically it attains "the utmost sanctity only when in use"
(Zenner, *Persistence and Flexibility*, 263).

tashmishey mitzvah: Judaica that does not in and of itself have sanctity
but "shares a measure of veneration" while being used to fulfill a
religious ritual (Zenner, *Persistence and Flexibility*, 263)

tzedakah: charity

Western Sephardic: a term used today to indicate Jews who migrated
from Iberia to Western Europe, particularly to Amsterdam, London,
and Hamburg. Between 1750 and 1850, they were typically referred
to as *nação*.

yeshivah (**yeshivot**, pl.): a Jewish day school or institute for rabbinic
study, with an emphasis on study of the Talmud

yichut: ancestry or lineage

yom tov (*yomim tovim*, pl.): holy day

Notes

1. Fernow, *Records of New Amsterdam*, 1. The average temperature in New York on September 10 is 64–78°F, compared to 75–84°F in Recife, with 97% humidity, according to www.weatherspark.com.
2. Moscow, *Book of New York Firsts*, 16–17; and Wiznitzer, "Exodus from Brazil," 93.
3. Leo Hershkowitz notes that many questions remain about the arrival of the first Jews in New York, and although I am emphasizing what we do not know about women here, he rightly notes that the entire story of early Jewish immigration is frustratingly patchy ("By Chance or Choice," 11). To be sure, all colonial records have been ravaged by time. My point in this book is that the uneven state of early American records is not always accidental but rather reflects both chance and deliberate pruning based on priorities of previous generations. These priorities sometime run counter to our own.
4. Sutton, *Capitalism and Cartography in the Dutch Golden Age*, 88. See also the painting by Zacharias Wagener, *Mercado de escravos no Recife* [Slave market in Recife, Brazil], ca. 1637–44, Kupferstich Kabinett, Dresden.
5. Leibman, "Poetics of the Apocalypse," 36; and Wiznitzer, *Jews in Colonial Brazil*, 101–3. The Jewish population of Recife in 1645 has been estimated at 1,000 out of a total (white) population of 1,700 (Klooster, "Networks of Colonial Entrepreneurs," 34).
6. Rock, *Haven of Liberty*, 12.
7. Moscow, *Book of New York Firsts*, 16–17.
8. Rock, *Haven of Liberty*, 12–13.
9. Fernow, *Records of New Amsterdam from 1653–1674*, 241.
10. Wiznitzer, "Exodus from Brazil," 93. See also Wiznitzer, "Minute Book of Congregations Zur Israel."

11. Shilstone, *Monumental Inscriptions in the Jewish Synagogue*, x. See also Samuel, "Review of the Jewish Colonists in Barbados," 18.

12. Verdooner and Snel, *Trouwen in mokum*, 731.

13. Stiefel, *Jewish Sanctuary in the Atlantic World*, 130; and Mark and da Silva Horta, "Catholics, Jews, and Muslims in Guiné," 186.

14. The years 1800 and 1850 are similarly covered in ninety-three pages (Marcus, *American Jewish Woman: A Documentary History*, 59–152).

15. Diner and Benderly, *Her Works Praise Her*. There is a similar trend in the 1992 edition of Umansky and Ashton's *Four Centuries of Jewish Women's Spirituality*, which spends only twenty-two pages on the period prior to 1800, none of which are dedicated to examples from the Americas (33–55). The 2009 edition of the text augments this section by adding more early voices reaching back into the medieval era. This edition includes eighty-eight pages of women's voices from 1523 to 1865; twelve pages of this addition (comprising seven authors) are from the Americas.

16. My language in this discussion owes much to Su and Wilkins, *Own the Room*, 9.

17. To be fair, most scholars today also specialize in American Jewish history after 1880, though the question of why this is the case remains.

18. The first women's studies department was established in the United States in 1970. The first journal in the field, *Feminist Studies*, began two years later, and the National Women's Studies Association came into being in 1977. See Salper, "San Diego State 1970."

19. Notably, even Aviva Ben-Ur, who has done remarkable work on both women's lives and early America, focuses primarily on the twentieth century in *Sephardic Jew in America*. Shari Rabin's ground-breaking study, *Jews on the Frontier: Religion and Mobility in Nineteenth-Century America*, in many ways begins with the 1840s and 1850s (which is the focus of the last chapter of *The Art of the Jewish Family*) and then moves forward through the rest of the nineteenth century even as it expands its gaze on American Jews past the Eastern Seaboard.

20. Ashton, *Rebecca Gratz*; and Franks, *Letters of Abigaill Levy Franks*.

21. Hoskins, abstract of "Afterword—Gendering Religious Objects," 110.

22. Smith, *Respectability as Moral Map and Public Discourse*, 119.

23. I am grateful to Michael Hoberman for pointing this out. See Ellis, Coulton, and Mauger, *Empire of Tea*, 8–12, 31, 44, and 164.

24. Smith, *Respectability as Moral Map and Public Discourse*, 119–20.

25. Ferguson, *Ceramics*, 157, 164, 166, 172, 178.

26. Hoberman, Leibman, and Surowitz-Israel, *Jews in the Americas*, 327.

27. Smith, *Respectability as Moral Map and Public Discourse*, 199.

28. Fuentes, *Dispossessed Lives*, 6.

29. Ibid., 146.

30. Hobuß, "Silence, Remembering, and Forgetting," 97.

31. Munrow, "Negotiating Memories and Silences," 175.

32. Spann, *New Metropolis*, 13–14, 121.

33. Kammen, *Colonial New York*, 279; Menard, *Handbook of Longitudinal Research*, 19; First census of the United States, 1790, record group 29, Records of the Bureau of the Census, NARA.

34.   Seventh census of the United States, 1850, record group 29, Records of the Bureau of the Census, NARA.

35.   Rosenwaike, *Population History of New York City*, 54.

36.   Ibid., 53.

37.   Rock, *Haven of Liberty*, 206.

38.   Cootz, *Marriage, a History*, 145–46.

39.   For the soul mates versus yoke mates language, see ibid.

40.   Perry, *Novel Relations*, 2; and Weinstein, *Family, Kinship, and Sympathy*, 9.

41.   Sarna, *American Judaism*, 27, 45.

42.   Martínez–San Miguel, *Coloniality of Diasporas*, 1–2, 12.

43.   Carroll, *American Masculinities*, 120.

44.   Lyons, *Sex Among the Rabble*, 152; Laqueur, *Making Sex*, 4-6.

45.   Lyons, *Sex Among the Rabble*, 152–53.

46.   Quoted in De Sola Pool, "Letters of Grace Seixas Nathan," 205.

47.   Noah, review of performance of *Richard III*, *National Advocate*, September 24, 1821, quoted in Gellman and Quigley, *Jim Crow New York*, 88.

48.   Carment and Sadjed, *Diaspora as Cultures of Cooperation*, 75.

49.   Sarah is referred to as a "Mulatto" in the will of Hannah Esther Lopez, Oct. 23, 1815, RL 1/6, BDA; and a "mulatto" in her baptismal record: Sarah Brandon, June 28, 1798, Barbados Church Records, 1637–1887, https://www.familysearch.org/search/collection/1923399; citing Baptism of Sarah Brandon, St. Michael's, Family History Library (FHL), microfilm 1,157,925.1,157,925, BDA. Hoberman, Leibman, and Surowitz-Israel, *Jews in the Americas*, 2.

50.   Fourth census of the United States, 1820, New York Ward 1, M33_77, image 18, p. 14, Records of the Bureau of the Census, NARA; *Soundex Index to Petitions for Naturalizations Filed in Federal, State, and Local Courts in New York City, 1792–1906*, M1674, roll 31.

51.   Marcus, *American Jewish Woman, 1654–1980*, 23.

52.   For more on the development of the term "sisterhood," see Nadell, "Synagog shall hear the Call of the Sister," 23.

53.   Simon, *Samuel Myer Isaacs*, 20.

CHAPTER ONE

Epigraph: Eliot, *Middlemarch*, 23.

1.   "Jacques Judah Lyons," xxiii–xxvi.

2.   From the *New-York Aurora*, "Interesting Jewish Marriage Ceremony," *Pittsburg Sun*, December 15, 1842, 1; "Items Relating to the Seixas Family"; Nathan, "Poetry Manuscript," 1805–30, Nathan family papers, AJHS.

3.   Unlike Dorothea and Casaubon in *Middlemarch* by George Eliot, there was no large age gap between the couple. In fact, Grace was four years older than Jacques (Stern, *First American Jewish Families*, 182, 226).

4.   Will of Benjamin Nathan, 1807, Record of Wills, 1665–1916, New York Surrogate's Court, vol. 204, 178.

5.   "Jacques Judah Lyons," xxvi–xxvii; Lyons, "From the Collections of the American Jewish Historical Society," 65–66; "Preface" (1913), x. The tra-

dition of giving to AJHS was continued by Grace and Jacques's daughter Sarah Lyons, who left several family portraits and miniatures to the society ("Report of Leon Hunter," xxi). My transcription of Hannah's letter owes a debt to Marcus, *American Jewry*, 89.

6.   The letters *I* and *j* were still interchangeable in written colonial English.

7.   Leibman and Watson, "Rediscovering an Important Link to American Jewish History."

8.   Aaron Lopez, for example, appears eighty-six times in the *Publications of the American Jewish Historical Society* (1893–1961), twenty-nine times in the *American Jewish Historical Quarterly* (1961–78), and two times in *American Jewish History* (1978–2010). Also see Bigelow, "Aaron Lopez"; Chyet, *Lopez of Newport*; Gutstein, *Aaron Lopez and Judah Touro*; and the letter books, shipping papers, account books, receipts, and shipping and journal books in the Aaron Lopez collection, microfilm nos. 1212–16, AJA. In contrast, Hannah Louzada appears four times in the *Publications of the American Jewish Historical Society* (three of which are in reference to the Lyons Collection), three times in the *American Jewish Historical Quarterly*, and not at all in *American Jewish History*.

9.   Bernfeld, *Poverty and Welfare*, 72, 60; Crenshaw, *Rembrandt's Bankruptcy*, 46; Cohen, *Jews in Another Environment*, 20–27, 94.

10.   Daniels, "Colonial Jewry," 383; and Marcus, *Colonial American Jew*, 2:1035, 1038–39.

11.   Bernfeld, *Poverty and Welfare*, 20–60, 72–73, 131–32.

12.   Lieberman, "From Charity to Philanthropy," 116–17, 121–22; Minute books of the Mahamad of Nidhe Israel, 1790–1826, 4521/D/01/01/002, 4521/D/01/01/003, 4521/D/01/01/004, 4521/D/01/01/008, LMA; Cohen, *Jews in Another Environment*, 20–24.

13.   It is worth noting that among non-Jews, women were also well represented among the poor in the colonies (Abramovitz, *Regulating the Lives of Women*, 58). Baugher likewise notes that in colonial New York, residents of almshouses were "mainly women, children, and the elderly, with an occasional injured or disabled man" ("Visible Charity," 198).

14.   Ben-Ur, "Still Life," 61–63; and Mays, *Women in Early America*, 66–69, 106–11.

15.   Minute books of the Mahamad of Nidhe Israel, 1790–1826, III.50, 4521/D/01/01/003, LMA; and Leibman, *Messianism, Secrecy, Mysticism*, 83. For an explanation of why so much was at stake surrounding ritual immersion, see Oron, "'No aksi mi fu libi yu.'"

16.   Minute books of the Mahamad of Nidhe Israel, 1790–1826, III.30, 4521/D/01/01/003, LMA. For more examples of "misbehavior" and punishment, see Ben-Ur and Roitman, "Adultery Here and There."

17.   Ulrich, "Vertuous Women Found," 20. See also Ulrich, *Well-Behaved Women Seldom Make History*.

18.   I am indebted to Julia Lieberman and her scholarship for bringing the idea of the deserving poor to my attention.

19.   Lieberman, "Founding of the London Bet Holim Hospital," 131.

20.   Ibid., 128, 131. Abramowitz notes similar ideas about "deserving poor" in colonial America, with women who complied with local notions of

family ethics receiving more favorable treatment (*Regulating the Lives of Women*, 52).

21. Minute books of the Mahamad of Nidhe Israel, 1790–1826, II.3, 22, 27, 29, 40, LMA/4521/D/01/01/002, LMA; and Marcus, *Colonial American Jew*, 2:1050.

22. Marcus, *Colonial American Jew*, 2:1033–40.

23. Hershkowitz, "Colonial Entrepreneurs"; and Prinz, *On the Chocolate Trail*, 48.

24. Marcus, *Colonial American Jew*, 2:1039.

25. Baugher, "Visible Charity," 183.

26. Ibid., 184.

27. Ibid.

28. Ibid., 176.

29. Hopper, *Reckoning with Homelessness*, 26.

30. Marcus, *Colonial American Jews*, 2:1040; and Quigley, "Reluctant Charity," 129–30.

31. Rockman, *Welfare Reform in the Early Republic*, 6; and Marcus, *Colonial American Jew*, 2:1033. The New York City government took over responsibility for caring for the poor in 1736 when it opened its first almshouse on the city commons. For surviving records for the city's almshouses to 1758, see "Almshouse Collection, 1758–1952 (Finding Aid)," NYC Records and Information Service, https://www1.nyc.gov/assets/records/pdf/featured -collections/almhouse-ledger-collection-1758-1952.pdf.

32. Marcus, *Colonial American Jew*, 2:1033.

33. The first synagogue was established in 1848 (Friedenberg, "Jews of New Jersey," 42).

34. Marcus, *Colonial American Jew*, 2:1039.

35. Letter from Hannah Louzada to Aaron Lopez, 1770, Champlin Collection of Autographs, no. 596, NYSL; Letter from Hannah Louzada to Aaron Lopez, July 26, 1770, Champlin Collection of Autographs, no. 601, NYSL, photocopy AJA.

36. *OED Online*, s.v. "supplicant, n. and adj.," http://www.oed.com.proxy .library.reed.edu/view/Entry/194649?redirectedFrom=supplicant.

37. Emphasis added. This is a phrase she would repeat in her letter from July 26, 1770.

38. Dierks, "Familiar Letter and Social Refinement," 31–33.

39. Leibman, "Tradition and Innovation," 193–94.

40. Bannet, "Empire and Occasional Conformity," 76; and Westlake, *How to Write Letters*, 46.

41. Mary Occom to Eleazar Wheelock, Jan. 15, 1767, box Ayer MS 655, Newberry Library.

42. Schneider, "This Once Savage Heart of Mine," 234.

43. Minute books of the Mahamad of Nidhe Israel, 1790–1826, VIII.42, 4521/D/01/01/008, LMA.

44. Ibid. Emphasis added.

45. Fairman, "English Pauper Letters," 63–71.

46. Schen, "Constructing the Poor," 457.

47. Lamb, *Rhetoric of Suffering*, 25, 275, 282.

48. "Earliest Extant Minute Books of the Spanish and Portuguese Congregation," 73.
49. Rozin, *The Rich and the Poor*, 11–12.
50. "Introduction to Volume I," xiii; and Marcus, *Studies in American Jewish History*, 45–46. I am grateful to Jonathan Sarna for calling this to my attention.
51. Almshouse Admissions, 1759–1818, vol. 212, Almshouse Ledger Collection, NYCRIS, http://nycma.lunaimaging.com/luna/servlet/detail /NYCMA~2~2~75~477973.
52. Fairman, "English Pauper Letters," 65.
53. Marcus, *American Jewry*, 89.
54. Fairman, "English Pauper Letters," 68–69.
55. Miller, "On the State of the Peruvian Empire," 42; and Ellis, *Plea for Phonetic Spelling*, 70.
56. George G. Champlin Autograph Collection, 1740–1938, SC9104-9509, NYSL, http://www.nysl.nysed.gov/msscfa/sc9104-9509.htm; and Chypet, "Aaron Lopez," 304.
57. Fairman, "English Pauper Letters," 68–69.
58. Leibman, *Messianism, Secrecy, and Mysticism*, 230.
59. Vink, *Creole Jews Negotiating Community*, 246–47; and Mirvis, "Sephardic Family Life in the Eighteenth-Century British West Indies," 68–69.
60. Earle, "Letters and Love in Colonial Spanish America," 30.
61. Ibid., 29–30; and Gil, "Estructura de las Cartas Marruecas," 131. Thank you to Julia Lieberman for calling my attention to early Spanish *epistolarios*.
62. Dworkin, *Guide to Old Spanish*, 22–23.
63. Studnicki-Gizbert, *Nation upon the Ocean Sea*, 19, 52.
64. Leibman, "Poetics of the Apocalypse," 54; and Bodian, *Hebrews of the Portuguese Nation*, 92.
65. Letter from Hannah Louzada to Aaron Lopez, July 26, 1770, Champlin Collection of Autographs, no. 601, NYSL, photocopy AJA.
66. Chyet, "Aaron Lopez," 304.
67. As Jennifer Monaghan notes, prior to 1770, women's education commonly prioritized reading over writing, even in Massachusetts, which was considered progressive with respect to women's education ("Literacy Instruction and Gender," 27).
68. Vink, *Creole Jews Negotiating Community*, 73.
69. Ben-Ur and Roitman, "Adultery Here and There," 188, 208, 212, 215–16.
70. Carr, "Nineteenth-Century Girls and Literacy," 51.
71. Stretton and Kesselring, "Introduction," 8. Lindsay Moore claims that contrary to the large body of historiography arguing otherwise, women did not have "more legal independence than their English counterparts" ("Women and Property Litigation," 115). As Linda Kerber notes, "Both the constraining and the protective aspects of coverture retained their vitality in the early Republic," that is, including after the era of Hannah's death (*Women of the Republic*, 139).
72. Hoberman, Leibman, and Surowitz-Israel, *Jews in the Americas*, 181.
73. Schaefer, *Hidden Half of the Family*, 178–79.

74. De Sola Pool, *Portraits Etched in Stone*, 240.

75. Only about a quarter of men in early New York wrote wills. See Morgan, *Laboring Women*, 70; and Gunderson, "Women and Inheritance in America," 93–94.

76. Schaefer, *Hidden Half of the Family*, 178.

77. Jamoussi, *Primogeniture and Entail in England*, 19.

78. In her novel *Dream-Life*, Cora differentiated between the poor who dressed "in rags and tatters, that lives in a hovel and can ask for 'cold victuals,'" and the "genteel" poor "who would rather starve than beg" (quoted in Sarna, "Jewish Women Without Money," 30). The novel was published serially, and this section appears in *Banner of Light* (Boston), Dec. 16, 1865, 1.

79. Gigantino, *Ragged Road to Abolition*, 180.

80. Deed of sale by Haym Myers to Samuel Jacobs of the "negro girl" Jenny, Aug. 5, 1786, Jacobs-Ermatinger Estate fonds 8:27A, 27B, LAC, MG19 A2; and Mackey, *Done with Slavery*, 537.

81. Hodges, *Slavery and Freedom in the Rural North*, 43–45.

82. Estate inventory of Moses Louzada, filed October 10, 1750, county of Middlesex, New Jersey, photocopy AJA.

83. Nelson, Honeyman, and Hutchinson, *Calendar of New Jersey Wills, Administrations, etc.* 1901, 7, 259–60, https://archive.org/details/calendarof newjer03newj.

84. Birmingham, *Grandees*, 7.

85. Ibid., 6.

86. Gilman, *Difference and Pathology*, 150–51.

87. Gilman, "Sibling Incest, Madness, and the 'Jews,'" 159.

88. Nalle, "On the Alumbrados," 118.

89. Ibid.

90. Hartogensis, "Rhode Island and Consanguineous Jewish Marriages," 139; and Nussbaum, *Liberty of Conscience*, 124.

91. "Mental Illness—Statistics," National Institute of Mental Health, https:// www.nimh.nih.gov/health/statistics/mental-illness.shtml; and Fischer, *Made in America*, 236.

92. Stern, *First American Jewish Families*, [insane:] 4, 29, 36, 44, 85, 97, 110, 151, 179, 263; [suicide:] 6, 12, 44, 120; [drowned or died in shipwreck:] 24, 29, 36 [3], 63, 155 [2], 163 [2], 172, 175, 216 [4], 218, 247, 264 [2], 296, 298; [duel:] 35, 39, 201 [2], 247.

93. Fischer, *Made in America*, 232.

94. Ibid.

95. Shaw and Raz, *Cousin Marriages*, 13–14.

96. McCarthy, Coleborne, O'Connor, and Knewstubb, "Lives in the Asylum Record," 369–70; and Sharkia, Azem, Kaiyal, Zelnik, and Mahajnah, "Mental Retardation," 91.

97. Eldridge, "Crazy Brained," 362.

98. Ibid., 361–67, 373.

99. McCarthy, Coleborne, O'Connor, and Knewstubb, "Lives in the Asylum Record," 371–72.

100. Stern, *First American Jewish Families*, [women:] 4, 29, 36, 85, 97, 110, 151,

263; [men:] 75, 179. In contrast, however, only men were recorded as committing suicide (ibid., 6, 12, 44, 120).

101. Ibid., [single:] 4, 29, 36, 75, 85, 110, 151, 179, 263; [married:] 97.

102. Fischer, *Made in America*, 231–32.

103. Shuger, *Don Quixote in the Archives*, 21–22.

104. Ibid., 20.

105. Ibid., 29.

106. Ibid., 34.

107. Ibid., 21.

108. Yanni, *Architecture of Madness*, 14.

109. Birmingham, *Grandees*, 197.

110. Grob, *Mental Institutions in America*, 8.

111. Ibid., 11.

112. Calendar of wills from "Louwada, Jacob of Middlesex Co., 1762," "1762, April 22.," "1762, April 21. Abrahams, Abraham, guardian," and "1764, Feb. 24, Revocation," in Honeyman, *Documents Relating to the Colonial History*, 259–60, 267.

113. Wallace Hale, "List of Vessels Employed by the Crown, New York, 1781," Fort Havoc, Provincial Archive of New Brunswick (Canada), https://archives.gnb.ca/Exhibits/FortHavoc/html/Vessels.aspx?culture=fr-CA.

114. Roth, "Some Jewish Loyalists in the War," 43–44.

115. Marcus, *American Jewry*, 16; and Zola and Dollinger, *American Jewish History*, 28.

116. Corré and Stern, "Record Book of the Reverend Jacob Raphael Cohen," 29.

117. Marcus, *Colonial American Jew*, 2:562, 1055.

118. The National Alliance for the Mentally Ill estimates that 20 percent of all young people in the United States ages thirteen to eighteen live with a mental health condition. While we have better public support systems today than Hannah did, mental illness still has a devastating impact on Jewish American families, and talking about it is an important first step toward providing moral and financial support to families in need. While certainly mental illness has been used as a slander against Jews in the past, refusing to acknowledge its presence also has consequences, as do histories that ignore its impact. Model minority stereotypes not only contribute to the stress young people and their families feel today but also make them less likely to seek services. See Levine and Hochbaum, *Poor Jews*, 1–5; "Mental Health by the Numbers," National Alliance on Mental Illness.org, 2018, https://www.nami.org/Learn-More/Mental-Health-By-the-Numbers; Ritika Rastogi, "No Such Thing as a 'Positive' Stereotype: Consequences of the Model Minority Myth," *Psychology in Action*, Jan. 3, 2018, www.psychologyinaction.org/psychology-in-action-1/2018/1/4/no-such-thing-as-a-positive-stereotype-deleterious-consequences-of-the-model-minority-myth?rq=rastogi://.

119. Museus and Kiang, "Deconstructing the Model Minority Myth," 6.

120. Ibid.; and Museus, "Model Minority and the Inferior Minority Myths," 3.

121. A 2007 study showed that 15 percent of U.S. Jews are poor—more than in Israel (Ruth Sinai, "Study Claims Jewish Poverty Rate in the U.S. Is Higher

Than in Israel," *Haaretz*, Nov. 16, 2007, http://www.haaretz.com
/jewish/2.209/study-claims-jewish-poverty-rate-in-the-u-s-is-higher-than
-in-israel-1.233403). See also "Mental Health by the Numbers," National
Alliance on Mental Illness.org, 2018, https://www.nami.org/Learn-More
/Mental-Health-By-the-Numbers.

122. Sinai, "Study Claims Jewish Poverty Rate," http://www.haaretz.com
/jewish/2.209/study-claims-jewish-poverty-rate-in-the-u-s-is-higher-than-in
-israel-1.233403.

CHAPTER TWO

1.   McEvilley, introduction to *Inside the White Cube*, by Brian O'Doherty, 8.
2.   Duncan, *Civilizing Rituals*, 55.
3.   Barquist, *Myer Myers*, 36–37; Barquist, "Stylistic Distinctiveness of Colonial New York Silver," 40–42; Krill, *Early American Decorative Arts*, 13. As
Julia Lieberman so usefully pointed out to me, the only thing that marks
the beakers as Jewish in the description is the name of "Congregation
Shearith Israel," which may itself be unfamiliar to some visitors.
4.   Wees and Harvey, *Early American Silver*, 83.
5.   Ibid.
6.   Stern, *First American Jewish Families*, 159, 209; and Dunn, *People of the
American Frontier*, 148.
7.   "From the 2nd Volume of the Minute Books," 83, 85, 88, and 89.
8.   See *Notable American Women*, 474; and the Loeb Jewish Portrait Database,
2018, http://loebjewishportraits.com/paintings/isaac-moses/ and
http://loebjewishportraits.com/paintings/isaac-moses-2/.
9.   Stephen Girard papers, 1793–1857, mss. film. 1424, APS; and the PMFNY,
undated, 1767–1941, 1971, P-1, AJHS.
10.   Isaac Moses, receipt book, 1785–87, PMFNY, AJHS.
11.   Rosenbloom, *Biographical Dictionary of Early American Jews*, 95.
12.   Diner and Benderly, *Her Works Praise Her*, 52.
13.   For example, in the Ukraine, it was typical to give silver watches, tobacco
boxes, or copies of the Pentateuch bound in silver (Freeze, *Jewish Marriage and Divorce*, 44).
14.   Although in eighteenth-century England an heirloom stands apart from
the system of primogeniture and technically means "a chattel that, under
a will, settlement or custom, follows the devolution of real estate," and
cannot be sold off or separated from the entailed estate, the term was not
used this way in the United States (Dawson, "'Heirlooms,'" 2); accord-
ingly, I do not use it with that British legalistic sense here. Rather, by
"heirloom" I mean moveable property, handed down from generation to
generation within a family, which was intended to mark and preserve a
family's heritage. See also Blackstone, *Commentaries on the Laws of England*,
1287–88.
15.   I would like to thank Michael Hoberman for pointing out this problem.
16.   Schoenberger, "Ritual Silver Made by Myer Myers"; Gutmann, *Beauty in
Holiness*, 66–78; Barquist, *Myer Myers*; Rosenbaum, *Myer Myers, Goldsmith*,
25–34, 67–68.

17.   Hyde, *The Gift*, 53.
18.   Isaac Moses, receipt book, 1785–87, p. 56, PMFNY, AJHS.
19.   Barquist, *Myer Myers*, 256.
20.   Ensko, *American Silversmiths and Their Marks*, 149; Barquist, *Myer Myers*, 253; Martello, *Midnight Ride, Industrial Dawn*, 39.
21.   Kammen, *Colonial New York*, 279.
22.   Maerschalck, *Plan of the City of New York*; Ratzer, *Plan of the City of New York*.
23.   Menard, *Handbook of Longitudinal Research*, 19; First census of the United States, 1790, record group 29, Records of the Bureau of the Census, NARA.
24.   Stern, *First American Jewish Families*, 159, 217.
25.   Rosenbloom, *Myer Myers, Goldsmith*, 25–27; Barquist, *Myer Myers*, 27–28; "Earliest Extant Minute Books of the Spanish and Portuguese Congregation," 31; Joel, Isaacs, and Phillips, "Items Relating to Congregation Shearith Israel," 1.
26.   *New York City Directory, 1786*, pp. 37–40, NYPL Digital Collections, Rare Book Division, http://digitalcollections.nypl.org/items/70bcc910-d5c9 -0134-fbe5-00505686d14e; Stern, *First American Jewish Families*, 159, 217; Rosenbloom, *Biographical Dictionary of Early American Jews*, 59; Tatsch, *Moses Michael Hays*.
27.   Rock, *Haven of Liberty*, 37, 56; Kohler, "Phases of Jewish Life in New York," 86–87.
28.   Rosenbloom, *Biographical Dictionary of Early American Jews*, 106; Singleton and Sturgis, *Furniture of Our Forefathers*, 303; Rosenbaum, *Myer Myers, Goldsmith*, 25–27.
29.   Stern, *First American Jewish Families*, 184, 217.
30.   Will of Isaac Moses, 1818, PMFNY, AJHS.
31.   Nutt, quoted in Sotheby's, *The Collection of Roy and Ruth Nutt: Important Americana & Decorative Arts*, Jan. 23, 2015, 13, http://www.sothebys.com /en/auctions/2015/nutt-americana-n09305.html.
32.   Kelly, *Election Day*, 9. Between 1737 and 1747, Jews were prohibited from voting in New York regardless of how much property they owned (Eisenstadt, *Encyclopedia of New York State*, 1501).
33.   Gurock, *Colonial and Early National Period*, 13–14; and *A Copy of the Poll List of the Election for Representatives for the City and County of New-York, 1761, 1768, 1769* (1880), Tomball, TX: Genealogical Publications, 1977.
34.   Rock, *Haven of Liberty*, xv, 78, 84–85; and Hühner, "Jews Interested in Privateering," 173.
35.   Barquist, *Myer Myers*, 128–29.
36.   Advertisement, *New-York Gazette*, March 23–30, 1767, 3; and Stern, *First American Jewish Families*, 104, 217.
37.   Barquist, *Myer Myers*, 60–61, 99, 128, 198–99.
38.   Jewish Museum, New York, "Circumcision Shield and Probe (1765–75)," https://thejewishmuseum.org/collection/28349-circumcision-shield-and -probe; Zimmerman, "Letter and Memorandum on Ritual Circumcision," 59; Stern, *First American Jewish Families*, 154, 159, 165, 190, 217, 263.
39.   Stern, *First American Jewish Families*, 159, 209; and Ben-Ur, "The Exceptional and the Mundane," 51.

40. De Sola Pool, *Portraits Etched in Stone*, 384.

41. *American National Biography*, 396.

42. Ibid.

43. Stern, *First American Jewish Families*, 159.

44. *American National Biography*, 396.

45. Advertisement, *New-York Journal*, May 23, 1771, 352; and advertisement, *New York Packet and the American Advertiser*, August 26, 1784, 4.

46. *American National Biography*, 396; and Reiss, *Jews in Colonial America*, 7.

47. Liberles, "On the Threshold of Modernity," 25–27.

48. Ibid., 25, 31, 42–43.

49. Ibid., 25.

50. Ibid., 27–29, 31, 33, 39.

51. Marcus, *Jew in the American World*, 140–41.

52. Pappenheim, *Jewish Wedding*, 46.

53. Russell, *Gender and Jewelry*, 24.

54. Marcus, *Jew in the American World*, 140–41.

55. Ibid.

56. Metropolitan Museum of Art, New York, "Myer Myers, Beaker (1770–90)," https://www.metmuseum.org/art/collection/search/431; and Schmitt-Korte and Price, "Nabataean Coinage," 130.

57. Geller, "New Sources for the Origins," 227; and De Sola Pool, *Portraits Etched in Stone*, 384.

58. Gyllenbok, *Encyclopaedia of Historical Metrology*, 1:2214.

59. Hyde, *The Gift*, 53.

60. Ibid., 52.

61. By the eighteenth century in some Ashkenazi and Mizrahi communities, the infant would be brought into the ceremony on such a tray, typically made of silver or copper, and the adult participants would bless and drink wine, typically from silver cups. These trays were often finely decorated with biblical scenes, particularly the Akedah, or binding of Isaac. The silver tray and wine glasses used at the ceremony echoed the coins' silver. The trays often belonged to the community rather than to individuals, in part because the expenses of the ceremony were beyond the finances of most members of Atlantic World Jewish communities. Regardless of who technically owned the silver, the metal symbolized transformation. In general, trays were not used for holding the firstborn in Western Sephardic communities, though silver trays were used in other ceremonies involving the Kohanim and ritual change. Thank you to Zachary Edinger, Shalom Vaz Dias, Aron Sterk, and Shalom Morris for answering questions about the use of silver trays in various Western Sephardic congregations and about the trays currently in synagogue collections. See Wein, *Living Jewish*, 20–21; Kadden and Kadden, *Teaching Jewish Life Cycle*, 5; Cardozo, *Jewish Family Celebrations*, 195; Klein, *Time to Be Born*, 225. See also the *Sacrifice of Isaac* tray owned by Pascal Jonnaert from Vienna (late eighteenth to early nineteenth century), http://www.ascasonline.org/ARTICOLOJUDAICA.html.

62. Hyde, *The Gift*, 54.

63. Barquist, *Myer Myers*, 186–87, 256.

64. Jewish Museum, New York, "Circumcision Shield and Probe (1765–75)," https://thejewishmuseum.org/collection/28349-circumcision-shield-and -probe.

65. Barquist, *Myer Myers*, 47, 137, 240.

66. Ibid., 241.

67. Ibid., 240.

68. Swierenga, *Forerunners*, 51.

69. Barquist, *Myer Myers*, 198–99.

70. Isaac Moses, receipt book, April 23 and September 31, 1786, pp. 51 and 80, PMFNY, AJHS.

71. Will of Isaac Moses, 1818, PMFNY, AJHS.

72. Ibid.; Will of Reyna Moses, 1824, *Record of Wills, 1665–1916*, vol. 58, 1821–25, pp. 487–90, New York Surrogate's Court (New York County), in *New York, Wills and Probate Records, 1659–1999*, https://www.ancestry.com /search/collections/usprobateny/; Isaac Moses estate inventory, 1818, PMFNY, AJHS. See also De Sola Pool, *Portraits Etched in Stone*, 390; and Krill, *Early American Decorative Arts*, 163.

73. De Sola Pool, *Portraits Etched in Stone*, 389.

74. Fitzroy Road was a country road in "the Bowery." According to Valentine's Manual, it "ran north from Greenwich Village; it started at the Southampton Road about the present 14th St. between 7th and 8th Aves. . . . ending at the cross road about the present 42nd St., midway between 8th and 9th Aves." (Brown, *Valentine's Manual of Old New York*, 102).

75. Will of Isaac Moses, 1818, PMFNY, AJHS; Will of Reyna Moses, 1824, https://www.ancestry.com/search/collections/usprobateny/; Isaac Moses estate inventory, 1818, PMFNY, AJHS.

76. "Items Relating to the Moses and Levy Families," 340.

77. De Sola Pool, *Portraits Etched in Stone*, 390–91.

78. Daiches-Dubens, "Eighteenth Century Anglo-Jewry," 143–69.

79. *Map of the City of New York*, 1860, https://www.loc.gov/item/2011593667/; Reed, *New York Elevated*, 20–21; Poor, *History of the Railroads and Canals of the United States*, 1:267.

80. Dawson, "'Heirlooms,'" 2–3.

81. Narrett, *Inheritance and Family Life in Colonial New York City*, 8.

82. Lillios, "Objects of Memory," 236.

83. Ibid.

84. Leibman, *Messianism, Secrecy, and Mysticism*, 172; and Groll, *Dutch Overseas*, 383.

85. Wees and Harvey, *Early American Silver*, 83.

86. Studnicki-Gizbert, *Nation upon the Ocean Sea*, 68.

87. Garraty and Carnes, *American National Biography*, 397; Marcus, *United States Jewry*, 1.63–64, 142–43; advertisement, *Daily Advertiser* (New York), January 2, 1795.

88. For more on Ashkenazi networks and merchant families during this era, see Pitock, "Separated from Us as Far as West," and her dissertation, "Commerce and Connection."

89. Stern, *First American Jewish Families*, 87, 209.

90. "Rachel Gratz Moses," in the Loeb Jewish Portrait Database, 2018,

http://loebjewishportraits.com/paintings/rachel-gratz-moses/.

91. Gilbert Stuart's portrait, *Rachel Gratz [Moses]* (1806), is located in the Rosenbach Museum and Library in Philadelphia. For other portraits, see London, *Miniatures and Silhouettes of Early American Jews*, 38, 39, 40, 41, 65, 123; and London, *Portraits of Jews by Gilbert Stuart*, 45, 53, 54, 66, 69, 71, plates 155 and 169.

92. Mordecai, *Recollections of My Aunt*, 12.

93. Rachel Gratz to Rebecca Gratz, June 21, 1803, Rachel Gratz, Letters (1802–5), Gratz family collection, APS.

94. Mordecai, *Recollections of My Aunt*, 16.

95. See Gratz family papers, AJHS.

96. Rachel Gratz to Rebecca Gratz, May 15, 1805, Gratz family papers, AJHS.

97. Rachel Gratz to Rebecca Gratz, May 22, 1806, Gratz family collection, APS.

98. Rachel Gratz to Rebecca Gratz, May 22, 1806, and May 29, 1806, Gratz family collection, APS.

99. Sarah is referred to in the letters as Saly, a common nickname.

100. Susan Sklaroff, *Rebecca Gratz and 19th-Century America*, http://rebeccagratz.blogspot.com/2010/04/gratz-sisters-solomon-moses.html.

101. Stern, *First American Jewish Families*, 87, 209.

102. Mordecai, *Recollections of My Aunt*, 16.

103. Ibid.

104. Stern, *First American Jewish Families*, 159, 209.

105. Ibid., 209.

106. Isaac Moses, receipt book, 1785–87, PMFNY, AJHS.

107. Joel, Isaacs, and Phillips, "Items Relating to Congregation Shearith Israel," 55.

108. Austen, *Emma*, 57.

109. Austen, *Pride and Prejudice*, 364.

110. To be sure, the new emphasis on romance meant some Jewish men also remained single, a point Jonathan Sarna brings home ("Louisa B. Hart," 96).

111. Sarna, *American Judaism*, 27, 45.

112. Stern, *First American Jewish Families*.

113. Hart, quoted in Sarna, "Louisa B. Hart," 96.

114. Fraser, *Gender, Race, and Family*, 153.

115. Ibid.

116. Shelly Zegart, "Old Maid, New Woman," *Quilt Digest* 4 (1986): 54–65.

117. Ashton, *Rebecca Gratz*, 92, 127, 247–48; and Congregation Shearith Israel, "Association for the Moral & Religious Instruction of Children of the Jewish Faith Meeting Minutes, 1838–1846," Sisterhood Records, CSIA.

118. For example, see the letters of the Gratz and Mordecai families: Mordecai family papers, 1649–1947, collection 00847, Wilson Library, University of North Carolina at Chapel Hill; Gratz family collection, no. 72, APS; Gratz family papers (Philadelphia), P-8, AJHS.

119. This trend can be seen in both the Gratz and Moses families (Ashton, *Rebecca Gratz*, 121).

120. Will of Isaac Moses, 1818, PMFNY, AJHS.

121. Will of Reyna Moses, 1824, https://www.ancestry.com/search/collec tions/usprobateny/.

122. "Measuring Worth—Relative Worth Comparators and Data Sets," 2019, https://measuringworth.com/.

123. Will of Reyna Moses, 1824, https://www.ancestry.com/search/collec tions/usprobateny/.

124. Ibid., 489.

125. Will of Sarah Moses, 1860, *Record of Wills, 1665–1916*, vol. 131–32, 1858–62, pp. 109–13, New York Surrogate's Court (New York County), in *New York, Wills and Probate Records, 1659–1999*, https://www.ancestry.com /search/collections/usprobateny/.

126. Mordecai, *Recollections of My Aunt*, 16–17; Fifth census of the United States, 1830, New York Ward 5, 96.316, record group 29, Records of the Bureau of the Census, NARA, https://www.ancestry.com/search/collectio ns/1830usfedcenancestry/; Stern, *First American Jewish Families*, 209.

127. Will of Sarah Moses, 1860, *Record of Wills, 1665–1916*, vol. 131–32, 1858–62, pp. 109–13, New York Surrogate's Court (New York County), in *New York, Wills and Probate Records, 1659–1999*, https://www.ancestry.com /search/collections/usprobateny/.

128. Stern, *First American Jewish Families*, 27.

129. Will of Abraham Rodriguez Brandon, 1860, *Record of Wills, 1665–1916*, vol. 129–130, 1858–62, p. 418, New York Surrogate's Court (New York County), in *New York, Wills and Probate Records, 1659–1999*, https://www .ancestry.com/search/collections/usprobateny/.

130. Jennifer Lewis, email messages to the author, Feb. 8 and 10, 2018.

131. Will of Esther Benazaken, 1790, Wills and Administrations, vols. 39–42, 1786–99, pp. 382–83, https://www.ancestry.com/search/collections /usprobateny/. See further examples in Hershkowitz, "Wills of Early New York Jews," 109, 119, 132, 135, 138, 141; and Brandmark, "Study of Wills in New York City."

132. Wees and Harvey, *Early American Silver*, 84.

133. Stern, *First American Jewish Families*, 209.

134. Ibid., 264.

135. Lionel Moses, "McKim, Mead, and White: A History," *American Architect and Building News*, May 24, 1922, 424; and Bradley, "Tribeca North Historic District Designation Report," 141–42.

136. Clearwater and Avery, *American Silver*, xxiii.

137. Stern, *First American Jewish Families*, 209; Wees and Harvey, *Early American Silver*, 84.

138. Barquist, *Myer Myers*, 186; "Lot 108. A Silver Beaker. Mark of Myer Myers, New York, 1770–90," Christie's, 2019, https://www.christies.com/lotfind er/Lot/a-silver-beaker-mark-of-myer-myers-5867593-details.aspx; "Catalog of 1959 Exhibits," 31.

139. Lindsey, "Displaying Islamic Art at the Metropolitan" and "Medieval Art and The Cloisters," Metropolitan Museum of Art, 2019, https://www .metmuseum.org/about-the-met/curatorial-departments/medieval-art -and-the-cloisters.

140. The Metropolitan Museum is not alone in this practice of display: with the exception of historical or ethnic museums, Jewish objects are almost unilaterally situated next to non-Jewish objects. The North Carolina Museum of Art is an exception to this trend in that it has a "Jewish wing." I am grateful to the planners and participants of the *Wandering Objects: Collecting and Interpreting Jewish Things* conference at the University of North Carolina (November 11–13, 2018) for this insight, particularly the keynote address of Barbara Kirshenblatt-Gimblett.

141. Wees and Harvey, *Early American Silver*, 83.

142. Heckscher, *Metropolitan Museum of Art*, 54.

143. Michael Kimmelman, "Avoiding the Clean-White-Box Syndrome," *New York Times*, Aug. 13, 1991, H32.

144. A wonderful exception to this is Jane Weitzman, a collector who primarily collects objects by women.

145. John Cotton Dana (from *The New Museum*, 1917), quoted in Duncan, *Civilizing Rituals*, 65.

146. Ibid.

147. Sandlin, "Consumption, Gender Stereotypes," 160.

148. Fischer and Arnold, "More Than a Labor of Love," 334.

CHAPTER THREE

1. Series XII, photographs, undated, 1865–88, PMFNY, AJHS.

2. Gelber, *Hobbies*, 5, 63, 100–106, 157–61; and Smith, "Family Webs," 7.

3. Blanche Moses correspondence, PMFNY, AJHS.

4. Gregory Rodriguez, "Roots of Genealogy Craze," *USAToday*, May 12, 2014.

5. Sorin, *Time for Building*; and Rischin, *Jews in North America*, 15.

6. As Roger Daniels notes, prior to 1924, people from parts of Asia also experienced both restriction and anti-Asian violence clearly intended to discourage immigration and settlement (*Guarding the Golden Door*, 20–21, 23, 40–41).

7. Weil, *Family Trees*, 112.

8. Ibid.

9. Ibid., 135.

10. Blanche Moses correspondence, PMFNY, AJHS. For more on the role of AJHS in the colonial revival, see Hoberman, *Hundred Acres of America*, 32–34.

11. Blanche Moses correspondence, PMFNY, AJHS.

12. Blanche Moses genealogy research, PMFNY, AJHS.

13. Stern, *First American Jewish Families*, 27.

14. Will of George Gill, Nov. 25, 1801, RB 4 53.133, BDA; Will of Hannah Esther Lopez, Oct. 23, 1815, RL 1/6, BDA. Hoberman, Leibman, and Surowitz-Israel, *Jews in the Americas*, 2.

15. Fourth census of the United States, 1820, New York Ward 1, M33_77, image 18, p. 14, Records of the Bureau of the Census, NARA.

16. Kenvin, *This Land of Liberty*, 1.

17. Fields and Fields, *Racecraft*, 18.

18. Ibid., 19.
19. Leibman, "Material of Race," forthcoming.
20. Colwill, "Sex, Savagery, and Slavery," 199.
21. Brodkin, *How Jews Became White Folks*, 60.
22. Goldstein, *Price of Whiteness*, 16–18; and Leibman, "Material of Race," forthcoming.
23. Leibman, "Material of Race," forthcoming.
24. Gilman, *Franz Kafka*, 14; and Thackeray, *Vanity Fair*, 4, 162.
25. Gilman, *Franz Kafka*, 14.
26. Fields and Fields, *Racecraft*, 25. Emphasis original.
27. Barbados Church Records, 1637–1887, https://www.familysearch.org/search/collection/1923399.
28. Will of George Gill, Nov. 25, 1801, RB 4 53.133, BDA; Will of Hannah Esther Lopez, Oct. 23, 1815, RL 1/6, BDA; Deed between Hannah Esther Lopez and George Gill, entered Oct. 15, 1801, written August 17, 1801, deeds 218 (1801): 22. R/1, BDA.
29. Watson, "Shifting Identities," 207–8.
30. Will of Hannah Esther Lopez, Oct. 23, 1815, RL 1/6, BDA; Will of George Gill, Nov. 25, 1801, RB 4 53.133, BDA.
31. The first time that she appears with the last name Brandon is in the minute books of Congregation Mikveh Israel of Philadelphia in 1818 ("Correspondence 1820–1830," Minute Book and Correspondence 1782–1890, 222/51, Philadelphia, PA—Congregation Mikve Israel. Manuscript Collection no. 552, AJA). Despite the name change, there is no *ketubah* for her and Abraham Rodrigues Brandon in Barbados, Suriname, London, Amsterdam, New York, or Philadelphia.
32. Handler, *Unappropriated People*, 201; and Forde, "Family Inheritance Provisions," 115–25.
33. Deed between Hannah Esther Lopez and Abraham Rodrigues Brandon, entered Aug. 20, 1800, deeds 212 (1801): 459, R/1, BDA; Deed between Hannah Esther Lopez and Abraham Rodrigues Brandon, entered Aug. 5, 1802, deeds 219 (1801): 9, R/1, BDA. If Esther had been freed before her children were born, they would not have been enslaved to Hannah Esther Lopez.
34. Minutes of the Mahamad, NPIGS, Dec. 29, 1812, inv. nr. 5, NA; and Minute books of the Mahamad of Nidhe Israel, 1790–1826, III.6, 4521/D/01/01/003, LMA.
35. Marley, *Historic Cities of the Americas*, 811; Vink, *Creole Jews Negotiating Community*, 141, 263–64; Cohen, *Jews in Another Environment*, 164–70.
36. Abraham Rodrigues Brandon would go on to have an extensive family with Sarah Simpson Wood after Esther's death. These children were also raised as Jews. In addition, slave registers, manumission records, and his will suggest that Abraham Rodrigues Brandon would have several other natural children by enslaved women on the island (Slave Registers of Former British Colonial Dependencies, 1813–34, https://www.ancestry.com/search/collections/britishslaves/; and Will of Abraham Rodrigues Brandon, June 17, 1831, BDA).

37. Minute books of the Mahamad of Nidhe Israel, 1790–1826, II.27, 29, 44; III.29, 30, 31, 40, 41, 44, 45, 79, 94, 123, 124, 125, 126, 127, 130, 133, 136, 4521/D/01/01/002, 4521/D/01/01/003, LMA; and Watson, "Shifting Identities," 212, 220–21.

38. London, *Miniatures and Silhouettes of Early American Jews*, 34; and Lucien Wolf, "Recollections of a Veteran," *Jewish Chronicle*, September 15, 1893, 12.

39. Rothery and French, *Making Men*, 15.

40. Fields and Fields, *Racecraft*, 25.

41. Rothery and French, *Making Men*, 15.

42. Glover, *Elite Women and Polite Society*, 27.

43. Ibid., 27–28, 32.

44. Kirsch, *Benjamin Disraeli*, 131; Endelman, *Broadening Jewish History*, 78, 106–8, 205; Wolf, "Recollections of a Veteran," 12; Black, *JFS*, 17.

45. Glover, *Elite Women and Polite Society*, 27, 32.

46. Minute books of the Mahamad of Nidhe Israel, 1790–1826, II.34, 4521/D/01/01/002, LMA. See also Mocatta, *Address to the Congregation of Portuguese Jews*, 10, 24.

47. Harris, "Anglo-Jewry's Experience of Secondary Education," 106; and Brown, "Jews of Gravesend," 121–22.

48. And hence so did the grandchildren of London's Moses Vita [Haim] Montefiore (1712–89).

49. Land and Greener, "Lineage of the Montefiore Family."

50. For a later example of these connections in work, see Kleeblatt, Wertkin, and Black, *Jewish Heritage in American Folk Art*, 49–50.

51. Brown, "Jews of Gravesend," 121–23; and Census returns of England and Wales, 1841, Kew, Surrey, England: National Archives of the UK, Public Record Office, https://www.ancestry.com/search/collections/uki1841/.

52. Ashton, *Rebecca Gratz*, 20.

53. De Sola Pool, *Old Faith in the New World*, 362–63. Emphasis original.

54. Congregation Shearith Israel, "Association for the Moral & Religious Instruction of Children of the Jewish Faith Meeting Minutes, 1838–1846," Sisterhood Records, CSIA; and Stern, *First American Jewish Families*, 159, 209.

55. Caffrey, "Jewels Above All Prize," 161; and Barratt and Zabar, *American Portrait Miniatures*, 38.

56. Lloyd, *Portrait Miniatures from Scottish Private Collections*, 9; and Frank, *Love and Loss*, 190.

57. See, for example, the instance of Mary Todd Lincoln's parents and Kitty and James Madison (Sheumaker, *Love Entwined*, 15; and Broadwater, *James Madison*, 114).

58. Grootenboer, *Treasuring the Gaze*, 11, 22–23, 42–46.

59. Whittock, *Miniature Painter's Manual*, 30–32.

60. Ibid., 31–32.

61. Elena Arias Riera, "The Collection of Miniatures in the Museo del Prado," Museo Nacional del Prado, 2019, https://www.museodelprado.es/en/learn/research/studies-and-restorations/resource/the-collection-of-miniatures-in-the-museo-del/e8b31ab8-746e-46d7-a031-329d808a4b4e.

62. "Making a Miniature," Gibbes Museum of Art, 2016, http://www.gibbes museum.org/miniatures/; "Portrait Miniatures: Materials & Techniques."

63. "Making a Miniature," Gibbes Museum of Art, 2016, http://www.gibbes museum.org/miniatures/.

64. John Robinson in Philadelphia, who painted both miniatures and full-sized oils from 1817 to 1824, charged $25–$200 for miniatures and only $20–$100 for larger portraits in oil (Barratt and Zabar, *American Portrait Miniatures*, 75).

65. Loeb Jewish Portrait Database, http://loebjewishportraits.com/paint ings/; and Brilliant, *Facing the New World*, 23–97.

66. Rubens, "Francis Town of Bond Street," 102–4; and Edgar Samuel, "Costa [*née* Mendes], Catherine [Rachel] da," *Oxford Dictionary of National Biography*, https://doi.org/10.1093/ref:odnb/72024.

67. Whittock, *Miniature Painter's Manual*, 8, 33.

68. Ibid., 35.

69. Riera, "Collection of Miniatures," https://www.museodelprado.es/en /learn/research/studies-and-restorations/resource/the-collection-of -miniatures-in-the-museo-del/e8b31ab8-746e-46d7-a031-329d808a4b4e; and Whittock, *Miniature Painter's Manual*, 36.

70. Whittock, *Miniature Painter's Manual*, 35–36.

71. Ibid., 40.

72. Riera, "Collection of Miniatures," https://www.museodelprado.es/en /learn/research/studies-and-restorations/resource/the-collection-of -miniatures-in-the-museo-del/e8b31ab8-746e-46d7-a031-329d808a4b4e.

73. Ibid.

74. Gilman, *Making the Body Beautiful*, 89.

75. Barratt and Zabar, *American Portrait Miniatures*, 32; Kelly, *Republic of Taste*, 105; Johnson, *American Portrait Miniatures in the Manney Collection*, 21–22.

76. See the portrait of Mrs. Pierre Toussaint by Anthony Meucci from ca. 1825 at NYHS, and the portrait of Elizabeth Freeman, "Mumbet," by Susan Anne Livingston Redley Sedwick from 1811 at the Massachusetts Historical Society.

77. For an example in oil, see Jacques Guillaume Lucien Amans, *Creole in a Red Headdress* (ca. 1840) in the Historic New Orleans Collection; and for an example in pastel, see *Portrait of a Young Woman* by an unknown artist from the late eighteenth century, at the Saint Louis Art Museum. Likewise, the *casta* paintings of eighteenth-century New Spain tended to be painted in oil on canvas (see examples in Katzew, *Casta Painting*, 12, 31, 100, 132, 157).

78. For examples of the perfected Indian miniatures, see the display titled "Twelve miniatures depicting Mughal rulers of India" at the Victoria and Albert Museum, London. An early exception is John Smart's *An Indian Prince* (1788), which displays a similar technique to that used by later artists. Ironically, Smart's technique was developed while painting portraits of princes under house arrest (Eaton, "Art of Colonial Despotism," 88).

79. Whittock, *Miniature Painter's Manual*, 52–53.

80. Ibid., 36.

81. Ibid., 41; King, *Essence of Liberty*, 203; Hodges and Brown, *"Pretends to Be Free,"* 32, 158, 189, 191. The use of the term "yellow" as a descriptor for the skin color of runaway slaves can also be seen in other areas of the Americas; see Forbes, *Africans and Native Americans*, 227–28.
82. Whittock, *Miniature Painter's Manual*, 30, 54.
83. Lafont, "How Skin Color Became a Racial Marker," 90, 95, 98.
84. Fields and Fields, *Racecraft*, 27.
85. John Wesley Jarvis, *Abraham Rodrigues Brandon* (ca. 1824), oil on canvas, 30¼ × 25 in., Museum of the City of New York.
86. Whittock, *Miniature Painter's Manual*, 41.
87. Ibid., 44.
88. Ibid., 54.
89. Fields and Fields, *Racecraft*, 25.
90. Leibman, "Material of Race."
91. Cunnington, *English Women's Clothing*, 34, 38–54.
92. Byrde, *Nineteenth Century Fashion*, 23.
93. Ibid.
94. Leibman, "Material of Race," forthcoming; Hollander, *Sex and Suits*, 92; Kelly, *Beau Brummell*, 101–2; Bindman, *Ape to Apollo*, 225.
95. Zieseniss and Le Bourhis, *Age of Napoleon*, vii–xi, 71, 199–200, 231–32; DeLorme and Chevallier, *Joséphine and the Arts of the Empire*, 167–69; Jaher, *Jews and the Nation*, 103–6. For examples of other images, see also Firmin Massot, *Portrait de l'Impératrice Joséphine de France* (1812), private collection, https://commons.wikimedia.org/wiki/File:Firmin_Massot_-_Jos%C3%A9phine_de_France.jpg; François Gérard, *Joséphine en costume de sacre* [Joséphine in coronation costume] (1807–8), Musée national du Château de Fontainebleau; Pierre-Paul Prud'hon, *L'impératrice Joséphine* [The empress Josephine] (ca. 1805), Louvre.
96. "Items Relating to the Moses and Levy Families," 23–24.
97. Cunnington, *English Women's Clothing*, 28.
98. *La Belle Assemblée*, March 1808, 4:95, quoted in Ribeiro, *Art of Dress*, 118.
99. Thomas Sully, *Sally Etting* (1808), Jewish Museum of New York; Anna Claypoole Peale, *Sally Etting* (ca. 1815–18), Rosenbach Museum and Library, Philadelphia; Gilbert Stuart, *Eliza Myers* (ca. 1808), Chrysler Museum of Art, Norfolk, VA.
100. DuPlessis, "Sartorial Sorting in the Colonial Caribbean," 351, 355–57, 365. See also Martin, *Caribbean History*, 84–86. Gage argues that in Brazil, enslaved women's clothing normally covered the chest and that images suggesting otherwise are part of anti-slavery propaganda or exoticizing efforts; notably, descriptions of women's chests were placed in advertisements for runaway slaves ("Forced Crossing," 112, 120, 124).
101. Whittock, *Miniature Painter's Manual*, 50.
102. Ibid., 52–53.
103. Ibid., 40.
104. Toledano, Christovich, and Derbes, *New Orleans Architecture*, 97; and Borelli, *She Is Cuba*, 34–35.
105. Shelly, "Black and Catholic," 6.

106. Lee, *Memoir of Pierre Toussaint*, 16, 121–22.

107. Cady and Webber, *Year with American Saints*, 199. See also Shelley, "Black and Catholic in Nineteenth Century New York," 13.

108. Hoberman, Leibman, and Surowitz-Israel, *Jews in the Americas*, 110–11.

109. Wegenstein, *Cosmetic Gaze*, 192.

110. Brilliant, *Facing the New World*, 66–67.

111. Vink, *Creole Jews Negotiating Community*, 165.

112. Grootenboer, *Treasuring the Gaze*, 11.

113. Hartman, *Scenes of Subjection*, 81.

114. Nichols on Laura Mulvey's analysis of the gaze, quoted in Nichols, *Movies and Methods*, 304.

115. Reiman, *Power of Body Language*, 58, 95–96, 254.

116. Bastiaans, "Detecting Difference," 245. See also Hartman, *Scenes of Subjection*, 88–89.

117. Reiman, *Power of Body Language*, 86–87, 109–10.

118. Ibid., 62, 253–54.

119. Grootenboer, *Treasuring the Gaze*.

120. Whittock, *Miniature Painter's Manual*, 56–57.

121. Marriage license of Joshua Moses and Sarah Rodrigues Brandon, March 17, 1817, 4521/A/02/03/009, LMA; and Joshua Moses, family record book, 1817–20, PMFNY, AJHS.

122. Will of Abraham Rodrigues Brandon, June 17, 1831, BDA; and "Measuring Worth—Relative Worth Comparators and Data Sets," 2019, https://measuringworth.com/.

123. Phillips, "Sketch of the Spanish and Portuguese Congregation," 212.

124. Sale of seats of the synagogue, March 6, 1820, minutes of the trustees, records of Congregation Shearith Israel, 1759–1932, MF-1e, microfilm, reel 2, microdex 1, AJA.

125. *Longworth's American Almanac*, 107, 415; and De Sola Pool, *Portraits Etched in Stone*, 426–27.

126. Sale of seats of the synagogue, March 3, 1828, minutes of the trustees, records of Congregation Shearith Israel, 1759–1932, MF-1e, microfilm, reel 2, microdex 1, AJA. Only members could purchase seats. At the same meeting Brandon purchased a seat in the women's section for his wife that was adjacent to the seats of her unmarried sisters. For more on the story of Isaac Lopez Brandon and his bid for civil rights in Barbados, see Leibman and May, "Making Jews."

127. Fourth census of the United States, 1820, New York Ward 1, M33_77, image 18, p. 14, Records of the Bureau of the Census, NARA.

128. I am grateful to Hasia Diner for making this distinction clear to me. In 1706, the provincial assembly passed a law stating, "Negroes only shall be slaves" (Harris, *In the Shadow of Slavery*, 28).

129. Wilkie, "United States Population by Race," 141; and Hickman, "Devil and the One Drop Rule," 1187.

130. Isaac applied for citizenship on June 27, 1826, and was naturalized on April 22, 1829 (*Soundex Index to Petitions for Naturalizations Filed in Federal, State, and Local Courts in New York City, 1792–1906*, M1674, NARA).

131. According to Isaac Moses's receipt book (1785–87), the family had once

owned slaves, though they do not appear in the 1790 census (PMFNY, AJHS). See also First census of the United States, 1790, record group 29, Records of the Bureau of the Census, NARA; Fourth census of the United States, 1820, New York Ward 1, M33_77, image 18, p. 14, Records of the Bureau of the Census, NARA; Third census of the United States, 1810, record group 29, Records of the Bureau of the Census, NARA.

132. Bacchus, *Utilization, Misuse, and Development of Human Resources*, 118; and Handler, Newton, Welch, and Wiltshire, *Freedmen of Barbados*, 2.

133. Ingersoll, *Mammon and Manon in Early New Orleans*, 403.

134. Stern, *First American Jewish Families*, 27, 209.

135. Series VII: Isaac Moses Jr. (1819–1889), 1833–89 (box 2, folder 2); Series VIII: Israel Moses, M.D. (1821–1870), 1847–91 (box 2, folder 3), PMFNY, AJHS.

136. Vietrogoski, "Case of Mr. J. P. Barnett," 1–3. Barnett's experience points to how temporally bound Sarah's story was in history and how the fluidity she experienced would evaporate ten to fifteen years after her death. I am grateful to Hasia Diner for reinforcing this point.

137. Stern, *First American Jewish Families*, 209, 264; and *Metropolis Explained and Illustrated*, 37.

138. As Robin DiAngelo notes, "Much of white supremacy's power is drawn from its invisibility, the taken-for-granted aspects that underwrite all other political and social contracts" (*White Fragility*, 29).

139. De Sola Pool, *Portraits Etched in Stone*, 386–89.

140. For an example of this issue, see Hobbs, *Chosen Exile*, 4, 37, 62; and Cross, *Secret Daughter*, 130.

141. *OED Online*, s.v. "[P]ass, v.," https://www.oed.com/view/Entry/138429?rs key=mskNNh&result=6&isAdvanced=false#eid.

142. Joel, Isaacs, and Phillips. "Items Relating to Congregation Shearith Israel," 55.

143. Fields and Fields, *Racecraft*, 25. Emphasis mine.

144. Fernheimer, *Stepping into Zion*, 65. Recent outrage at the Israeli rabbinate for possibly using "DNA tests in cases where the Jewishness of individuals seeking to marry is in doubt" suggests there may be a time when the use of DNA blurs religious lines (Judy Maltz, "Israeli Rabbinate Accused of Using DNA Testing to Prove Jewishness," *Haaretz*, February 4, 2019, https://www.haaretz.com).

145. Kahn, "Who Are the Jews?," 923; and Gilman, "Thilo Sarrazin and the Politics of Race," 49.

146. Cohen, "Sephardic Phenomenon," 43.

147. For more on the subject of "pure Sephardi," or *Sefardi tahor*, see Cohen and Stein, *Sephardi Lives*, 346; Haskell, "From the Editor," 1; Efron, *German Jewry and the Allure of the Sephardic*, 50.

CHAPTER FOUR

1. Climate Data Online for NY City Central Park, NY US, Usw0009472, National Centers for Environmental Education, information for June 6,

1892, sent to author in email, March 10, 2019.

2.   Kaganoff, "AJHS at 90," 466–67.

3.   Ibid., 466; "Constitution," 138–43.

4.   As Mordecai herself notes, Simon was one of the "richest and most promi-nent Indian [*sic*] traders in the province" (Mordecai, "Notes," 121–22). Although Miriam's younger brother, Gratz, would publish an article in the journal in 1897, a woman would not author a full article in the *Publica-tions of the American Jewish Historical Society* until 1909, when Rosalie S. Philips wrote "A Burial Place for the Jewish Nation Forever."

5.   Stern, *First American Jewish Families*, 106.

6.   Mordecai, *Recollections of My Aunt.*

7.   Ibid.; and Stern, *First American Jewish Families*, 106.

8.   Mordecai, *Recollections of My Aunt*, 9.

9.   Irving and M. J. K., "Rebecca Gratz," 189–90.

10.   Philipson, "Some Unpublished Letters of Rebecca Gratz," 53–60. Intrigu-ingly, Rose (Schloss) Frank did appear in the Necrology section in 1910 (Friedenwald, "Rose S. Frank," 201–2). I am also not counting the 1914 article on "The Original of Scott's Rebecca," as the primary interest in the piece is on the *male* writer as a lens for thinking about which women are interesting.

11.   Lifschutz, review of *Union Pioneer*, by Abraham Bisno and Joel Seidman.

12.   Porter, "Rosa Sonnenschein and 'The American Jewess.'"

13.   Wenger, review of *Sweatshop Strife*, by Ruth A. Frager; and McCune, "Social Workers in the 'Muskeljudentum.'"

14.   Stern, *First American Jewish Families*, 87, 106.

15.   Sarah Ann donated the book she wrote about her aunt and a report writ-ten by her husband to the AJHS in December of 1892, but it is unclear who donated the other items related to her or when. It is possible that Sarah Ann donated them herself. Tanya Elder, email message to author, March 13, 2019.

16.   Galvin, "Commentary," 311.

17.   Allan, *Commonplace Books and Reading*, 35–45, 266; Hess, "Commonplace-Book Stylistics," 16; Katz, *Cuneiform to Computer*, 71.

18.   Havens, *Commonplace Books*, 8.

19.   Ibid.; Cerezo-Román, Wessman, and Williams, "Introduction," 17; An-drews and Freund, *Copious and Critical Latin-English Lexicon*, 1062.

20.   Havens, *Commonplace Books*, 8.

21.   To be sure, men also created commonplace books during this era as well (Hess, "Commonplace-Book Stylistics," 5–6).

22.   Cootz, *Marriage, a History*, 145–46. See also Ashton, *Rebecca Gratz*, 55–56, 239, 242, 252; the letters between the Gratz sisters and between Rebecca Gratz and her friend Maria Fenno in the Gratz family collection, APS; and the Gratz family papers, AJHS, respectively.

23.   Austen, *Emma*, 75–82.

24.   Havens, *Commonplace Books*, 54.

25.   Ibid., 14.

26.   Sarah Ann Hays Mordecai collection, 1823–88, P-70, AJHS.

27. Rosenthal, *Race Mixture*, 102. A famous proponent of such a view of flowers is Emily Dickinson, whose "herbarium" was published and whose interest in botany has been richly analyzed. Although not as extensive as Dickinson's collection, a small "herbarium" owned by Sarah Ann was donated to AJHS. See Dickinson, *Emily Dickinson's Herbarium*; Farr and Carter, *Gardens of Emily Dickinson* "Material used for illustration," n.d., box 1, folder 5, Sarah Ann Hays Mordecai collection, AJHS.

28. Benedict, "Paradox of the Anthology," 233.

29. Woodgate, Pratt, Makinson, Lim, Reynolds, and Chittka, "Life-Long Radar Tracking of Bumblebees."

30. Marcus, *American Jewish Woman: 1654–1980*, 23.

31. Stern, *First American Jewish Families*, 106.

32. Rosenbloom, *Biographical Dictionary of Early America Jews*, 60.

33. As Sarah Ann herself notes, her aunt Rebecca was "the head of her brothers' establishment" and ran their household just a few doors down from where the Hayses lived (Mordecai, *Recollections of My Aunt*, 18).

34. Bingham, *Mordecai*, 242.

35. Singer, *Jewish Encyclopedia*, 12:267.

36. Ibid.

37. Census of the State of New York, 1865, New York State Archives, Microfilm, https://www.ancestry.com/search/collections/general-7218/.

38. "Temple Beth Shalom Marks Centennial," *Troy Record*, March 5, 1966.

39. Mordecai, *Recollections of My Aunt*, 11; and Ashton, *Rebecca Gratz*, 121–70.

40. Straub, *Rise of New Media*, 30–31. Like Victorian literary anthologies, these collections were "designed for 'dip, sip, and skip' reading," or in this case, dip, sip, and clip (Benedict, "Paradox of the Anthology," 232).

41. Havens, *Commonplace Books*, 58.

42. Lange was an older, married gentleman who lived nearby (Fourth census of the United States, 1820, Philadelphia, Lower Delaware Ward, p. 252, Records of the Bureau of the Census, NARA). The handwriting is smeared, but he is my best guess as the writer. Dr. Lange's office was also nearby at 256 Front St. (*Philadelphia Directory and Stranger's Guide*, 82).

43. Segura, quoted in Ambrose and Harris, *Fundamentals of Typography*, 50.

44. Rabinowitz Deer, *Exploring Typography*, 14.

45. Jones, *Gothic Effigy*, 182.

46. Nesbitt, *Lettering*, 118–20, 146–47.

47. Thornton, *Handwriting in America*, 65.

48. This quote from Voltaire is cited in "Points in Composition," *Godey's Lady's Book*, October 1833.

49. Robinson, *Philadelphia Directory for 1804*.

50. Salm, *Women's Painted Furniture*, 43.

51. Ibid.; and Laura Fecych Sprague, "Schoolgirl Art from the Misses Martin's School for Young Ladies in Portland, Maine," *AFA News*, September 6, 2011.

52. Salm, *Women's Painted Furniture*, 43–44, 179–81.

53. Francia, *Series of Progressive Lessons*, 28, plate 12.

54. "Written in the First Leaf of a Friend's Album," *London Magazine*, Mar.

1821, 267–68; later reprinted in Barton, *Poetic Vigils*, 118.

55. Parker, *Literary Magazines and British Romanticism*, 15.

56. Ibid.

57. Ibid.

58. Ashton, "Shifting Veils," 96.

59. Mordecai, *Recollections of My Aunt*, 14; and Ashton, *Rebecca Gratz*, 21.

60. Jewish women who earned their living as educators included not only Sarah Ann and her daughters but her sisters-in-law in the Mordecai family. Other famous (but unrelated) Jewish female educators in Philadelphia include Simha Peixotto and Rachel Peixotto Pyke. Gratz also advised Jewish women in Charleston, Savannah, and Baltimore on how to open Jewish schools (Ashton, *Rebecca Gratz*, 21).

61. Bingham, *Mordecai*, 260.

62. Reis, *Damned Women*, 2–3, 5, 12–54.

63. Petrino, "Nineteenth-Century American Women's Poetry," 123.

64. Ibid.

65. Camfield, "Moral Aesthetics of Sentimentality," 325, 339.

66. Ibid., 336.

67. Ibid.

68. Manuscript commonplace book, pp. 15–16, Sarah Ann Hays Mordecai Collection, box 1, folder 1, AJHS.

69. Rachel Gratz to Rebecca Gratz, May 22, 1806, and May 29, 1806, Gratz family papers, APS.

70. McMahon, "While Our Souls Together Blend," 67.

71. Ibid.

72. Ibid.

73. Castronovo, *Oxford Handbook of Nineteenth-Century American Literature*, 258.

74. De Jong, introduction to *Sentimentalism in Nineteenth-Century America*, 1.

75. Philipson, *Letters of Rebecca Gratz*, 85.

76. Hess, "Common-Place Stylistics," [death and mourning:] 5, 24, 51, 119; [immortality and afterlife:] 35, 58, 128, 131; [resurrection:] 131; [relics:] 50, 185.

77. Sontag, *Illness as Metaphor*, 32.

78. Day, *Consumptive Chic*, 149; and Dubos and Dubos, *White Plague*, 58.

79. Bewell, *Romanticism and Colonial Disease*, 185.

80. Ibid.

81. This belief in the productivity of sharing pain almost certainly has roots in Protestant American visions of the work of Christ. Most Jewish discussions of martyrdom emphasize *overcoming* or enduring pain, yet to be sure, the prophetic works that inspired the Christian understanding of the messiah do emphasize the important role that sharing pain plays in cosmic redemption (Shepkaru, *Jewish Martyrs*, 60, 73, 258–59, 270; and Ozarowski, "'Bikur Cholim,'" 64).

82. De Jong, introduction to *Sentimentalism in Nineteenth-Century America*, 1.

83. Hendler, *Public Sentiments*, 125.

84. Ibid.

85. McMahon, "While Our Souls Together Blend," 70.

86. Ibid., 71.

87. Ashton, *Rebecca Gratz*, 46.

88. Mordecai, *Recollections of My Aunt*, 7.

89. See the many examples included in the Mordecai family papers, University of North Carolina at Chapel Hill; Miriam Gratz Moses Cohen papers, 1824–64, #2639, Southern Historical Collection, University of North Carolina at Chapel Hill; Philipson, *Letters of Rebecca Gratz*; Rebecca Gratz papers, 1797–1863, NYHS, AJHS, and University of North Carolina at Chapel Hill.

90. Sarna, *American Judaism*, 27, 45.

91. Hoberman, Leibman, and Surowitz-Israel, *Jews in the Americas*, 401; and Stern, *First American Jewish Families*, 106.

92. Castronovo, *Oxford Handbook of Nineteenth-Century American Literature*, 258.

93. Ibid.

94. Straub, *Rise of New Media*, 31.

95. See the English tea caddy lid with an insect motif painted by a young woman of the same era with a nearly identical butterfly (Salm, *Women's Painted Furniture*, 87).

96. Marcus, *American Jewish Woman: 1654–1980*, 23.

97. Disraeli, *Vivian Grey*, 2:475.

98. Schwartz, *Disraeli's Fiction*, 10.

99. Along with her six siblings, Miriam lived with Rebecca Gratz after her mother's death in 1823 (Ashton, *Rebecca Gratz*, 138; Stern, *First American Jewish Families*, 87; Mordecai, *Recollections of My Aunt*, 16).

100. As Molendijk notes, da Costa saw no conflict between these two identities, claiming, "I remained (no, I first truly became) an Israelite at the moment that I—through the grace of God and Saviour of my fathers—confessed to be a Christian" ("Rhetorics and Politics of the Conversion," 74, 81).

101. These inclusions are from men such as Mr. Murray, Joshua Barney, Mr. James Caldwell, Antonio Rousseau, W. F. Krumbhaar, Dillon Drake, Charles Fenno Hoffman, Dr. R. E. Griffiths, R. Emmet Robinson, Mr. Lee, Edmund Byrne, and "Her Doctor."

102. Ashton, *Rebecca Gratz*, 66, 79–82.

103. Manuscript commonplace book, p. 108, Sarah Ann Hays Mordecai Collection, box 1, folder 1, AJHS.

104. Not all of the entries were signed by the author or annotated by Sarah Ann to indicate who wrote them. Either Alfred did not write in the book, or his handwriting was clear enough that Sarah Ann did not need to worry she would forget over time who wrote it.

105. Ashton, *Rebecca Gratz*, 13.

106. Alfred was not the only one in his family to grow up indifferent to Judaism. Several of his siblings and their children either converted to Christianity or flirted with conversion (Bingham, *Mordecai*, 100–101, 134–36, 155, 177, 195–96, 207, 312).

107. Ibid., 105–6.

108. Bingham, "American, Jewish, Southern, Mordecai," 62.

109. Bingham, *Mordecai*, 237. See also Berman, *Last of the Jews?*, 91; Marcus, *United States Jewry*, 1:713.

110. Bingham, *Mordecai*, 237.
111. Kaplan, "Jewish Profile of the Spanish-Portuguese Community," 236.
112. Mordecai, *Recollections of My Aunt*, 9; and Philipson, *Letters of Rebecca Gratz*, 325, respectively.
113. Philipson, *Letters of Rebecca Gratz*, 397.
114. Bingham, *Mordecai*, 242–43; Philipson, *Letters of Rebecca Gratz*, xvi.
115. Bingham, *Mordecai*, 236.
116. Ibid., 242; and Davis, *Papers of Jefferson Davis*, 5:124–25.
117. Bingham, *Mordecai*, 242–43. Jefferson Davis and Sarah Ann Hays Mordecai had exchanged letters before the war.
118. Ibid., 243, 245.
119. Ibid., 247.
120. Ibid.
121. Ibid.
122. Elizabeth Blair Lee to Samuel Phillips Lee, June 1, 1861, in Laas, *Wartime Washington*, 41.
123. Bingham, *Mordecai*, 248.
124. Evans, *American Experience*, 25.
125. Bingham, *Mordecai*, 248, 250.
126. Ibid., 260.
127. Ibid., 250; see also p. 236.
128. Today, Alfred is even featured on the cemetery's sign at the Federal Street Burial Ground, second Mikveh Israel cemetery, Philadelphia.
129. Stern, *First American Jewish Families*, 200.
130. Faust, *This Republic of Suffering*, 3, 102, 180, 274; Eighth census of the United States, 1860, M653 722, Records of the Bureau of the Census, NARA.
131. Stern, *First American Jewish Families*, 87, 88.
132. Ibid., 167.
133. Ibid., 200.
134. Mordecai, *Rebecca Gratz*, 23, 25.
135. Ibid., 5.
136. Ibid., 9.
137. Ibid., 5.

CHAPTER FIVE

1.   Helen Laughon, "August Edouart: A Quaker Album of American and English Duplicate Silhouettes, 1827–1845," *Pennsylvania Magazine of History and Biography* 109, no. 3 (1985): 387–88.
2.   Trotten, "Thacher-Thatcher Genealogy," 261.
3.   Jackson, *Ancestors in Silhouette*; and London, *Shades of My Forefathers*.
4.   Jackson, *History of Silhouettes*, 97.
5.   Advertisement, *Southern Patriot*, Dec. 20, 1845, 3; Advertisement, *New York Herald*, Nov. 24, 1844, 1.
6.   "The Fine Arts," *New York Herald*, Dec. 5, 1844, 1.
7.   Advertisement, *New York Herald*, Nov. 24, 1844, 4.
8.   Ibid.

9.   "The Fine Arts," *New York Herald*, Dec. 5, 1844, 1.

10. Ibid.

11. Ibid.

12. Simon, *Samuel Myer Isaacs*, 8; Swierenga, *Forerunners*, 356.

13. Sherman, *Orthodox Judaism in America*, 104.

14. Dr. DeSola Mendes, Rabbi Isaacs's successor, quoted in Simon, *Samuel Myer Isaacs*, 63.

15. Samuel Myer Isaacs, "The Reform Agitation," *Occident* 2, no. 6 (1844): 284. See also Simons, *Samuel Myer Isaacs*, 169.

16. Simons, *Samuel Myer Isaacs*, 168–70; Isaacs, "Reform Agitation," 283–91; "Address to the Brethren of the House of Israel," *Jewish Messenger*, Jan. 2, 1857, 4.

17. Leeser, "The Frankfort Reform Society," *Occident* 2, no. 6 (1844): 305–6; and Isaacs, "Reform Agitation," 283–91.

18. Carroll, *American Masculinities*, 120.

19. Rock, *Haven of Liberty*, 151; Anbinder, *Five Points*, 42–43, 45–46.

20. Rock, *Haven of Liberty*, 154.

21. These congregations include Ansche Chesed (1828), Shaaray Zedek (1837), Shaaray Hashamayim (1839), Rodeph Shalom (1842), Shaaray Tefila (1845), Beth Israel (1845), and Temple Emanu-El (1845).

22. Rock, *Haven of Liberty*, 181–82.

23. Moore, Gurock, Polland, Rock, Soyer, and Linden, *Jewish New York*, 43, 155.

24. Rock, *Haven of Liberty*, 206.

25. Polland and Soyer, *Emerging Metropolis*, 82; and Rock, *Haven of Liberty*, 159, 186, 212. Wise first innovated mixed seating in 1851 (Sarna, "Debate over Mixed Seating," 366).

26. Polland and Soyer, *Emerging Metropolis*, 82; Cohn-Sherbok, *Judaism*, 264; Simons, *Samuel Myer Isaacs*, 168.

27. Eleff, *Modern Orthodox Judaism*, xxxviii.

28. Antoun, *Understanding Fundamentalism*, 2. See also Marty and Appleby, *Fundamentalisms Observed*, ix–x.

29. Leeser," "Frankfort Reform Society," 305–6.

30. Ibid. See also Isaacs, "Reform Agitation," 283–91.

31. Pred, "Manufacturing in the American Mercantile City," 321, 323–24.

32. Glanz, "German Jewish Mass Emigration," 52.

33. Ibid., 58–60, 66.

34. Jonathan Sarna has suggested to me that an alternate theory for including the whole family in the silhouette is that copies were made to send to Samuel Myer Isaacs's very transnational family, which included relatives in London, Holland, and Australia. Many other Jews who ordered silhouettes had family who lived more locally and hence only included individuals. While this suggestion is entirely possible, it does not help explain the other details of the silhouette, such as the unusual positioning of the family members and their headgear. What makes the Isaacs's silhouette distinctive is the way the family is presented.

35. Isaacs, "Reform Agitation," 286.

36.   Saunders, *American Faces*, 36.

37.   Samuel Myer Isaacs, quoted in Simon, *Samuel Myer Isaacs*, 8.

38.   Swierenga, *Forerunners*, 77.

39.   Judging by the names of the other twenty-six passengers, it is highly unlikely there was a minyan on board (United States Immigration and Naturalization Service, *Passenger Lists of Vessels Arriving at New York*, 1839, M237, roll 040, line 1, list number 670, NARA; and Simon, *Samuel Myer Isaacs*, 7–8).

40.   United States Immigration and Naturalization Service, *Passenger Lists of Vessels Arriving at New York*, 1839, M237, roll 040, line 1, list number 670, NARA.

41.   Isaac Samuel Isaacs was born Nov. 1, 1845, so Jane was a little over two months pregnant at the time. He went on to marry Estelle Solomon (Stern, *First American Jewish Families*, 127).

42.   Endelman, *Jews of Georgian England*, 171–72.

43.   Ibid., 171–72, 174.

44.   Ibid., 174.

45.   Ibid., 181–82; and Rozin, *The Rich and the Poor*, 39.

46.   Endelman, *Jews of Georgian England*, 182.

47.   Rozin, *The Rich and the Poor*, 39.

48.   Leibman, "Material of Race," forthcoming. Contrast this emphasis on physiognomy with the slightly earlier silhouette by William Bache, *Jew Pedlar–Dutch* (London, *Miniatures and Silhouettes of Early American Jews*, 95).

49.   Rozin, *The Rich and the Poor*, 11. An important exception to this is the recently rediscovered work of Cora Wilburn (Sarna, "Jewish Women Without Money").

50.   Rozin, *The Rich and the Poor*, 11–12.

51.   The German for cake baker is *Kuchenbäcker*.

52.   Shire, *Great Synagogue Marriage Records*.

53.   Endelman, *Jews of Georgian England*, 166.

54.   Ibid.

55.   New York, New York City Municipal Deaths, 1795–1949 (database), NYCMA, https://www.familysearch.org/search/collection/2240477; and Simon, *Samuel Myer Isaacs*, 6–7.

56.   Endelman, *Jews of Georgian England*, 187.

57.   Rozin, *The Rich and the Poor*, 69.

58.   Ibid., 68–71.

59.   Swierenga, *Forerunners*, 74.

60.   Mendelsohn, "Sacrifices of the Isaacs," 17.

61.   Swierenga, *Forerunners*, 74.

62.   Marriage certificate of Samuel Myer Isaacs and Jane Symons, 1839, General Register Office of London. Copy included in Simon, *Samuel Myer Isaacs*, 6.

63.   Simon, *Samuel Myer Isaacs*, 6–7.

64.   Higginbotham, *Children's Homes*, 168.

65.   Swierenga, *Forerunners*, 77–78.

66.   Ibid.

67. Goldstein, *Century of Judaism in New York*, 83–89.

68. Isaacs, "Reform Agitation," 285.

69. Goldstein, *Century of Judaism in New York*, 86–87.

70. Ibid., 88–89; and Oron, "'*No aksi mi fu libi yu*,'" 48, 53, 65.

71. Swierenga, *Forerunners*, 73; and Simon, *Samuel Myer Isaacs*, 9.

72. Like the other congregations, Shaaray Tefila would gradually migrate up-town over the course of the nineteenth century. During Samuel's tenure, the congregation moved a second time to the Armory building on West 36th Street and Broadway in 1864, and then they moved a third time to West 44th Street in 1869. After his death, the congregation would con-tinue uptown to West 82nd Street, and finally to the current location at 250 East 79th Street (Olitzky and Raphael, *American Synagogue*, 258–60).

73. Loeb Portrait Database, http://loebjewishportraits.com/silhouettes/; Shadur and Shadur, *Traditional Jewish Papercuts*, 185. Despite what her name might seem to suggest, Isabel Harris was Jewish (Stern, *First Ameri-can Jewish Families*, 94, 214).

74. She arrived on the Elisinore from Liverpool on Dec. 22, 1846 (*Registers of Vessels Arriving at the Port of New York from Foreign Ports, 1789–1919*, M237, roll 65, NARA, https://www.ancestry.com/search/collections/newy ork273/).

75. Augustin-Amant-Constant-Fidèle Edouart and Luther Bradish, broadside beginning, "469 Broadway, 5 doors above Grand St. Monsieur Edouart begs to inform the citizens of New York that he has returned from Sarato-ga Springs after having taken upwards of 1500 likenesses, amongst which are many eminent characters of the church, the army, the bench, the bar, and private life . . . ," 1840, SY1840, no. 38, NYHS.

76. The Hendricks family went to Congregation Shearith Israel. Mary Ann Wheeler, [Dressmaker's] account book 1848–54, p. 52, Mss Collection, NYHS.

77. Portraits that did have sisters standing and brothers sitting were typically of infant boys (Hemphill, *Siblings*, 98–99).

78. Brilliant, Weinstein, Delamaire, and Vedder, *Group Dynamics*, 6.

79. Hemphill, *Siblings*, 99.

80. This age is reflected in Jacob's bodily proportions despite his unusual height.

81. Simon, *Samuel Myer Isaacs*, 20.

82. Carroll, *American Masculinities*, 120.

83. Congregation Shearith Israel, "Association for the Moral & Religious Instruction of Children of the Jewish Faith Meeting Minutes, 1838–1846," Sisterhood Records, CSIA.

84. Simons, *Samuel Myer Isaacs*, 12.

85. Ibid., 123.

86. Council of Ten, "Public Examination of the Pupils of Miss Palache's Academy," *Occident* 2, no. 4 (1844): 209–10; and Sophia Daniels, "Sunday School of Barbadoes," *Occident* 2, no. 7 (1844): 338–39.

87. Hemphill, *Siblings*, 99.

88. Loeb Portrait Database, http://loebjewishportraits.com/silhouettes/.

89. Horace Bushnell, quoted in Perry, *Young America*, 50–51.

90.   Nayder, *Dickens, Sexuality, and Gender*, 611. Handkerchiefs were valued possessions in the first half of the nineteenth century, hence their appearance in portraits (Kurella, *Whitework Embroidered Lace Handkerchiefs*, 8).

91.   Bernstein, *Racial Innocence*, 10.

92.   Boyarin, *Unheroic Conduct*. Although the New York Haggadah of 1837 was not illustrated, other nineteenth-century American images at the time present good Jewish sons as being subdued and studious, while the *rasha* (evil son) either carries or smokes a "male authority stick." For example, in the 1879 Haggadah printed in Chicago, the *rasha* smokes a cigarette, thereby conflating "authority sticks" with those who violate the laws of the *yomim tovim*. Likewise, the 1823 Haggadah from Vienna reuses an old drawing in which the *rasha* dresses as a Roman soldier carrying a sword. Images of these scenes can be found in Zion and Dishon, *Different Night*, 62–71.

93.   For example, see the two silhouettes of John Moss in the Loeb Portrait Database, http://loebjewishportraits.com/silhouettes/john-moss/ and http://loebjewishportraits.com/silhouettes/john-moss-rebecca-lyons -moss-samuel-lyons-moss-and-baby/. Notably, he wears a hat when alone but not when with women, in keeping with nineteenth-century hat etiquette.

94.   For example, see Auguste Edouart, *Boy with Dog*, n.d., paper and ink on paper, Smithsonian American Art Museum, gift of Mrs. Florence R. Perry, 1981.172.31.

95.   Juhasz, "Head Covering, Men."

96.   Joseph Wood, *Silhouette of Gershom Mendes Seixas*, New York, 1813, http:// www.sothebys.com/en/auctions/ecatalogue/2013/judaica-n09060 /lot.149.html.

97.   In making this argument, I am augmenting Lawrence Grossman's assertion, "For American Jews up until the late nineteenth century there could be no such attribution of religious significance to male head covering" (Grossman, "Kippah Comes to America," 132). While I agree with Grossman that during the colonial era neither Western Sephardim nor Ashkenazim of Central Europe who primarily settled in the Americas "came from cultures that stressed head covering," I argue here that head covering—specifically a soft cap—became an important symbol for the emergent "orthodox" Ashkenazi congregations of the late 1840s–1850s. For a history of the laws regarding head covering, see also Zimmer, "Men's Headcovering."

98.   "Opinions of the Religious Press," *New York Herald*, Aug. 29, 1875, 61, quoted in Eleff, *Who Rules the Synagogue?*, 177. For Jewish reactions to this editorial, see "A Sound Opinion," *Jewish Times*, Sept. 3, 1875, 424; and "More Litigation," *Jewish Messenger*, Sept. 3, 1875, 4.

99.   Crane, *Fashion and Its Social Agendas*, 83.

100.   Hughes, *Hats*, 96–97.

101.   Ibid., 97.

102.   Posey, *Alabama in the 1830's*, 43.

103.   Hughes, *Hats*, 112.

104. Martin, *All Things Dickinson*, 425; and Joselit, *Perfect Fit*, 107.
105. *Shulchan Aruch, Yoreh Deah*, 178, quoted in Dynner, "Garment of Torah," 99–100.
106. In silhouettes by Edouart, top hats were worn by August Belmonte (1939) and John Moss (n.d.), and the stovepipe hat was worn by Joseph Andrade John Moss (1865). Although today the top hat is favored in many Western Sephardic congregations, up until the 1863, Sephardic *hazzanim* at Bevis Marks wore the tricorne, as did their counterparts like Rev. Isaac Lopez in Jamaica. This hat was also standard at Shearith Israel (prior to 1842), and even early ministers at Ansche Chesed wore it (Landman, *Cantor*, 82; and De Breffny, *Synagogue*, 153).
107. Kleeblatt, Wertkin, and Black, *Jewish Heritage in American Folk Art*, 49.
108. See, for example, the etchings by Isaac Mendes Belisario: *Rev. Isaac Lopez* (1846; included in Gerber, *Jews in the Caribbean*, plate 7.9) and *Interior of the Bevis Marks Synagogue* (1812).
109. Apple, *Great Synagogue*, 144.
110. Isaac Leeser, "The Chief Rabbi of England," *Occident* 2, no. 7 (October 1844), 350.
111. Quoted in Steinhauer, "Holy Headgear," 12.
112. Severa, *Dressed for the Photographer*, 24.
113. During the mid-1840s, American women typically wore bonnets and caps, saving hats for "the garden or on the most informal occasions in the garden or at the seaside" (De Courtais, *Women's Hats, Headdresses, and Hairstyles*, 120; see also p. 116). See also Dalrymple, *American Victorian Costume in Early Photographs*, 1.
114. De Courtais, *Women's Hats, Headdresses, and Hairstyles*, 116.
115. Cunnington, *English Women's Clothing in the Nineteenth Century*, 99–104, 124–26, 158–65.
116. Hoberman, Leibman, and Surowitz-Israel, *Jews in the Americas*, 111.
117. Ibid.
118. Ibid.; and Olsen, *Daily Life in 18th-Century England*, 99.
119. De Courtais, *Women's Hats, Headdresses, and Hairstyles*, 114–15.
120. I am indebted to Zev Eleff for pointing me toward this controversy in New York. Cohn, "Leo Merzbacher," 22.
121. Ibid.; and Sarna, *American Judaism*, 93.
122. Brilliant, *Facing the New World*, 67.
123. Ibid.
124. Russel-Henar, *Angisa Tori*, 23, 27, 33–34, 131–32.
125. Benoit's caption reads: "Five female slaves on their way to church on a holiday. On the right a Lutheran woman, next to a Jewess, a Calvinist, and a Moravian woman. In the center a young Christian creole slave, on her way to church on Palm Sunday" (*Voyage à Surinam*, plate xi, fig. 20).
126. The Haskalah was a precursor to the Reform movement.
127. Obituary, *American Hebrew*, May 23, 1884, 26.
128. Basch, *In the Eyes of the Law*, 136, 138, 161.
129. Ibid., 122.
130. Ibid., 122, 235.

CONCLUSION

1.   Stern, *First American Jewish Families*, 209; and National Park Service, "The Civil War," https://www.nps.gov/civilwar/.

2.   To be sure, the size, quality, and materials used to commemorate the dead varied greatly. For extreme examples of the way wealth impacted Jewish memorials, see Lufkin, "Home Between Death and Life"; and Stern, *Rise and Progress of Reform Judaism*, 201, 204–5, and photos at the end of the volume.

3.   For example, today one can be denied burial in some Jewish cemeteries for being cremated or tattooed. Between 1750 and 1850, Jews in the Atlantic World were sometimes denied burial owing to conversion to Christianity, for marrying a non-Jew, for misbehavior, or because they or their families crossed the synagogue board. Many communities, however, had a separate section for such cases, rather than denying renegades burial altogether. For examples of these decrees and decisions, see the minute books of the Mahamad of Nidhe Israel, 1790–1826, III.45, 130, 131, 142; VIII.30–31, 55, 90, 100, 4521/D/01/01/003, 4521/D/01/01/008, LMA. For more on how conflicts within the synagogue impacted who was buried and how, see Emmanuel and Emmanuel, *History of the Jews*, 196–201.

4.   De Sola Pool, *Portraits Etched in Stone*, 128. Emphasis in the original.

5.   This mistress was Sarah Simpson Wood (1802–92). Although descendants claim that Wood and Brandon married in 1823, there is no record of their marriage in either the synagogue or any of the island's churches. Moreover, in his will, Abraham Rodrigues Brandon refers to her as "Sarah Simpson Wood of St. Michael's Parish" rather than as his wife or with his last name. Regardless of the nature of their relationship, they had numerous children together, including Julia Rodrigues Brandon, who was born in 1824 (Will of Abraham Rodrigues Brandon, June 17, 1831, BDA).

6.   De Sola Pool, *Portraits Etched in Stone*, 127. Emphasis in the original.

7.   Ibid., 137.

8.   Ibid., 126–29.

9.   Coleborne, "Reading Insanity's Archive," https://prov.vic.gov.au/index .php/explore-collection/provenance-journal/provenance-2010/reading -insanitys-archive.

10.   Ibid.

11.   Almshouse Admissions, Discharges and Death Ledger, 1759–1813, vol. 160, p. 69, Almshouse Ledger Collection, NYCRIS, http://nycma.lunaim aging.com/luna/servlet/detail/NYCMA~2~2~75~477683.

12.   Stern, *First American Jewish Families*, 179.

13.   Marcus, *Colonial American Jew*, 2:1039.

14.   Aboim, *Plural Masculinities*, 47; and Greenebaum, "Placing Jewish Women into the Intersectionality."

15.   I am indebted to Ellen Smith for this observation.

16.   Harris, *In the Shadow of Slavery*, 70, 94; and Stern, *First American Jewish Families*, 159.

17.   Noah argued, "It is perfectly ridiculous to give them ["blacks"] the right

of suffrage—a right which they cannot value, and which in this city, particularly in the federal wards, is a mere vendible article" (Noah, "The Convention," *National Advocate*, September 24, 1821). As Jonathan Sarna notes, Noah's views on African Americans seem to have developed later in his life (*Jacksonian Jew*, 108–14).

18. Papers of Mordecai Manuel Noah (1785–1851), AJHS; and Records of Congregation Shearith Israel, 1759–1932, AJHS.

19. Hartman, "Venus in Two Acts," 2.

20. Patterson, *Slavery and Social Death*, 5, quoted in Cavitch, *American Elegy*, 186.

21. Mauss, *The Gift*, viii.

22. Manumission of Sarah and Isaac Lopez (1801/2), entered Aug. 5, 1801, deeds 219:9, BDA.

23. *New York City Directory*, 1870, vol. 84, p. 15, NYPL Digital Collections, Rare Book Division, https://digitalcollections.nypl.org/items/3e73f720-58c9 -0134-ada6-00505686a51c.

24. Mann made this point in her official response to my third lecture at Bard Graduate Center, April 12, 2018, on which chapter 4 is based.

25. Bilski and Braun, *Jewish Women and Their Salons*, 15; and Nadell, *America's Jewish Women*, 61.

26. Bilski and Braun, *Jewish Women and Their Salons*, 4–5; and Nadell, *America's Jewish Women*, 61–65.

27. Benedict, "Paradox of Anthology," 242.

28. Shlomo Yehuda Rechnitz, "There *IS* No Shidduch Crisis," *Mishpacha*, Aug. 6, 2014, 60.

29. Ibid., 63.

30. Sections of this paragraph are a revised version of Leibman, "When Women Don't Marry: Single Blessedness and the Shidduch Crisis," *Religion in American History*, September 15, 2014, http://usreligion.blogspot.com.

31. Sarna, "Louisa B. Hart," 96.

32. Fuentes, *Dispossessed Lives*, 6.

33. Kroker, "Archive Drift," 137.

34. Chaudhuri, *Feminist Film Theorists*, 32.

35. Silverman, "Dis-Embodying the Female Voice," 309.

36. Gay, "Preparing for Culturally Responsive Teaching," 109.

37. Ibid., 106.

Bibliography

Archives, Museums, and Cemeteries

American Jewish Archives (AJA). Cincinnati, OH.
American Jewish Historical Society (AJHS). New York.
American Philosophical Society (APS). Philadelphia.
Barbados Department of Archives (BDA). Bridgetown.
Bard Graduate Center (BGC). New York.
Beth Olam Cemetery. Ridgewood, Queens, NY.
Congregation Shearith Israel Archives (CSIA). Newark, NJ.
The Jewish Museum (JM). London.
The Jewish Museum (JMNY). New York.
Library and Archives Canada (LAC), Ottawa.
Library of Congress. Washington, DC.
London Metropolitan Archives (LMA).
Metropolitan Museum of Art (Met). New York.
National Archives and Records Administration (NARA), Washington, DC.
National Archives of the Netherlands [Nationaal Archief] (NA). The Hague.
National Museum of American Jewish History. Philadelphia.
Newberry Library. Chicago.
New York City Municipal Archives (NYCMA). New York.
New York City Records and Information Service (NYCRIS). New York.
New-York Historical Society (NYHS). New York.
New York Public Library (NYPL). New York, NY.
New York State Archives. Albany, NY.
New York State Library (NYSL). Albany, NY.
North Carolina Museum of Art (NCMA). Raleigh, NC.
Provincial Archive of New Brunswick, Canada.
Salem Field Cemetery. Ridgewood, Queens, NY.

Twenty-First Street Cemetery. New York.
West Eleventh Street Cemetery. New York.
Wilson Library. University of North Carolina at Chapel Hill.
Winterthur Museum, Garden and Library. Winterthur, DE.
Victoria and Albert Museum (V&A). London.
Yeshiva University. New York.

Periodicals

The American Hebrew (New York). 1879–1902.
Christian Register and Boston Observer. 1835–43.
The Clothiers' and Haberdashers' Weekly (New York). 1892–1901.
Godey's Lady's Book (Philadelphia). 1830–98.
Jewish Messenger (New York). 1857–1902.
The London Magazine. 1820–29.
National Advocate (New York). 1812–29.
New York Herald. 1835–1924.
New-York Journal. 1937–66.
The New York Packet and the American Advertiser. 1776–84.
The New York Times. 1851–present.
The New Yorker: A Weekly Journal of Literature, Politics and General Intelligence. 1838–39.
The Occident and American Jewish Advocate (Philadelphia). 1843–69.
Southern Patriot (Charleston, SC). 1831–48.
The State (Columbia, SC). 1891–present.

Books, Chapters, Articles, and Online Sources

Aboim, Sofia. *Plural Masculinities: The Remaking of the Self in Private Life.* London: Taylor and Francis, 2016.

Abramovitz, Mimi. *Regulating the Lives of Women: Social Welfare Policy from Colonial Times to the Present.* New York: Routledge, 2018.

Allan, David. *Commonplace Books and Reading in Georgian England.* Cambridge: Cambridge University Press, 2014.

Ambrose, Gavin, and Paul Harris. *Fundamentals of Typography.* Lausanne: AVA Academia, 2006.

American National Biography: With a Cumulative Index by Occupations and Realms of Renown. Supplement 2. New York: Oxford University Press, 2005.

Anbinder, Tyler. *Five Points: The 19th-Century New York City Neighborhood That Invented Tap Dance, Stole Elections, and Became the World's Most Notorious Slum.* New York: Free Press, 2001.

Andrews, E. A., and William Freund. *A Copious and Critical Latin-English Lexicon, Founded on the Larger Latin-German Lexicon of Dr. William Freund: With Additions and Corrections from the Lexicons of Gesner, Facciolati, Scheller, Georges, etc.* London: Sampson Low, 1851.

Antoun, Richard T. *Understanding Fundamentalism: Christian, Islamic, and Jewish Movements.* Walnut Creek, CA: AltaMira Press, 2001.

Apple, Raymond. *The Great Synagogue: A History of Sydney's Big Shule.* Sydney: University of New South Wales Press, 2008.

Ashton, Dianne. *Rebecca Gratz: Women and Judaism in Antebellum America.* Detroit: Wayne State University Press, 1997.

———. "Shifting Veils: Religion, Politics, and Womanhood in the Civil War Writings of American Jewish Women." In *Women and American Judaism: Historical Perspectives,* edited by Pamela Susan Nadell and Jonathan D. Sarna, 81–106. Hanover, NH: University Press of New England, 2001.

Austen, Jane. *Emma.* Edited by Richard Cronin and Dorothy McMillan. Cambridge: Cambridge University Press, 2005.

———. *Pride and Prejudice.* Edited by Joseph Pearce. San Francisco: Ignatius Press, 2008.

Bacchus, M. K. *Utilization, Misuse, and Development of Human Resources in the Early West Indian Colonies.* Waterloo, ON: Wilfrid Laurier University Press, 1990.

Bagneris, Mia L. *Colouring the Caribbean: Race and the Art of Agostino Brunias.* Manchester, UK: Manchester University Press, 2018.

Balducci, Temma. *Gender, Space, and the Gaze in Post-Haussmann Visual Culture: Beyond the Flâneur.* New York: Routledge, 2017.

Bannet, Eve Tavor. "Empire and Occasional Conformity: David Fordyce's 'Complete British Letter-Writer.'" *Huntington Library Quarterly* 66, nos. 1/2 (2003): 55–79.

Barnett, Lionel David, ed. *Abstracts of the Ketubot or Marriage-Contracts of the Congregation from Earliest Times until 1837.* Part 2 of *Bevis Marks Records.* Oxford: Oxford University Press, 1949.

Barquist, David L., ed. *Myer Myers: Jewish Silversmith in Colonial New York.* New Haven, CT: Yale University Press, 2001.

———. "The Stylistic Distinctiveness of Colonial New York Silver." In *Stories in Sterling: Four Centuries of Silver in New York,* edited by Margaret K. Hofer et al., 34–47. New York: New-York Historical Society, 2011.

Barratt, Carrie Rebora, and Lori Zabar. *American Portrait Miniatures in the Metropolitan Museum of Art.* New York: Metropolitan Museum of Art, 2010.

Barton, Bernard. *Poetic Vigils.* London: Baldwin, Cradock, and Joy, 1824.

Barton, David, and Nigel Hall, eds. *Letter Writing as a Social Practice.* Philadelphia: John Benjamins, 2000.

Bastiaans, Aisha D. "Detecting Difference in *Devil in a Blue Dress*: The Mulatta Figure, Noir, and the Cinematic Reification of Race." In *Mixed Race Hollywood,* edited by Camilla Fojas and Mary Beltrán, 223–47. New York: New York University Press, 2008.

Baugher, Sherene. "Visible Charity: The Archaeology, Material Culture, and Landscape Design of New York City's Municipal Almshouse Complex, 1736–1797." *International Journal of Historical Archaeology* 5, no. 2 (2001): 175–202.

Benedict, Barbara M. "The Paradox of the Anthology: Collecting and Difference in Eighteenth-Century Britain." *New Literary History* 34, no. 2 (2003): 231–56.

Benoit, Pierre Jacques. *Voyage à Surinam: Description des possessions néerlandaises dans la Guyane; Cent dessins pris sur nature par l'auteur.* Brussels: Société des Beaux-Arts, 1839.

Ben-Ur, Aviva. "The Exceptional and the Mundane: A Biographical Portrait of Rebecca Machado Phillips." In *Women and American Judaism: Historical Perspectives,* edited by Pamela Susan Nadell and Jonathan D. Sarna, 48–80. Hanover, NH: University Press of New England, 2001.

———. *Sephardic Jews in America: A Diasporic History.* New York: New York University Press, 2009.

———. "Still Life: Sephardi, Ashkenazi, and West African Art and Form in Suriname's Jewish Cemeteries." *American Jewish History* 92, no. 1 (2004): 31–79. http://www.jstor.org/stable/23887431.

Ben-Ur, Aviva, and Jessica Vance Roitman. "Adultery Here and There: Crossing Sexual Boundaries in the Dutch Jewish Atlantic." In *Dutch Atlantic Connections, 1680–1800: Linking Empires, Bridging Borders,* edited by Gert Oostindie and Jessica V. Roitman, 185–223. Leiden: Brill, 2014.

Berman, Myron. *The Last of the Jews?* Lanham, MD: University Press of America, 1998.

Bernfeld, Tirtsah Levie. *Poverty and Welfare Among the Portuguese Jews in Early Modern Amsterdam.* Portland, OR: Littman Library of Jewish Civilization, 2011.

Bernstein, Robin. *Racial Innocence: Performing American Childhood and Race from Slavery to Civil Rights.* New York: New York University Press, 2012.

Bewell, Alan. *Romanticism and Colonial Disease: Medicine & Culture.* Baltimore: Johns Hopkins University Press, 2000.

Bigelow, Bruce. "Aaron Lopez: Merchant of Newport." *New England Quarterly* 4, no. 1 (1931): 757–76.

Bilski, Emily D., and Emily Braun, eds. *Jewish Women and Their Salons: The Power of Conversation.* New Haven, CT: Yale University Press, 2005.

Bindman, David. *Ape to Apollo: Aesthetics and the Idea of Race in the 18th Century.* Ithaca, NY: Cornell University Press, 2002.

Bingham, Emily. "American, Jewish, Southern, Mordecai: Constructing Identities to 1865." In *Jewish Roots in Southern Soil: A New History,* edited by Marcie Cohen Ferris and Mark I. Greenberg, 46–71. Waltham, MA: Brandeis University Press, 2006.

———. *Mordecai: An Early American Family.* New York: Hill and Wang, 2003.

Birmingham, Stephen. *The Grandees: America's Sephardic Elite.* New York: Harper and Row, 1971.

Black, Gerry. *JFS: A History of the Jews' Free School, London, Since 1732.* London: Tymsder, 1998.

Blackstone, William. *Commentaries on the Laws of England.* Edited by William Carey Jones. San Francisco: Bancroft-Whitney, 1915.

Bodian, Miriam. *Hebrews of the Portuguese Nation: Conversos and Community in Early Modern Amsterdam.* Bloomington: Indiana University Press, 1997.

Borelli, Melissa Blanco. *She Is Cuba: A Genealogy of the Mulata Body.* New York: Oxford University Press, 2016.

Boyarin, Daniel. *Unheroic Conduct: The Rise of Heterosexuality and the Invention of the Jewish Man*. Berkeley: University of California Press, 1997.

Bradley, Betsy. "Tribeca North Historic District Designation Report." New York: NYC Landmarks Preservation Commission, 1992.

Brilliant, Richard, ed. *Facing the New World: Jewish Portraits in Colonial and Federal America*. New York: Jewish Museum, 1997.

Brilliant, Richard, Amy Weinstein, Marie-Stephanie Delamaire, and Lee Vedder. *Group Dynamics: Family Portraits and Scenes of Everyday Life at the New-York Historical Society*. New York: New Press, 2006.

Broadwater, Jeff. *James Madison: A Son of Virginia and a Founder of the Nation*. Chapel Hill: University of North Carolina Press, 2012.

Brock, Jim P., and Kenn Kaufman. *Field Guide to Butterflies of North America*. Boston: Houghton Mifflin, 2006.

Brodkin, Karen. *How the Jews Became White Folks and What That Says About Race in America*. New Brunswick, NJ: Rutgers University Press, 1999.

Brown, Henry Collins. *Valentine's Manual of Old New York*. New York: Valentine's Manual, 1919.

Brown, Malcolm. "The Jews of Gravesend Before 1915." *Jewish Historical Studies* 35 (1996): 119–39.

Brown, Tammy L. *City of Islands: Caribbean Intellectuals in New York*. Jackson: University Press of Mississippi, 2015.

Burtinshaw, Kathryn M., and John R. F. Burt. *Lunatics, Imbeciles and Idiots: A History of Insanity in Nineteenth-Century Britain and Ireland*. Barnsley, South Yorkshire, UK: Pen and Sword Archaeology, 2017.

Byrde, Penelope. *Nineteenth Century Fashion*. London: Batsford, 1992.

Cady, G. Scott, and Christopher Webber. *A Year with American Saints*. New York: Church, 2006.

Caffrey, Paul. "Jewels Above All Prize: Portrait Miniatures on Enamel and Ivory." In *Ireland: Crossroads of Art and Design, 1690–1840*, edited by William Laffan, Christopher Monkhouse, and Leslie Fitzpatrick, 161–66. New Haven, CT: Yale University Press, 2015.

Camfield, Gregg. "The Moral Aesthetics of Sentimentality: A Missing Key to *Uncle Tom's Cabin*." *Nineteenth-Century Literature* 43, no. 3 (1988): 319–45.

Cardozo, Arlene. *Jewish Family Celebrations: The Sabbath, Festivals, and Ceremonies*. New York: St. Martin's Press, 1982.

Carment, David, and Ariane Sadjed. *Diaspora as Cultures of Cooperation: Global and Local Perspectives*. Basingstoke, UK: Palgrave Macmillan, 2018.

Carr, Jean Ferguson. "Nineteenth-Century Girls and Literacy." In *Girls and Literacy in America: Historical Perspectives to the Present*, edited by Jane Greer, 51–78. Santa Barbara, CA: ABC Clio, 2003.

Carroll, Bret E. *American Masculinities: A Historical Encyclopedia*. Thousand Oaks, CA: Sage Publications, 2003.

Castronovo, Russ. *The Oxford Handbook of Nineteenth-Century American Literature*. New York: Oxford University Press, 2014.

"Catalog of 1959 Exhibits on American Jewish History." Washington, DC: B'nai B'rith, 1959.

Cavitch, Max. *American Elegy: The Poetry of Mourning from the Puritans to Whitman.* Minneapolis: University of Minnesota Press, 2007.

Cerezo-Román, Jessica, Anna Wessman, and Howard Williams. "Introduction: Archaeologies of Cremation." In *Cremation and the Archaeology of Death*, edited by Jessica Cerezo-Román, Anna Wessman, and Howard Williams, 1–26. Oxford: Oxford University Press, 2017.

Chaudhuri, Shohini. *Feminist Film Theorists: Laura Mulvey, Kaja Silverman, Teresa De Lauretis, Barbara Creed.* Routledge Critical Thinkers. London: Routledge, 2006.

Chyet, Stanley F. "Aaron Lopez: A Study in Buenafama." *American Jewish Historical Quarterly* 52, no. 4 (1963): 295–309.

——. *Lopez of Newport: Colonial American Merchant Prince.* Detroit: Wayne State University Press, 1970.

Clearwater, Alphonso Trumpbour, and C. Louise Avery. *American Silver of the XVII and XVIII Centuries: A Study Based on the Clearwater Collection.* New York: Metropolitan Museum of Art, 1920.

Cohen, Julia Phillips, and Sarah Abrevaya Stein. *Sephardi Lives: A Documentary History, 1700–1950.* Palo Alto, CA: Stanford University Press, 2014.

Cohen, Martin A. "The Sephardic Phenomenon: A Reappraisal." In *Sephardim in the Americas: Studies in Culture and History*, edited by Martin A. Cohen and Abraham J. Peck, 1–80. Tuscaloosa, AL: American Jewish Archives, 1993.

Cohen, Robert. *Jews in Another Environment: Surinam in the Second Half of the Eighteenth Century.* Leiden: E. J. Brill, 1991.

Cohen, Simon. *Shaaray Tefila: A History of Its Hundred Years, 1845–1945.* New York: Greenberg, 1945.

Cohn, Bernard. "Leo Merzbacher." *American Jewish Archives* 6 (1954): 21–24.

Cohn-Sherbok, Dan. *Judaism: History, Belief, and Practice.* New York: Routledge, 2003.

Coleborne, Catharine. "Reading Insanity's Archive: Reflections from Four Archival Sites." *Provenance: The Journal of Public Record Office Victoria* 9 (2010). https://prov.vic.gov.au/index.php/explore-collection/provenance-journal /provenance-2010/reading-insanitys-archive.

Colwill, Elizabeth. "Sex, Savagery, and Slavery in the Shaping of the French Body Politic." In *From the Royal to the Republican Body: Incorporating the Political in Seventeenth- and Eighteenth-Century France*, edited by Sara E. Melzer and Kathryn Norberg, 198–223. Berkeley: University of California Press, 1998.

"Constitution." *Publications of American Jewish Historical Society* 1 (1893): 137–43.

Cootz, Stephanie. *Marriage, a History: How Love Conquered Marriage.* New York: Penguin, 2005.

Corré, Alan D., and Malcolm H. Stern. "The Record Book of the Reverend Jacob Raphael Cohen." *American Jewish Historical Quarterly* 59, no. 1 (1969): 23–82.

Crane, Diana. *Fashion and Its Social Agendas: Class, Gender, and Identity in Clothing.* Chicago: University of Chicago Press, 2000.

Cranny-Francis, Anne. *Multimedia Texts and Contexts.* London: Sage, 2005.

Crenshaw, Paul. *Rembrandt's Bankruptcy: The Artist, His Patrons, and the Art Market in Seventeenth-Century Netherlands.* New York: Cambridge University Press, 2006.

Crittenden, A. F., and Samuel W. Crittenden. *An Inductive and Practical System of Double Entry Book-Keeping.* Philadelphia: Biddle, 1848.

Cross, June. *Secret Daughter: A Mixed-Race Daughter and the Mother Who Gave Her Away.* New York: Viking, 2006.

Cunnington, C. Willett. *English Women's Clothing in the Nineteenth Century: A Comprehensive Guide with 1,117 Illustrations.* New York: Dover Publications, 1990.

Daiches-Dubens, Rachel. "Eighteenth Century Anglo-Jewry In and Around Richmond, Surrey." *Transactions (Jewish Historical Society of England)* 18 (1953): 143–69.

Dalrymple, Priscilla Harris. *American Victorian Costume in Early Photographs.* New York: Dover Publications, 1991.

Daniels, Doris Groshen. "Colonial Jewry: Religion, Domestic and Social Relations." *American Jewish Historical Quarterly* 66, no. 3 (1977): 375–400.

Daniels, Roger. *Guarding the Golden Door: American Immigration Policy and Immigrants Since 1882.* New York: Farrar, Straus and Giroux, 2013.

Davis, Jefferson. *The Papers of Jefferson Davis.* Vol. 5, *1853–1855,* edited by Lynda L. Crist and Mary S. Dix. Baton Rouge: Louisiana State University Press, 1985.

Dawson, Norma. "'Heirlooms': The Evolution of a Legal Concept (United Kingdom)." *Northern Ireland Legal Quarterly* 51, no. 1 (2000): 1–24.

Day, Carolyn A. *Consumptive Chic: A History of Beauty, Fashion, and Disease.* London: Bloomsbury Academic, 2017.

De Breffny, Brian. *The Synagogue.* New York: Macmillan, 1978.

De Courtais, Georgine. *Women's Hats, Headdresses, and Hairstyles: With 453 Illustrations, Medieval to Modern.* Mineola, NY: Dover Publications, 2006.

De Jong, Mary G. Introduction to *Sentimentalism in Nineteenth-Century America: Literary and Cultural Practices,* edited by Mary De Jong and Paula Bernat Bennett, 1–12. Madison, NJ: Fairleigh Dickinson University Press, 2013.

De Sola Pool, David. *Book of Prayer: According to the Custom of the Spanish and Portuguese Jews.* New York: Union of Sephardic Congregations, 1960.

———. *An Old Faith in the New World; Portrait of Shearith Israel, 1654–1954.* New York: Columbia University Press, 1955.

———. *Portraits Etched in Stone: Early Jewish Settlers, 1682–1831.* New York: Columbia University Press, 1953.

———. "Some Letters of Grace Seixas Nathan, 1814–1821." *Publications of the American Jewish Historical Society* 37 (1947): 203–11. http://www.jstor.org/stable/43058337.

DeLorme, Eleanor P., and Bernard Chevallier. *Joséphine and the Arts of the Empire.* Los Angeles: J. P. Getty Museum, 2005.

Desilver, Robert. *The Philadelphia Index, or Directory, for 1823.* Philadelphia: R. Desilver, 1823.

DiAngelo, Robin J. *White Fragility: Why It's So Hard for White People to Talk About Racism.* Boston: Beacon Press, 2018.

Dickinson, Emily. *Emily Dickinson's Herbarium: A Facsimile Edition.* Cambridge, MA: Belknap Press of Harvard University Press, 2006.

Diebel, James, Jacob Norda, and Orna Kretchmer. *Weather Spark.* Accessed August 31, 2018. http://weatherspark.com/.

Dierks, Konstantin. "The Familiar Letter and Social Refinement in America, 1750–1800." In *Letter Writing as a Social Practice,* edited by David Barton and Nigel Hall, 31–41. Philadelphia: John Benjamins, 2000.

Dimand, Maurice Sven. *A Handbook of Mohammedan Decorative Arts.* New York: Metropolitan Museum of Art, 1930.

Diner, Hasia R., and Beryl Lieff Benderly. *Her Works Praise Her.* New York: Basic Books, 2003.

Disraeli, Benjamin. *Vivian Grey.* London: H. Colburn, 1826.

Dubos, René J., and Jean Dubos. *The White Plague: Tuberculosis, Man, and Society.* New Brunswick, NJ: Rutgers University Press, 1987.

Duncan, Carol. *Civilizing Rituals: Inside Public Art Museums.* New York: Routledge, 1995.

Dunn, Walter Scott. *People of the American Frontier: The Coming of the American Revolution.* Westport, CT: Praeger, 2005.

DuPlessis, Robert. "Sartorial Sorting in the Colonial Caribbean and North America." In *The Right to Dress: Sumptuary Laws in a Global Perspective, 1200–1800,* edited by Giorgio Riello and Ulinka Rublack, 346–74. New York: Cambridge University Press, 2019.

Dworkin, Steven Norman. A *Guide to Old Spanish.* New York: Oxford University Press, 2018.

Dynner, Glenn. "The Garment of Torah: Clothing Decrees and the Warsaw Career of the First Gerer *Rebbe.*" In *Warsaw, the Jewish Metropolis: Essays in Honor of the 75th Birthday of Professor Antony Polonsky,* edited by Glenn Dynner, François Guesnet, and Antony Polonsky, 91–127. Boston: Brill, 2015.

Earle, Rebecca. "Letters and Love in Colonial Spanish America." *Américas* 62, no. 1 (2005): 17–46.

"The Earliest Extant Minute Books of the Spanish and Portuguese Congregation Shearith Israel in New York, 1728–1786." *Publications of the American Jewish Historical Society* 21 (1913): 1–82.

Eaton, Natasha. "The Art of Colonial Despotism: Portraits, Politics, and Empire in South India, 1750–1795." *Cultural Critique* 70, no. 1 (2008): 63–93.

Efron, John M. *German Jewry and the Allure of the Sephardic.* Princeton, NJ: Princeton University Press, 2016.

Eisenstadt, Peter R. *The Encyclopedia of New York State.* Syracuse, NY: Syracuse University Press, 2005.

Eldridge, Larry D. "'Crazy Brained': Mental Illness in Colonial America." *Bulletin of the History of Medicine* 70, no. 3 (1996): 361–86.

Eleff, Zev. *Modern Orthodox Judaism: A Documentary History.* Philadelphia: Jewish Publication Society, 2016.

———. *Who Rules the Synagogue? Religious Authority and the Formation of American Judaism.* New York: Oxford University Press, 2016.

Eliot, George. *Middlemarch.* Chicago: Belford, Clarke, 1884.

Ellis, Alexander John. *A Plea for Phonetic Spelling; or, The Necessity of Orthographic Reform.* London: F. Pitman, 1848.

Ellis, Markman, Richard Coulton, and Matthew Mauger. *Empire of Tea: The Asian Leaf That Conquered the World.* London: Reaktion Books, 2018.

Elmaleh, Leon H., and Joseph Bunford Samuel. *The Jewish Cemetery, Ninth and Spruce Streets, Philadelphia.* Philadelphia: Congregation Mikveh Israel, 1962.

Emmanuel, Isaac S., and Suzanne A. Emmanuel. *History of the Jews of the Netherlands Antilles.* Cincinnati: American Jewish Archives, 1970.

Endelman, Todd M. *Broadening Jewish History: Towards a Social History of Ordinary Jews.* Oxford: Littman Library of Jewish Civilization, 2011.

————. *The Jews of Georgian England, 1714–1830: Tradition and Change in a Liberal Society.* Philadelphia: Jewish Publication Society of America, 1979.

Ensko, Stephen Guernsey Cook. *American Silversmiths and Their Marks: The Definitive (1948) Edition.* New York: Dover Publications, 1983.

Espinosa Martín, Carmen. *Las miniaturas en el Museo del Prado; Catálogo razonado.* Madrid: Museo Nacional del Prado, 2011.

Evans, Eli N. *An American Experience: Adeline Moses Loeb (1876–1953) and Her Early American Jewish Ancestors.* New York: Sons of the Revolution in the State of New York, 2009.

Fairman, Tony. "English Pauper Letters, 1800–34, and the English Language." In *Letter Writing as a Social Practice,* edited by David Barton and Nigel Hall, 63–82. Amsterdam: John Benjamins, 1999.

Farr, Judith, and Louise Carter. *The Gardens of Emily Dickinson.* Cambridge, MA: Harvard University Press, 2004.

Faust, Drew Gilpin. *This Republic of Suffering: Death and the American Civil War.* New York: Vintage Books, 2008.

Ferguson, Patricia F. *Ceramics: 400 Years of British Collecting in 100 Masterpieces.* London: Philip Wilson, 2016.

Fernheimer, Janice W. *Stepping into Zion: Hatzaad Harishon, Black Jews, and the Remaking of Jewish Identity.* Tuscaloosa: University of Alabama Press, 2014.

Fernow, Berthold, ed. *The Records of New Amsterdam from 1653 to 1674 Anno Domini.* Baltimore: Genealogical Publishing, 1976.

Fields, Karen E., and Barbara Jeanne Fields. *Racecraft: The Soul of Inequality in American Life.* London: Verso, 2014.

Fischer, Claude S. *Made in America: A Social History of American Culture and Character.* Chicago: University of Chicago Press, 2010.

Fischer, Eileen, and Stephen J. Arnold. "More Than a Labor of Love: Gender Roles and Christmas Gift Shopping." *Journal of Consumer Research* 17, no. 3 (1990): 333–45. http://www.jstor.org/stable/2626799.

Foner, Nancy. *Islands in the City: West Indian Migration to New York.* Berkeley: University of California Press, 2001.

Forbes, Jack D. *Africans and Native Americans: The Language of Race and the Evolution of Red–Black Peoples.* Urbana: University of Illinois Press, 1993.

Forde, Norma Monica. "Family Inheritance Provisions in the Barbados Succession Act: Redefining 'The Family.'" *Lawyer of the Americas* 9, no. 1 (1977): 115–25.

Francia, François-Thomas-Louis. *A Series of Progressive Lessons Intended to Elu-cidate the Art of Flower Painting in Water Colours.* Early American Imprints, Second Series 45685. Philadelphia: M. Thomas, 1818.

Frank, Robin Jaffee. *Love and Loss: American Portrait and Mourning Miniatures.* New Haven, CT: Yale University Press, 2000.

Franks, Abigail. *The Letters of Abigail Levy Franks, 1733–1748.* Edited by Edith Gelles. New Haven, CT: Yale University Press, 2004.

Fraser, Rebecca J. *Gender, Race, and Family in Nineteenth Century America: From Northern Woman to Plantation Mistress.* New York: Palgrave Macmillan, 2013.

Freeze, ChaeRan Y. *Jewish Marriage and Divorce in Imperial Russia.* Hanover, NH: University Press of New England for Brandeis University Press, 2002.

Friedenberg, Albert M. "The Jews of New Jersey from the Earliest Times to 1850." *Publications of the American Jewish Historical Society* 17 (1909): 33–43. http://www.jstor.org/stable/43057791.

Friedenwald, Herbert. "Rose S. Frank." *Publications of the American Jewish Histori-cal Society* 19 (1910): 201–2. http://www.jstor.org/stable/43057863.

"From the 2nd Volume of the Minute Books of the Congn: Shearith Israel in New York." *Publications of the American Jewish Historical Society* 21 (1913): 83–171. http://www.jstor.org/stable/43057906.

Fuentes, Marisa J. *Dispossessed Lives: Enslaved Women, Violence, and the Archive.* Philadelphia: University of Pennsylvania Press, 2016.

Gage, Kelly Mohs. "Forced Crossing: The Dress of African Slave Women in Rio de Janeiro, Brazil, 1861." *Dress* 39, no. 2 (2013): 111–33.

Galvin, Kathleen M. "Commentary: The Pastiche of Gender and Family Com-munication." In *Gender in Applied Communication Contexts,* edited by Patrice M. Buzzanell, Helen M. Sterk, and Lynn H. Turner, 311–16. Thousand Oaks, CA: Sage Publications, 2004.

Garraty, John Arthur, and Mark C. Carnes. *American National Biography.* Putman-Roush 18. New York: Oxford University Press, 1999.

Gay, Geneva. "Preparing for Culturally Responsive Teaching." *Journal of Teacher Education* 53, no. 2 (2002): 106–16.

Gelber, Steven M. *Hobbies: Leisure and the Culture of Work in America.* New York: Columbia University Press, 1999.

Geller, Markham J. "New Sources for the Origins of the Rabbinic Ketubah." *Hebrew Union College Annual* 49 (1978): 227–45. http://www.jstor.org /stable/23506832.

Gellman, David N., and David Quigley, eds. *Jim Crow New York: A Documentary History of Race and Citizenship, 1777–1877.* New York: New York University Press, 2003.

Gerber, Jane S. *The Jews in the Caribbean.* Oxford: Littman Library of Jewish Civilization, 2014.

Gigantino, James J. *The Ragged Road to Abolition: Slavery and Freedom in New Jer-sey, 1775–1865.* Philadelphia: University of Pennsylvania Press, 2015.

Gil, Ángeles Ezama. "La estructura de las Cartas Marruecas: Viejos y nuevos formatos literarios." *Cuadernos de Estudios del Siglo* 18, no. 21 (2011): 119–48.

Gilman, Sander L. *Difference and Pathology: Stereotypes of Sexuality, Race, and Mad-ness.* Ithaca, NY: Cornell University Press, 1985.

———. *Franz Kafka, the Jewish Patient.* New York: Routledge, 1995.

———. *Making the Body Beautiful: A Cultural History of Aesthetic Surgery.* Princeton, NJ: Princeton University Press, 1999.

———. "Sibling Incest, Madness, and the 'Jews.'" *Jewish Social Studies,* n.s., 4, no. 2 (1998): 157–79. http://www.jstor.org/stable/4467524.

———. "Thilo Sarrazin and the Politics of Race in the Twenty-First Century." *New German Critique* 39, no. 117 (2012): 47–59.

Glanz, Rudolf. "The German Jewish Mass Emigration: 1820–1880." *American Jewish Archives* 22, no. 1 (1970): 49–66.

Glover, Katharine. *Elite Women and Polite Society in Eighteenth-Century Scotland.* Woodbridge, UK: Boydell Press, 2011.

Goldstein, Eric L. *The Price of Whiteness: Jews, Race, and American Identity.* Princeton, NJ: Princeton University Press, 2006.

Goldstein, Israel. *A Century of Judaism in New York: B'nai Jeshurun, 1825–1925; New York's Oldest Ashkenazic Congregation.* New York: Congregation B'nai Jeshurun, 1930.

Greenebaum, Jessica. "Placing Jewish Women into the Intersectionality of Race, Class, and Gender." *Race, Gender, and Class* 6, no. 4 (1999): 41–60.

Grob, Gerald N. *Mental Institutions in America: Social Policy to 1875.* New York: Free Press, 1973.

Groll, C. L. Temminck. *The Dutch Overseas: Architectural Survey; Mutual Heritage of Four Centuries in Three Continents.* Zwolle: Waanders, 2002.

Grootenboer, Hanneke. *Treasuring the Gaze: Intimate Vision in Late Eighteenth-Century Eye Miniatures.* Chicago: University of Chicago Press, 2012.

Grossman, Lawrence. "The Kippah Comes to America." In *Continuity and Change: A Festschrift in Honor of Irving (Yitz) Greenberg's 75th Birthday,* edited by Steven T. Katz and Steven Bayme, 129–50. Lanham, MD: University Press of America, 2010.

Gunderson, Joan R. "Women and Inheritance in America: Virginia and New York as a Case Study, 1700–1860." In *Inheritance and Wealth in America,* edited by Robert K. Miller and Stephen J. McNamee, 91–118. New York: Plenum Press, 1998.

Gurock, Jeffrey S. *The Colonial and Early National Period, 1654–1840: American Jewish History.* New York: Routledge, 2014.

Gutmann, Joseph. *Beauty in Holiness: Studies in Jewish Customs and Ceremonial Art.* New York: Ktav, 1970.

Gutstein, Morris Aaron. *Aaron Lopez and Judah Touro: A Refugee and a Son of a Refugee.* New York: Behrman's Jewish Book House, 1939.

Gyllenbok, Jan. *Encyclopaedia of Historical Metrology, Weights, and Measures.* Vol. 1. Basel: Birkhäuser, 2018.

Handler, Jerome S. *The Unappropriated People: Freedmen in the Slave Society of Barbados.* Kingston: University of the West Indies Press, 2009.

Handler, Jerome, Melanie Newton, Pedro L. V. Welch, and Ernest M. Wiltshire. *Freedmen of Barbados: Names and Notes for Genealogical and Family History Research.* Charlottesville: Virginia Foundation for the Humanities, 2007.

Harris, E. T. "Anglo-Jewry's Experience of Secondary Education from the 1830s until 1920." PhD diss., University of London, 2007.

Harris, Leslie M. *In the Shadow of Slavery: African Americans in New York City, 1626–1863*. Chicago: University of Chicago Press, 2003.

Hartman, Saidiya V. *Scenes of Subjection: Terror, Slavery, and Self-Making in Nineteenth-Century America*. New York: Oxford University Press, 1997.

———. "Venus in Two Acts." *Small Axe* 12, no. 2 (2008): 1–14.

Hartogensis, Benjamin H. "Rhode Island and Consanguineous Jewish Marriages." *Publications of the American Jewish Historical Society* 20 (1911): 137–46. http://www.jstor.org/stable/43057881.

Haskell, Guy H. "From the Editor." *Jewish Folklore and Ethnology Review* 15, no. 2 (1993): 1.

Havens, Earle. *Commonplace Books: A History of Manuscripts and Printed Books from Antiquity to the Twentieth Century*. New Haven, CT: Beinecke Rare Book and Manuscript Library, 2001.

Heckscher, Morrison H. *The Metropolitan Museum of Art: An Architectural History*. New York: Metropolitan Museum of Art, 1998.

Heilbrun, Carolyn G. *Writing a Woman's Life*. New York: Norton, 1988.

Heilman, Samuel. "Jews and Judaica: Who Owns and Buys What?" In *Persistence and Flexibility: Anthropological Perspectives on the American Jewish Experience*, edited by Walter P. Zenner, 260–80. Albany: State University of New York Press, 1988.

Hemphill, C. Dallett. *Siblings: Brothers and Sisters in American History*. New York: Oxford University Press, 2011.

Hendler, Glenn. *Public Sentiments: Structures of Feeling in Nineteenth-Century American Literature*. Chapel Hill: University of North Carolina Press, 2001.

Hershkowitz, Leo. "By Chance or Choice: Jews in New Amsterdam, 1654." *American Jewish Archives Journal* 57, nos. 1–2 (2005): 1–13.

———. "Colonial Entrepreneurs: A Quartet of Jewish Women." *Jewish Women: A Comprehensive Historical Encyclopedia*. March 1, 2009. Jewish Women's Archive, https://jwa.org/encyclopedia/article/colonial-entrepreneurs-quartet-of-jewish-women.

———. "Wills of Early New York Jews (1784–1799)." *American Jewish Historical Quarterly* 56, no. 2 (1966): 163–207.

Hess, Jillian Marissa. "Commonplace-Book Stylistics: Romantic and Victorian Technologies of Reading and Writing." PhD diss, Stanford University, 2012.

Hickman, Christine B. "The Devil and the One Drop Rule: Racial Categories, African Americans, and the U.S. Census." *Michigan Law Review* 95, no. 5 (1997): 1161–265.

Higginbotham, P. *Children's Homes: A History of Institutional Care for Britain's Young*. Barnsley, UK: Pen and Sword History, 2017.

Hobbs, Allyson. *A Chosen Exile: A History of Racial Passing in American Life*. Cambridge, MA: Harvard University Press, 2014.

Hoberman, Michael. *A Hundred Acres of America: The Geography of Jewish American Literary History*. New Brunswick, NJ: Rutgers University Press, 2019.

Hoberman, Michael, Laura Arnold Leibman, and Hilit Surowitz-Israel. *Jews in the Americas, 1776–1826*. London: Routledge, 2017.

Hobuß, Steffi. "Silence, Remembering, and Forgetting in Wittgenstein, Cage, and Derrida." In *Beyond Memory: Silence and the Aesthetics of Remembrance*, edited by Alexandre Dessingué and Jay M. Winter, 95–110. New York: Routledge, 2016.

Hodges, Graham Russell. *Slavery and Freedom in the Rural North: African Americans in Monmouth County, New Jersey, 1665–1865.* New York: Rowman and Littlefield, 1997.

Hodges, Graham Russell, and Alan Edward Brown, eds. *"Pretends to Be Free": Runaway Slave Advertisements from Colonial and Revolutionary New York and New Jersey.* New York: Fordham University Press, 1994.

Hofer, Margaret K., Debra Schmidt Bach, Kenneth L. Ames, and David L. Barquist. *Stories in Sterling: Four Centuries of Silver in New York.* New York: New-York Historical Society, 2011.

Hollander, Anne. *Sex and Suits.* New York: Knopf, 1994.

Honeyman, A. Van Doren, ed. *Documents Relating to the Colonial History of the State of New Jersey.* Vol. 4: *1761–1770.* Somerville, NJ: Union Gazette Association, 1928.

Hopper, Kim. *Reckoning with Homelessness.* Ithaca, NY: Cornell University Press, 2002.

Hoskins, Janet. "Afterword—Gendering Religious Objects: Placing Them as Agents in Matrices of Power." *Material Religion* 3, no. 1 (2007): 110–19.

Hughes, Clair. *Hats.* New York: Bloomsbury Visual Arts, 2017.

Hühner, Leon. "Jews Interested in Privateering in American During the Eighteenth Century." *Publications of the American Jewish Historical Society* 23 (1915): 163–76.

Hyde, Lewis. *The Gift: Creativity and the Artist in the Modern World.* New York: Vintage Books, 2007.

Idelson-Shein, Iris. *Difference of a Different Kind: Jewish Constructions of Race During the Long Eighteenth Century.* Philadelphia: University of Pennsylvania Press, 2014.

Ingersoll, Thomas N. *Mammon and Manon in Early New Orleans: The First Slave Society in the Deep South, 1718–1819.* Knoxville: University of Tennessee Press, 1999.

"Introduction to Volume I." *Publications of the American Jewish Historical Society* 21 (1913): xiii–xi.

Irving, Washington, and M. J. K. "Rebecca Gratz." *Publications of the American Jewish Historical Society* 11 (1903): 189–90. http://www.jstor.org/stable/43057650.

"Items Relating to the Moses and Levy Families, New York." *Publications of the American Jewish Historical Society* 27 (1920): 331–45. http://www.jstor.org/stable/43058016.

"Items Relating to the Seixas Family, New York." *Publications of the American Jewish Historical Society* 27 (1920): 346–70.

Jackson, Emily. *Ancestors in Silhouette, Cut by August Edouart.* Boston: Longwood Press, 1977.

———. *The History of Silhouettes.* London: Connoisseur, 1911.

"Jacques Judah Lyons." *Publications of the American Jewish Historical Society* 21 (1913): xxiii–xviii.

Jaher, Frederic Cople. *The Jews and the Nation: Revolution, Emancipation, State*

Formation, and the Liberal Paradigm in America and France. Princeton, NJ: Princeton University Press, 2003.

Jamoussi, Zouheir. *Primogeniture and Entail in England: A Survey of Their History and Representation in Literature*. Newcastle upon Tyne, UK: Cambridge Scholars Publishing, 2011.

Joel, Israel, Abraham Isaacs, and Jonas N. Phillips. "Items Relating to Congregation Shearith Israel, New York." *Publications of the American Jewish Historical Society* 27 (1920): 1–125.

Johnson, Dale T. *American Portrait Miniatures in the Manney Collection*. New York: Abrams, 1990.

Jones, David J. *Gothic Effigy: A Guide to Dark Visibilities*. Manchester, UK: Manchester University Press, 2018.

Joselit, Jenna Weissman. *A Perfect Fit: Clothes, Character, and the Promise of America*. New York: Metropolitan Books, 2001.

Juhasz, Esther. "Head Covering, Men." In *Encyclopedia of Jewish Folklore and Traditions*, edited by Haya Bar-Itzhak and Raphael Patai, 233–34. New York: Routledge, 2013.

Kadden, Barbara Binder, and Bruce Kadden. *Teaching Jewish Life Cycle: Traditions and Activities*. Denver: A.R.E., 1997.

Kaganoff, Nathan M. "AJHS at 90: Reflections on the History of the Oldest Ethnic Historical Society in America." *American Jewish History* 71, no. 4 (1982): 466–85.

Kahn, Susan Martha. "Who Are the Jews? New Formulations of an Age-Old Question." *Human Biology* 85, no. 6 (2013): 919–24.

Kammen, Michael G. *Colonial New York: A History*. History of the American Colonies. New York: Scribner, 1975.

Kaplan, Yosef. "The Jewish Profile of the Spanish-Portuguese Community of London During the Seventeenth Century." *Judaism* 41, no. 3 (1992): 229–40.

Kasinitz, Philip. *Caribbean New York: Black Immigrants and the Politics of Race*. Ithaca, NY: Cornell University Press, 1992.

Katz, William A. *Cuneiform to Computer: A History of Reference Sources*. London: Scarecrow, 1997.

Katzew, Ilona. *Casta Painting: Images of Race in Eighteenth-Century Mexico*. New Haven, CT: Yale University Press, 2004.

Kelly, Catherine E. *Republic of Taste: Art, Politics, and Everyday Life in Early America*. Philadelphia: University of Pennsylvania Press, 2016.

Kelly, Ian. *Beau Brummell: The Ultimate Man of Style*. New York: Free Press, 2006.

Kelly, Kate. *Election Day: An American Holiday, an American History*. New York: Asja Press, 2008.

Kenvin, Helene Schwartz. *This Land of Liberty: A History of America's Jews*. West Orange, NJ: Behrman House, 1986.

Kerber, Linda K. *Women of the Republic: Intellect and Ideology in Revolutionary America*. Chapel Hill: Published for the Institute of Early American History and Culture by the University of North Carolina Press, 1980.

King, Wilma. *The Essence of Liberty: Free Black Women During the Slave Era*. Columbia: University of Missouri Press, 2006.

Kirsch, Adam. *Benjamin Disraeli*. New York: Schocken, 2008.

Kirshenblatt-Gimblett, Barbara. "Keynote Address." Lecture presented at *Wandering Objects: Collecting and Interpreting Jewish Things* (Conference). North Carolina Museum of Art, Raleigh and Ackland Art Museum, UNC–Chapel Hill. Raleigh, NC, November 2018.

Kleeblatt, Norman L., Gerard C. Wertkin, and Mary Black. *The Jewish Heritage in American Folk Art*. New York: Universe Books, 1984.

Klein, Michele. *A Time to Be Born*. Philadelphia: Jewish Publication Society, 2000.

Klooster, Wim. "Networks of Colonial Entrepreneurs: The Founders of the Jewish Settlements in Dutch America, 1650s and 1660s." In *Atlantic Diasporas: Jews, Conversos, and Crypto-Jews in the Age of Mercantilism, 1500–1800*, edited by Richard L. Kagan and Philip D. Morgan, 33–49. Baltimore: Johns Hopkins University Press, 2009.

Kohler, Max J. "Phases of Jewish Life in New York Before 1800." *Publications of the American Jewish Historical Society* 3 (1895): 73–86.

Krill, Rosemary Troy. *Early American Decorative Arts, 1620–1860: A Handbook for Interpreters*. Walnut Creek, CA: AltaMira Press, 2010.

Kroker, Arthur. "Archive Drift." *Intermédialités* 18 (2011): 137–49. https://id.erudit.org/iderudit/1009078ar.

Kurella, Elizabeth M. *Whitework Embroidered Lace Handkerchiefs*. Whiting, IN: Lace Merchant, 2004.

Laas, Virginia Jeans, ed. *Wartime Washington: The Civil War Letters of Elizabeth Blair Lee*. Urbana: University of Illinois Press, 1991.

Lafont, Anne. "How Skin Color Became a Racial Marker: Art Historical Perspectives on Race." *Eighteenth-Century Studies* 51, no. 1 (2017): 89–113.

Lamb, Jonathan. *The Rhetoric of Suffering: Reading the Book of Job in the Eighteenth Century*. New York: Oxford University Press, 1995.

Land, Julian, and James Greener. "The Lineage of the Montefiore Family and Major Connected Families." Unpublished manuscript, last modified 2016. Microsoft Word file.

Landman, Leo. *The Cantor: An Historic Perspective, [Ma'amado shel he-ḥazan]; A Study of the Origin, Communal Position, and Function of the Hazzan*. New York: Yeshiva University, 1972.

Laqueur, Thomas. *Making Sex: Body and Gender from the Greeks to Freud*. Cambridge, MA: Harvard University Press, 1990.

Lee, Hannah Farnham Sawyer. *Memoir of Pierre Toussaint, Born a Slave in St. Domingo*. Boston: Crosby, Nichols, 1854.

Leibman, Laura Arnold. "The Material of Race: Clothing, Anti-Semitism, and Manhood in the Caribbean During the Era of Emancipation." In *Jews, Liberalism, Anti-Semitism: A Global History*, edited by Abigail Green and Simon Levis Sullam. Basingstoke, UK: Palgrave Macmillan, forthcoming.

———. *Messianism, Secrecy, and Mysticism: A New Interpretation of Early American Jewish Life*. London: Vallentine Mitchell, 2012.

———. "Poetics of the Apocalypse: Messianism in Early Jewish American Poetry." *Studies in American Jewish Literature* 33, no. 1 (2014): 35–62.

———. "Tradition and Innovation in a Colonial Wampanoag Family from Martha's Vineyard." In *Early Native Literacies in New England: A Documentary and Critical Anthology*, edited by Hilary Wyss and Kristina Bross, 174–97. Amherst: University of Massachusetts Press, 2008.

Leibman, Laura Arnold, and Sam May. "Making Jews: Race, Gender and Identity in Barbados in the Age of Emancipation." *American Jewish History* 99, no. 1 (2015): 1–26.

Levine, Naomi B., and Martin Hochbaum. *Poor Jews: An American Awakening.* New Brunswick, NJ: Transaction Books, 1974.

Liberles, Robert. "On the Threshold of Modernity: 1616–1780." In *Jewish Daily Life in Germany, 1618–1945*, edited by Marion A. Kaplan, 9–92. New York: Oxford University Press, 2005.

Lieberman, Julia Rebollo. "The Founding of the London Bet Holim Hospital in 1748 and the Secularization of Sedaca in the Spanish and Portuguese Jewish Community in the Eighteenth Century." *Jewish Historical Studies* 49, no. 1 (2017): 106–43.

———. "From Charity to Philanthropy Among the Jewish Elite: Emancipation, Modernization, Ethnicity, and Nationalism." In *Charity in Jewish, Christian, and Islamic Traditions*, edited by Julia Rebollo Lieberman and Michał Rozbicki, 105–30. Lanham, MD: Lexington Books, 2017.

———. *Sephardi Family Life in the Early Modern Diaspora.* Hanover, NH: Brandeis University Press, 2011.

Lieberman, Julia Rebollo, and Michał Rozbicki. *Charity in Jewish, Christian, and Islamic Traditions.* Lanham, MD: Lexington Books, 2017.

Lifschutz, Ezekiel. Review of *Union Pioneer: An Autobiographical Account of Bisno's Early Life and the Beginnings of Unionism in the Women's Garment Industry*, by Abraham Bisno and Joel Seidman. *American Jewish Historical Quarterly* 57, no. 3 (1968): 444–45.

Lillios, Katina T. "Objects of Memory: The Ethnography and Archaeology of Heirlooms." *Journal of Archaeological Method and Theory* 6, no. 3 (1999): 235–62.

Lindsey, Rebecca. "Displaying Islamic Art at the Metropolitan: A Retrospective Look." Metropolitan Museum of Art, February 2, 2012. https://www.metmuseum.org/blogs/now-at-the-met/features/2012/displaying-islamic-art-at-the-metropolitan.

Lloyd, Stephen. *Portrait Miniatures from Scottish Private Collections.* Edinburgh: National Galleries of Scotland, 2006.

London, Hannah Ruth. *Miniatures and Silhouettes of Early American Jews.* Rutland, VT: C. E. Tuttle, 1970.

———. *Portraits of Jews by Gilbert Stuart and Other Early American Artists.* Rutland, VT: C. E. Tuttle, 1969.

———. *Shades of My Forefathers.* Springfield, MA: Pond-Ekberg, 1941.

Longworth's American Almanac, New-York Register and City Directory for 1829. New York: Thomas Longworth, 1829.

Lufkin, Sophia C. "A Home Between Death and Life: Mausoleums as Liminal Spaces of Memory for Classical Reform Jews of Temple Emanu-El, 1890–1945." *American Jewish History* 101, no. 2 (2017): 121–61.

Lynn, Kimberly, and Erin Kathleen Rowe. *The Early Modern Hispanic World: Transnational and Interdisciplinary Approaches.* New York: Cambridge University Press, 2017.

Lyons, Clare A. *Sex Among the Rabble: An Intimate History of Gender and Power in the Age of Revolution.* Chapel Hill: University of North Carolina Press, 2006.

Lyons, Jacques J. "From the Collections of the American Jewish Historical Society." *American Jewish History* 97, no. 1 (2013): 65–73.

Mackey, Frank. *Done with Slavery: The Black Fact in Montreal, 1760–1840.* Montreal: McGill-Queens University Press, 2010.

Maerschalck, Francis W. *A Plan of the City of New York from an Actual Survey, Anno Domini, MDCCLV.* New York: G. Duyckinck, 1755. https://www.loc.gov /item/73691802/.

"Manuscript Material and Extracts from the Note Books of Rev. J. J. Lyons." *Publications of the American Jewish Historical Society* 27 (1920): 1.

Marcus, Jacob Rader. *The American Jewish Woman: A Documentary History.* New York: Ktav, 1981.

———. *The American Jewish Woman, 1654–1980.* Cincinnati: American Jewish Archives, 1981.

———. *American Jewry: Documents; Eighteenth Century; Primarily Hitherto Unpublished Manuscripts.* Cincinnati: Hebrew Union College Press, 1959.

———. *The Colonial American Jew, 1492–1776.* 3 vols. Detroit: Wayne State University Press, 1970.

———. *The Jew in the American World: A Source Book.* Detroit: Wayne State University Press, 1996.

———. *Studies in American Jewish History: Studies and Addresses.* Cincinnati: Hebrew Union College Press, 1969.

———. *United States Jewry.* Vol. 1: *1776–1985.* Detroit: Wayne State University Press, 2018.

Mark, Peter, and José da Silva Horta. "Catholics, Jews, and Muslims in Guiné." In *Atlantic Diasporas: Jews, Conversos, and Crypto-Jews in the Age of Mercantilism, 1500–1800,* edited by Richard L. Kagan and Philip D. Morgan, 170–94. Baltimore: Johns Hopkins University Press, 2009.

Marley, David. *Historic Cities of the Americas: An Illustrated Encyclopedia.* Vol. 1. Santa Barbara, CA: ABC-CLIO, 2005.

Martello, Robert. *Midnight Ride, Industrial Dawn: Paul Revere and the Growth of American Enterprise.* Baltimore: Johns Hopkins University Press, 2010.

Martin, Tony. *Caribbean History: From Pre-Colonial Origins to the Present.* Boston: Pearson, 2012.

Martin, Wendy. *All Things Dickinson: An Encyclopedia of Emily Dickinson's World.* Santa Barbara, CA: Greenwood, 2014.

Martínez–San Miguel, Yolanda. *Coloniality of Diasporas: Rethinking Intra-Colonial Migrations in a Pan-Caribbean Context.* New York: Palgrave Macmillan, 2014.

Marty, Martin E., and R. Scott Appleby, eds. *Fundamentalisms Observed.* Chicago: University of Chicago Press, 1991.

Mauss, Marcel. *The Gift: The Form and Reason for Exchange in Archaic Societies.* New York: W. W. Norton, 2000.

Mays, Dorothy A. *Women in Early America: Struggle, Survival, and Freedom in a New World.* Santa Barbara, CA: ABC-CLIO, 2004.

McCallum, James Dow. *The Letters of Eleazar Wheelock's Indians.* Hanover, NH: Dartmouth College Publications, 1932.

McCarthy, Angela, Catharine Coleborne, Maree O'Connor, and Elspeth Knewstubb. "Lives in the Asylum Record, 1864 to 1910: Utilising Large Data Collection for Histories of Psychiatry and Mental Health." *Medical History* 61, no. 3 (2017): 358–79.

McCune, Mary. "Social Workers in the 'Muskeljudentum': 'Hadassah Ladies,' 'Manly Men' and the Significance of Gender in the American Zionist Movement, 1912–1928." *American Jewish History* 86, no. 2 (1998): 135–65.

McEvilley, Thomas. Introduction to *Inside the White Cube: The Ideology of the Gallery Space*, by Brian O'Doherty, 7–12. Berkeley: University of California Press, 1999.

McMahon, Lucia. "'While Our Souls Together Blend': Narrating a Romantic Readership in the Early Republic." In *An Emotional History of the United States*, edited by Peter N. Stearns and Jan Lewis, 66–90. New York: New York University Press, 1998.

Menard, Scott W., ed. *Handbook of Longitudinal Research: Design, Measurement, and Analysis*. Burlington, MA: Elsevier / Academic Press, 2008.

Mendelsohn, Adam. "The Sacrifices of the Isaacs: The Diffusion of New Models of Religious Leadership in the English-Speaking Jewish World." In *Transnational Traditions: New Perspectives on American Jewish History*, edited by Ava Fran Kahn and Adam Mendelsohn, 11–37. Detroit: Wayne State University Press, 2014.

The Metropolis Explained and Illustrated in Familiar Form. New York: Devlin, 1871.

Miller, George J. "Early Jews in Middlesex County, New Jersey." *Publications of the American Jewish Historical Society* 33 (1934): 251–54.

Miller, Robert K., and Stephen J. McNamee. *Inheritance and Wealth in America.* New York: Plenum Press, 1998.

Miller, W. "On the State of the Peruvian Empire Previous to the Arrival of the Spaniards." *Fraser's Magazine* 30, no. 175 (1844): 37–47.

Mirvis, Stanley. "Sephardic Family Life in the Eighteenth-Century British West Indies." PhD diss., City University of New York, 2013.

Mocatta, J. *An Address to the Congregation of Portuguese Jews: Delivered at a Meeting of Their Elders, on the Examination of the Report, Presented by the Committee on the Ecclesiastical State.* London, 1803.

Molendijk, Arie L. "The Rhetorics and Politics of the Conversion of Isaac da Costa." In *Cultures of Conversions*, edited by Jan N. Bremmer, Wout Jac. van Bekkum, and Arie L. Molendijk, 65–82. Leuven: Peeters, 2006.

Monaghan, E. Jennifer. "Literacy Instruction and Gender in Colonial New England." *American Quarterly* 40, no. 1 (1988): 18–41.

Moore, Deborah Dash, Jeffrey S. Gurock, Annie Polland, Howard B. Rock, Daniel Soyer, and Diana L. Linden. *Jewish New York: The Remarkable Story of a City and a People.* New York: New York University Press, 2017.

Moore, Lindsay. "Women and Property Litigation in Seventeenth-Century England and North America." In *Married Women and the Law: Coverture in England and the Common Law World*, edited by Tim Stretton and Krista J. Kesselring, 113–38. Montreal: McGill-Queen's University Press, 2013.

Mordecai, Gratz. "Notice of Jacob Mordecai, Founder, and Proprietor from 1809 to 1818, of the Warrenton (N.C.) Female Seminary." *Publications of the American Jewish Historical Society* 6 (1897): 39–48.

Mordecai, Miriam Gratz. "Notes." *Publications of the American Jewish Historical Society* 1 (1893): 121–22.

Mordecai, Sarah Ann Hays. *Recollections of My Aunt, Rebecca Gratz.* Philadelphia, 1893.

Morgan, Jennifer L. *Laboring Women: Reproduction and Gender in New World Slavery.* Philadelphia: University of Pennsylvania Press, 2004.

Moscow, Henry. *The Book of New York Firsts.* Syracuse, NY: Syracuse University Press, 1995.

Munrow, Leanne. "Negotiating Memories and Silences: Museum Narratives of Transatlantic Slavery in England." In *Beyond Memory: Silence and the Aesthetics of Remembrance,* edited by Alexandre Dessingué and Jay M. Winter, 175–94. New York: Routledge, 2016.

Museus, Samuel D. "The Model Minority and the Inferior Minority Myths: Understanding Stereotypes and Their Implications for Student Involvement." *About Campus* 13, no. 3 (2008): 2–8.

Museus, Samuel D., and Peter N. Kiang. "Deconstructing the Model Minority Myth and How It Contributes to the Invisible Minority Reality in Higher Education Research." *New Directions for Institutional Research* 142 (2009): 5–15.

Nadell, Pamela Susan, ed. *American Jewish Women's History: A Reader.* New York: New York University Press, 2003.

———. *America's Jewish Women: A History from Colonial Times to Today.* New York: W. W. Norton, 2019.

———. "On Their Own Terms: America's Jewish Women, 1954–2004." *American Jewish History* 91, no. 3/4 (2003): 389–404.

———. "'The Synagog shall hear the Call of the Sister': Carrie Simon and the Founding of NFTS." In *Sisterhood: A Centennial History of Women of Reform Judaism,* edited by Carole B. Balin, Dana Herman, Jonathan D. Sarna, and Gary P. Zola, 19–48. Cincinnati: Hebrew Union College Press, 2013.

Nadell, Pamela Susan, and Jonathan D. Sarna, eds. *Women and American Judaism: Historical Perspectives.* Hanover, NH: University Press of New England, 2001.

Nalle, Sara Tilghman. "On the Alumbrados: Confessionalism and Religious Dissidence in the Iberian World." In *The Early Modern Hispanic World: Transnational and Interdisciplinary Approaches,* edited by Kimberly Lynn and Erin Kathleen Rowe, 91–120. New York: Cambridge University Press, 2017.

Narrett, David E. *Inheritance and Family Life in Colonial New York City.* Ithaca, NY: Cornell University Press, 1992.

Nayder, Lillian. *Dickens, Sexuality, and Gender: Library of Essays on Charles Dickens.* Burlington, VT: Ashgate, 2012.

Nesbitt, Alexander. *Lettering: The History and Technique of Lettering as Design.* New York: Prentice Hall, 1950.

New York City Directory, 1849/50. New York: John Doggett, Jr., 1849.

New York State. *Manual for the Use of the Legislature of the State of New York.* Albany: New York State Dept. of State, 1927.

Nichols, Bill. *Movies and Methods: An Anthology.* Berkeley: University of California Press, 1985.

Noah, Mordecai Manuel. *She Would Be a Soldier, or, The Plains of Chippewa, an Historical Drama in Three Acts: Performed for the First Time on the 21st of June,*

1819. Early American Imprints, second ser. 48940. New York: Longworth's Dramatic Repository, 1819.

Notable American Women: The Modern Period; A Biographical Dictionary. Cambridge, MA: Belknap Press of Harvard University Press, 1980.

Nussbaum, Martha Craven. *Liberty of Conscience in Defense of America's Tradition of Religious Equality*. New York: Basic Books, 2010.

O'Doherty, Brian. *Inside the White Cube: The Ideology of the Gallery Space*. Berkeley: University of California Press, 1999.

Olitzky, Kerry M., and Marc Lee Raphael. *The American Synagogue: A Historical Dictionary and Sourcebook*. Westport, CT: Greenwood Press, 1996.

Olsen, Kirstin. *Daily Life in 18th-Century England*. Santa Barbara, CA: Greenwood, 2017.

Oron, H. A. "'*No aksi mi fu libi yu*': A View on the Halakhic Status of the Congregation '*Siva Darkhey Y'Sharim*'—the Judeo-Creoles of Suriname." MA thesis, Leiden University, 2009.

Ozarowski, Joseph S. "*Bikur Cholim*: A Paradigm for Pastoral Caring." In *Jewish Pastoral Care: A Practical Handbook from Traditional and Contemporary Sources*, edited by Dayle A. Friedman, 56–74. Woodstock, VT: Jewish Lights Publishing, 2010.

Pappenheim, Shlomo. *The Jewish Wedding*. Exhibition at Yeshiva University Museum. New York: The Museum, 1977.

Parker, Mark Louis. *Literary Magazines and British Romanticism*. Cambridge: Cambridge University Press, 2000.

Patterson, Orlando. *Slavery and Social Death: A Comparative Study*. Cambridge, MA: Harvard University Press, 1982.

Perry, Claire. *Young America: Childhood in 19th-Century Art and Culture*. New Haven, CT: Yale University Press, 2006.

Perry, Ruth. *Novel Relations: The Transformation of Kinship in English Literature and Culture, 1748–1818*. New York: Cambridge University Press, 2004.

Petrino, Elizabeth. "Nineteenth-Century American Women's Poetry." In *The Cambridge Companion to Nineteenth-Century American Women's Writing*, edited by Dale M. Bauer and Philip Gould, 122–42. Cambridge: Cambridge University Press, 2001.

The Philadelphia Directory and Stranger's Guide, for 1825. Philadelphia: Thomas Wilson and William D. Vanbaun, John Bioren, 1825.

Philipson, David, ed. *Letters of Rebecca Gratz*. Philadelphia: Jewish Publication Society of America, 1929.

———. "Some Unpublished Letters of Rebecca Gratz." *Publications of the American Jewish Historical Society*, no. 29 (1925): 53–60.

Phillips, Naphtali. "Sketch of the Spanish and Portuguese Congregation Shearith Israel Written About 1855." *Publications of the American Jewish Historical Society* 21, no. 1 (1913): 174–228.

Pitock, Toni. "Commerce and Connection: Jewish Merchants, Philadelphia, and the Atlantic World, 1736–1822." PhD diss., University of Delaware, 2016.

———. "'Separated from Us as Far as West Is from East': Eighteenth-Century Ashkenazi Immigrants in the Atlantic World." *American Jewish History* 102, no. 2 (2018): 173–93.

Polland, Annie, and Daniel Soyer. *Emerging Metropolis: New York Jews in the Age of Immigration, 1840–1920*. New York: New York University Press, 2015.

Poor, Henry V. *History of the Railroads and Canals of the United States*. Vol. 1. New York: J. H. Schultz, 1860.

Porter, Jack Nusan. "Rosa Sonnenschein and 'The American Jewess': The First Independent English Language Jewish Women's Journal in the United States." *American Jewish History* 68, no. 1 (1978): 57–63.

"Portrait Miniatures: Materials & Techniques." London: Victoria and Albert Museum, 2016. http://www.vam.ac.uk/content/articles/p/portrait-miniatures -on-vellum/.

Posey, Walter Brownlow. *Alabama in the 1830's: As Recorded by British Travellers*. Birmingham, AL: Southern University Press, 1988.

Pred, Allan. "Manufacturing in the American Mercantile City: 1800–1840." *Annals of the Association of American Geographers* 56, no. 2 (1966): 307–38.

"Preface." *Publications of the American Jewish Historical Society*, no. 21 (1913): ix–xii.

Prinz, Deborah. *On the Chocolate Trail: A Delicious Adventure Connecting Jews, Religions, History, Travel, Rituals, and Recipes to the Magic of Cacao*. Woodstock, VT: Jewish Lights Publishing, 2013.

Quigley, William P. "Reluctant Charity: Poor Laws in the Original Thirteen States." *University of Richmond Law Review* 31 (1997): 111–78.

Rabin, Shari. *Jews on the Frontier: Religion and Mobility in Nineteenth-Century America*. New York: New York University Press, 2017.

Rabinowitz Deer, Tova. *Exploring Typography*. Clifton Park, NY: Thomson Delmar Learning, 2006.

Ranston, Jackie. *Belisario: Sketches of Character; A Historical Biography of a Jamaican Artist*. Kingston: Mills Press, 2018.

Reed, Robert C. *The New York Elevated*. South Brunswick, NJ: Barnes, 1978.

Reiman, Tonya. *The Power of Body Language: How to Succeed in Every Business and Social Encounter*. New York: Pocket Books, 2007.

Reis, Elizabeth Sarah. *Damned Women: Sinners and Witches in Puritan New England*. Ithaca, NY: Cornell University Press, 1999.

"Report of Leon Hunter, Curator, and Edward D. Coleman, Librarian." *Publications of the American Jewish Historical Society* 34 (1937): xvi–xvii.

Ribeiro, Aileen. *The Art of Dress: Fashion in England and France, 1750–1820*. New Haven, CT: Yale University Press, 1995.

Riello, Giorgio, and Ulinka Rublack, eds. *The Right to Dress: Sumptuary Laws in a Global Perspective, 1200–1800*. New York: Cambridge University Press, 2019.

Rischin, Moses. *The Jews in North America*. Detroit: Wayne State University Press, 1987.

Robinson, James. *The Philadelphia Directory for 1804 Containing the Names, Trades and Residence of the Inhabitants of the City, Southwark, Northern Liberties, and Kensington: To Which Is Prefixed a Brief Sketch of the Origin and Present State of the City of Philadelphia*. Early American Imprints, Second Series 7044. Philadelphia: John H. Oswald, 1804.

———. *Robinson's Original Annual Directory for 1817, Being an Alphabetical List of More Than 22,000 Merchants, Mechanicks, Traders, &c. of Philadelphia and Suburbs; with Useful Information, &c*. Whitehall, PA, 1817.

Rock, Howard B. *Haven of Liberty: New York Jews in the New World, 1654–1865.* New York: New York University Press, 2015.

Rockman, Seth. *Welfare Reform in the Early Republic: A Brief History with Documents.* Boston: Bedford / St. Martin's, 2003.

Rosenbach, Isabella H., and Abraham S. Wolf Rosenbach. "Aaron Levy." *Publications of the American Jewish Historical Society,* no. 2 (1894): 157–63.

Rosenbaum, Jeanette W. *Myer Myers, Goldsmith, 1723–1795.* Philadelphia: Jewish Publication Society of America, 1954.

Rosenbloom, Joseph R. *A Biographical Dictionary of Early American Jews: Colonial Times Through 1800.* Lexington: University of Kentucky Press, 1960.

Rosenthal, Debra J. *Race Mixture in Nineteenth-Century U.S. and Spanish American Fictions: Gender, Culture, and National Building.* Chapel Hill: University of North Carolina Press, 2004.

Rosenwaike, Ira. *Population History of New York City.* Syracuse, NY: Syracuse University Press, 1972.

Roth, Cecil. "Some Jewish Loyalists in the War of American Independence." In *American Jewish History: The Colonial and Early National Periods, 1654–1840,* edited by Jeffrey S. Gurock, 21–48. New York: Routledge, 1998.

Rothery, Mark, and Henry French, eds. *Making Men: The Formation of Elite Male Identities in England, c. 1660–1900; A Sourcebook.* Basingstoke, UK: Palgrave Macmillan, 2012.

Rozin, Mordechai. *The Rich and the Poor: Jewish Philanthropy and Social Control in Nineteenth-Century London.* Brighton, UK: Sussex Academic Press, 1999.

Russel-Henar, Christine van. *Angisa Tori: De Geheimtaal van Suriname's Hoofddoeken* [Angisa Tori: The secret code of Surinamese headkerchiefs]. Paramaribo: de Stichting / Foundation Fu Memre Wi Afo, 2008.

Russell, Rebecca Ross. *Gender and Jewelry: A Feminist Analysis.* Scotts Valley, CA: CreateSpace Independent Publishing Platform, 2010.

Salm, Betsy Krieg. *Women's Painted Furniture, 1790–1830: American Schoolgirl Art.* Hanover, NH: University Press of New England, 2010.

Salper, Roberta. "San Diego State 1970: The Initial Year of the Nation's First Women's Studies Program." *Feminist Studies* 37, no. 3 (2011): 658–82. http://www.feministstudies.org/aboutfs/history.html.

Samuel, Wilfred S. "A Review of the Jewish Colonists in Barbados in the Year 1680." *Transactions (Jewish Historical Society of England)* 13 (1932): 1–111.

Sandlin, Jennifer A. "Consumption, Gendered Stereotypes, and the Struggle for Respect: Controlling Images of Poor Women as Consumer in Popular, Political, and Adult Education Courses." In *Learning for Economic Self Sufficiency: Constructing Pedagogies of Hope Among Low-Income, Low-Literate Adults,* edited by Mary V. Alfred, 155–74. Charlotte, NC: Information Age Publishing, 2014.

Sarna, Jonathan D. *American Judaism: A History.* New Haven, CT: Yale University Press, 2004.

———. "The Debate over Mixed Seating in the American Synagogue." In *The American Synagogue: A Sanctuary Transformed,* edited by Jack Wertheimer, 363–94. New York: Cambridge University Press, 1987.

———. *Jacksonian Jew: The Two Worlds of Mordecai Noah.* New York: Holmes and Meier, 1981.

———. "Jewish Women Without Money: The Case of Cora Wilburn (1824–1906)." *Nashim: A Journal of Jewish Women's Studies and Gender Issues* 32 (2018): 23–37.

———. "Louisa B. Hart: An Orthodox Jewish Woman's Voice from the Civil War Era." In *You Arose a Mother in Israel: A Festschrift in Honor of Blu Greenberg*, edited by Devorah Zlochower, 95–102. New York: Jewish Orthodox Feminist Alliance, 2017.

Saunders, Richard H. *American Faces: A Cultural History of Portraiture and Identity*. Hanover, NH: University Press of New England, 2016.

Schaefer, Christina K. *The Hidden Half of the Family: A Sourcebook for Women's Genealogy*. Baltimore: Genealogical Publishing, 1999.

Schen, Claire S. "Constructing the Poor in Early Seventeenth-Century London." *Albion: A Quarterly Journal Concerned with British Studies* 32, no. 3 (2000): 450–63.

Schmitt-Korte, Karl, and Martin Price. "Nabataean Coinage—Part III. The Nabataean Monetary System." *Numismatic Chronicle* 154 (1994): 67–131.

Schneider, Tammy. "This Once Savage Heart of Mine: Joseph Johnson, Wheelock's 'Indians,' and the Construction of Christian/Indian Identity, 1764–1776." In *Reinterpreting New England Indians and the Colonial Experience*, edited by Colin G. Calloway and Neal Salisbury, 232–63. Boston: Colonial Society of Massachusetts, 2003.

Schoenberger, Guido. "The Ritual Silver Made by Myer Myers." *Publications of the American Jewish Historical Society* 43, no. 1 (1953): 1–9.

Schwarz, Daniel R. *Disraeli's Fiction*. London: Macmillan, 1979.

Severa, Joan L. *Dressed for the Photographer: Ordinary Americans and Fashion, 1840–1900*. Kent, OH: Kent State University Press, 1995.

Shadur, Joseph, and Yehudit Shadur. *Traditional Jewish Papercuts: An Inner World of Art and Symbol*. Hanover, NH: University Press of New England, 2002.

Sharkia, Rajach, Abdussalam Azem, Qassem Kaiyal, Nathanel Zelnik, and Muhammad Mahajnah. "Mental Retardation and Consanguinity in a Selected Region of the Israeli Arab Community." *Central European Journal of Medicine* 5, no. 1 (2010): 91–96.

Shaw, Alison, and Aviad E. Raz, eds. *Cousin Marriages: Between Tradition, Genetic Risk, and Cultural Change*. New York: Berghahn Books, 2015.

Shelley, Thomas J. "Black and Catholic in Nineteenth Century New York: The Case of Pierre Toussaint." *Records of the American Catholic Historical Society of Philadelphia* 102, no. 4 (1991): 1–17.

Shepkaru, Shmuel. *Jewish Martyrs in the Pagan and Christian Worlds*. Cambridge: Cambridge University Press, 2006.

Sherman, Moshe D. *Orthodox Judaism in America: A Biographical Dictionary and Sourcebook*. Westport, CT: Greenwood Press, 1996.

Sheumaker, Helen. *Love Entwined: The Curious History of Hairwork in America*. Philadelphia: University of Pennsylvania Press, 2007.

Shilstone, E. M. *Monumental Inscriptions in the Jewish Synagogue at Bridgetown, Barbados: With Historical Notes from 1630*. Roberts Stationery, Barbados: Macmillan, 1988.

Shire, Angela, ed. *Great Synagogue Marriage Records, 1791–1850*. Rev. ed. Exeter, UK: Frank J. Gent, 2001.

Shuger, Dale. *Don Quixote in the Archives: Madness and Literature in Early Modern Spain*. Edinburgh: Edinburgh University Press, 2012.

Silverman, Kaja. "Dis-Embodying the Female Voice." In *Issues in Feminist Film Criticism*, ed. Patricia Erens, 309–29. Bloomington: Indiana University Press, 1990.

Simon, E. Yechiel. "Samuel Myer Isaacs: A 19th Century Jewish Minister in New York City." PhD diss., Yeshiva University, 1974.

Singer, Isidore. *The Jewish Encyclopedia: A Descriptive Record of the History, Religion, Literature, and Customs of the Jewish People from the Earliest Times to the Present Day*. 12 vols. New York: Funk and Wagnalls, 1901.

Singleton, Esther, and Russell Sturgis. *The Furniture of Our Forefathers*. Garden City, NY: Doubleday, Page, 1916.

Smith, Amy M. "Family Webs: The Impact of Women's Genealogy on Family Communication." PhD diss., Bowling Green State University, 2008.

Smith, Woodruff D. *Respectability as Moral Map and Public Discourse in the Nineteenth Century*. New York: Routledge, 2018.

Sontag, Susan. *Illness as Metaphor; and, AIDS and Its Metaphors*. New York: Doubleday, 1990.

Sorin, Gerald. *A Time for Building: The Third Migration, 1880–1920*. Baltimore: Johns Hopkins University Press, 1992.

Spann, Edward K. *The New Metropolis: New York City, 1840–1857*. New York: Columbia University Press, 1981.

Steele, Valerie. *The Corset: A Cultural History*. New Haven, CT: Yale University Press, 2001.

Steinhauer, Harry. "Holy Headgear." *Antioch Review* 48, no. 1 (1990): 4–25.

Stern, Malcolm H. *First American Jewish Families: 600 Genealogies, 1654–1977*. Cincinnati: American Jewish Archives, 1978.

Stern, Myer. *The Rise and Progress of Reform Judaism: Embracing a History Made from the Official Records of Temple Emanu-El of New York, with a Description of Salem Field Cemetery, Its City of the Dead, with Illustrations of Its Vaults, Monuments, and Landscape Effects*. New York: M. Stern, 1895.

Stiefel, Barry. *Jewish Sanctuary in the Atlantic World: A Social and Architectural History*. Columbia: University of South Carolina Press, 2014.

Stolzman, Henry, Tami Hausman, and Daniel Stolzman. *Synagogue Architecture in America: Faith, Spirit, and Identity*. Mulgrave, Australia: ACC Distribution, 2004.

Straub, Julia. *The Rise of New Media, 1750–1850: Transatlantic Discourse and American Memory*. New York: Palgrave Macmillan, 2017.

Stretton, Tim, and Krista J. Kesselring. "Introduction: Coverture and Continuity." In *Married Women and the Law: Coverture in England and the Common Law World*, edited by Tim Stretton and Krista J. Kesselring, 3–23. Montreal: McGill-Queen's University Press, 2013.

Studnicki-Gizbert, Daviken. *A Nation upon the Ocean Sea: Portugal's Atlantic Diaspora and the Crisis of the Spanish Empire, 1492–1640*. New York: Oxford University Press, 2007.

Su, Amy Jen, and Muriel Maignan Wilkins. *Own the Room: Discover Your Signature Voice to Master Your Leadership Presence*. Boston: Harvard Business Review Press, 2013.

Sutton, Elizabeth A. *Capitalism and Cartography in the Dutch Golden Age.* Chicago: University of Chicago Press, 2015.

Swierenga, Robert P. *The Forerunners: Dutch Jewry in the North American Diaspora.* Detroit: Wayne State University Press, 1994.

Sztokman, Elana Maryles. *War on Women in Israel: A Story of Religious Radicalism and the Women Fighting for Freedom.* Naperville, IL: Sourcebooks, 2014.

Tatsch, J. Hugo. *Moses Michael Hays: Merchant, Citizen, Freemason, 1739–1805.* Boston: Masonic Craftsman, 1937.

Thackeray, William Makepeace. *Vanity Fair: A Novel Without a Hero.* London: Bradbury and Evans, 1853.

Thornton, Tamara Plakins. *Handwriting in America: A Cultural History.* New Haven, CT: Yale University Press, 1996.

Toledano, Roulhac, Mary Louise Christovich, and Robin Derbes. *New Orleans Architecture: Faubourg Tremé and the Bayou Road.* Gretna, LA: Pelican, 2003.

Trotten, John R. "Thacher-Thatcher Genealogy." *New York Genealogical and Biographical Record* 47 (1916): 257–80.

Ulrich, Laurel Thatcher. "Vertuous Women Found: New England Ministerial Literature, 1668–1735." *American Quarterly* 28, no. 1 (1976): 20–40.

———. *Well-Behaved Women Seldom Make History.* New York: Alfred A. Knopf, 2007.

Umansky, Ellen M., and Dianne Ashton. *Four Centuries of Jewish Women's Spirituality: A Sourcebook.* Boston: Beacon Press, 1992; rev. ed., Hanover, NH: Brandeis University Press, 2009.

Verdooner, Dave, and Harmen Snel. *Trouwen in mokum* [Jewish marriage in Amsterdam], *1598–1811.* 's-Grevenhage, Netherlands: Warray, 1991.

Vink, Wieke. *Creole Jews Negotiating Community in Colonial Suriname.* Leiden: Brill, 2010.

Walling, George W. *Recollections of a New York Chief of Police.* Montclair, NJ: Patterson Smith, 1972.

Watson, Karl. "Shifting Identities: Religion, Race, and Creolization Among the Sephardi Jews of Barbados, 1654–1900." In *The Jews in the Caribbean,* edited by Jane S. Gerber, 195–222. Portland, OR: Littman Library, 2014.

Wees, Beth Carver, and Higgins Medill Harvey. *Early American Silver in the Metropolitan Museum of Art.* New York: Metropolitan Museum of Art, 2013.

Wegenstein, Bernadette. *The Cosmetic Gaze: Body Modification and the Construction of Beauty.* Cambridge, MA: MIT Press, 2012.

Weil, François. *Family Trees: A History of Genealogy in America.* Cambridge, MA: Harvard University Press, 2013.

Wein, Berel. *Living Jewish: Values, Practices, and Traditions.* Brooklyn: Shaar Press, 2002.

Weinstein, Cindy. *Family, Kinship, and Sympathy in Nineteenth-Century American Literature.* New York: Cambridge University Press, 2004.

Wenger, Beth S. Review of *Sweatshop Strife: Class, Ethnicity, and Gender in the Jewish Labour Movement of Toronto, 1900–1939,* by Ruth A. Frager. *American Jewish History* 83, no. 1 (1995): 126–29. http://www.jstor.org/stable/23885550.

Westlake, J. Willis. *How to Write Letters: A Manual of Correspondence, Showing the Correct Structure, Composition, Punctuation, Formalities, and Uses of the Various Kinds of Letters, Notes, and Cards.* Philadelphia: Sower and Potts, 1882.

Whitely, Edward. *The Philadelphia Directory and Register, for 1820. By E. Whitely.* : Philadelphia: M'Carty and Davis, 1820.

Whittock, Nathaniel. *The Miniature Painter's Manual: Containing Progressive Lessons on the Art of Drawing and Painting Likenesses from Life on Card-Board, Vellum, and Ivory: With Concise Remarks on the Delineation of Character and Caricature.* London: Sherwood, Gilbert, and Piper, 1844.

Wilkie, Jane Riblett. "The United States Population by Race and Urban-Rural Residence, 1790–1860: Reference Tables." *Demography* 13, no. 1 (1976): 139–48.

Wiznitzer, Arnold. "The Exodus from Brazil and Arrival in New Amsterdam of the Jewish Pilgrim Fathers, 1654." *Publications of the American Jewish Historical Society* 44, no. 2 (1954): 80–97.

——. *Jews in Colonial Brazil.* New York: Columbia University Press, 1960.

——. "The Minute Book of Congregations Zur Israel of Recife and Magen Abraham of Maurica, Brazil." *Publications of the American Jewish Historical Society* 42, no. 3 (1953): 217–302.

Woodgate, Joseph L., Stephen C. Pratt, James C. Makinson, Ka S. Lim, Andrew M. Reynolds, and Lars Chittka. "Life-Long Radar Tracking of Bumblebees." *PLOS ONE* 11, no. 8 (2016). https://doi.org/10.1371/journal.pone.0160333.

Yanni, Carla. *The Architecture of Madness: Insane Asylums in the United States.* Minneapolis: University of Minnesota Press, 2007.

Zenner, Walter P., ed. *Persistence and Flexibility: Anthropological Perspectives on the American Jewish Experience.* Albany: State University of New York Press, 1988.

Zieseniss, Charles-Otto, and Katell Le Bourhis. *The Age of Napoleon: Costume from Revolution to Empire, 1789–1815.* New York: H. N. Abrams, 1989.

Zimmer, Eric. "Men's Headcovering: The Metamorphosis of the Practice." In *Reverence, Righteousness, and Rahamanut: Essays in Memory of Rabbi Dr. Leo Jung,* edited by Jacob J. Schacter, 325–52. Northvale, NJ: J. Aronson, 1992.

Zimmerman, Frank. "A Letter and Memorandum on Ritual Circumcision, 1772." *Publications of the American Jewish Historical Society* 44, no. 1 (1954): 58–63. http://www.jstor.org/stable/43058871.

Zion, Noam, and David Dishon. *A Different Night: The Family Participation Haggadah.* Jerusalem: Shalom Hartman Institute, 1997.

Zola, Gary Phillip, and Marc Dollinger. *American Jewish History: A Primary Source Reader.* Waltham, MA: Brandeis University Press, 2014.

Index